ORIENTAL AND ASIAN BIBLIOGRAPHY

ORIENTAL AND ASIAN BIBLIOGRAPHY

AN INTRODUCTION
WITH SOME REFERENCE TO AFRICA

J. D. PEARSON M.A.

Librarian, School of Oriental and African Studies
University of London

ARCHON BOOKS
HAMDEN, CONNECTICUT: 1966

Published in the United States of America by
Archon Books, The Shoe String Press, Inc.
60 Connolly Parkway, Hamden,
Connecticut 06514

Printed in Great Britain by
Fletcher & Son Ltd, Norwich and bound by
Richard Clay (The Chaucer Press) Ltd, Bungay, Suffolk

CONTENTS

Preface   ix

Introduction   xi

PART I: PRODUCERS OF THE LITERATURE

1 Oriental, Asian and African Studies: their scope and range   3

     Major regions and countries of Asia; Near and Middle East; South Asia; South-East Asia; Far East; Soviet Asia; Oceania; Africa; Realm of the Orientalist

     Content of Oriental studies
         LANGUAGES; RELIGIONS; HISTORY; OTHER SUBJECTS

2 History of Oriental Studies   21

     General; France; Italy; U.S.S.R.; Other European countries; U.S.A.; United Kingdom; Branches of Oriental studies

3 Recent developments in Oriental Studies in the United Kingdom   34

4 Organizations interested in Oriental, Asian and African Studies   43

     International organizations:

     National Directories; U.S.A.; Canada; United Kingdom; Japan; Taiwan; Korea; India; Czechoslovakia; Eastern Europe; France; West Germany; Italy

     Types of organization:

     Universities; professional associations; learned societies; congresses. Individual scholars

PART II: THE LITERATURE AND ITS CONTROLS

5 Manuscripts   69

     European MSS. relating to Asia
     Cataloguing of Oriental MSS.; Palaeography
     Lists of collections and catalogues
     Union catalogues

6 Reference Books   86
    Lists of reference books
    Encyclopaedias; 'Handbücher'
    Other reference books

7 Periodicals   104
    History of the Orientalist periodical
    Reviewing journals
    Lists of Orientalist periodicals
    Catalogues of periodical articles
    Indexes to periodicals
    Newspapers
    News Summaries
    Newspaper cuttings
    Gazettes

8 General Bibliographies   123
    World bibliographies by subject
    Principal subject bibliographies in the humanities and social sciences, and the proportion of items relating to Asia and Africa
    HISTORY OF RELIGIONS; PHILOSOPHY; HISTORY OF SCIENCE, ART AND ARCHAEOLOGY; GEOGRAPHY; HISTORY; SOCIAL SCIENCES; LAW
    General Orientalist bibliographies
    PERIODICALLY ISSUED BIBLIOGRAPHIES
    National Orientalist Bibliographies
    GERMANY; POLAND; ITALY; HUNGARY; SCANDINAVIA; U.S.S.R.; CZECHOSLOVAKIA; JAPAN

9 Bibliographies of parts of Asia   148
    Colonial bibliographies; British Commonwealth; Other colonial powers

10 Select Bibliographies   156

PART III: STOREHOUSES OF THE LITERATURE

11 Libraries   163
    Orientalist libraries of the United Kingdom
    BRITISH MUSEUM
    BODLEIAN; OTHER OXFORD LIBRARIES
    UNIVERSITY LIBRARY, CAMBRIDGE; OTHER CAMBRIDGE LIBRARIES
    INDIA OFFICE LIBRARY
    SCHOOL OF ORIENTAL AND AFRICAN STUDIES
    ROYAL ASIATIC SOCIETY
    ROYAL COMMONWEALTH SOCIETY

INDIA HOUSE LIBRARY
UNIVERSITY LIBRARY, DURHAM: ORIENTAL SECTION
JOHN RYLANDS LIBRARY, MANCHESTER
SELLY OAK COLLEGES LIBRARY, BIRMINGHAM
OTHER LIBRARIES IN U.K.
CHESTER BEATTY LIBRARY, DUBLIN
THE HAYTER REPORT AND LIBRARY CO-OPERATION

12 American Libraries   192
  Library of Congress
  Public libraries
  University and college libraries
  American Oriental Society Library
  Co-operation among American libraries
  Public Law 480 programmes

13 Orientalist Libraries in U.S.S.R.   206

14 Rest of Europe   209
  France; Germany; Other countries

15 Asia   215
  *Middle East; Turkey; Israel; India; Pakistan; Burma; Ceylon; Far
  East; Library associations in Asia*

16 Special problems affecting Orientalist Libraries   223
  Acquisition of books
  Processing

  NAMES
  Recruitment of staff

Appendix A: Booksellers in Asia; compiled by K. B. Gardner   235
Appendix B: List of works referred to in the text   241
Index   257

PREFACE

The present work has developed out of notes given to students attending courses of lectures which I have been invited to give over the last five years in the School of Librarianship and Archives in University College, London. It has all the defects of a pioneer work in the field which it covers, and as such, is set up as a kind of Aunt-Sally to be shied at by specialists, in the hope that the shying will consist of more detailed and thorough expositions of the various topics here dealt with. It is intended to be an introduction to the subject of Oriental and Asian bibliography as a whole and is, therefore, primarily concerned with institutions, books and libraries which relate to the whole of, or substantial parts of, the Asian continent: works concerned with individual countries or smaller regions are, however, from time to time cited as interesting examples of the bibliographer's or librarian's art, worthy of imitation in respect of other countries or regions. It is hoped to follow it up with a series of volumes of a more specialist nature dealing with areas more limited geographically: Africa, the Islamic Near East, the non- and pre-Islamic Near East, South Asia, South-East Asia and Oceania, and Central Asia and the Far East.

Many centuries ago the Preacher addressed his son in the following words: 'And further, by these, my son, be admonished: of making many books there is no end: and much study is weariness of the flesh?'[1] It has been estimated[2] that in the last two centuries over forty thousand books have been published on the Near and Middle East alone: Theodore Bestermann listed in the third edition of *A world bibliography of bibliographies* some 2,730 titles among the 84,403 there recorded which relate to Asia, Africa, or both continents. Many more relevant works have been published as contributions to periodicals and other collective works and in Oriental languages, categories which are omitted by Bestermann. It is in his desire to provide a guiding cord through the labyrinth of these bibliographies and of sparing other students some

[1] Eccles. xii, 12 (Revised version).
[2] By the compiler of the bibliography in *Social forces in the Middle East*, ed. S. N. Fisher (Cornell U.P., 1955), p. 263.

weariness of flesh that the author hopes that this particular addition to the 'literature explosion' may find its justification. It is not a 'bibliography of bibliographies', but a statement of the position reached in the provision of bibliographical aids up to the Spring of 1965.

With great satisfaction I acknowledge my debt of gratitude owed to the students who have attended my courses over the past five years. The majority of them being visitors from countries in Asia and Africa, they have contributed greatly to my own knowledge of their subjects. That the present work will assist their successors who attend courses in this and other countries is my earnest and sincere hope. To my wife, my secretary, Joan Crouchman, and my former secretary, Mrs Trixie Overman, my best thanks are due for the ever-cheerful and patient way in which they typed and improved long passages in an illegible hand of a text that could have been of no conceivable interest to them.

J. D. PEARSON

St Albans, 10 April, 1965

INTRODUCTION

Under the revised regulations for the Academic Postgraduate Diploma in Librarianship of the University of London which were approved by the University in May, 1959, the subject 'Palaeography and Diplomatics of English Archives', or its alternative, 'Oriental Palaeography', ceased to be compulsory for all candidates for Part I of the Diploma. In its place, English Palaeography became one of four optional papers, the others being:

(1) Oriental and African Bibliography, with special reference to an approved field of study. The title of this option was later changed to 'The bibliography of Asia and Africa'.
(2) History and Literature of Science.
(3) Advanced Historical Bibliography and Modern Book Production[1].

Oriental palaeography may no longer be offered as a subject.

Until session 1963-64 two papers on the bibliography of Asia and Africa were set in the examination for Part I of the Diploma held at the end of the first year: one of these was on the general bibliography of Asia and Africa and the other on the bibliography of the region in which the student chose to specialize. Since that session one examination paper only has been set, but the student's final class in the examination has depended also upon performance in class work and in bibliographical exercises or essays set from time to time.

The reason for establishing this course was said to be that 'the student from an Oriental or African country will gain more from a study of the development of libraries and book-production in the particular region where he intends in due course to work'.[2] Studies of the 'developing', as well as the already developed countries of Asia and Africa are, however, being pursued much more intensively at the present time both in the older-established universities and in newly-formed ones in all countries of the world. As a result of this many

[1] University of London School of Librarianship and Archives, Occasional publications, no. 11. *Report on the work of the School for the period 1956–62*, p.7.
[2] Ibid.

libraries are finding that their collections in the Asian and African fields need to be considerably strengthened to cater for these studies and that it becomes increasingly desirable to appoint to their staffs assistants who have some knowledge of the bibliography of these areas.

The new syllabus created in 1963 for the Part II Examination for the Associateship of Librarianship has since 1964 included papers on the Bibliography and librarianship of Africa (South of the Sahara), of the Near East, of South Asia, and of the Far East. The details of the syllabus for these papers show that questions may be set on the following topics:

Bibliographical apparatus: bibliographies, catalogues, abstracts, reference works. Principal works and editions.

Special types of materials.

Classification and cataloguing: treatment of the subject in general bibliographical classification schemes: special schemes of classification: special problems of classification and cataloguing within the subject field.

Outstanding collections in the field, their contents, special features and availability.

Societies and bibliographical and other organizations in the field, and their publications.

Selection of material. Exploitation of the collection. Production of bibliographical aids.

The present work will, it is hoped, go some of the way toward supplying the need for a text-book on the general aspects of these subjects for the benefit of students sitting for either of these examinations, as well as providing a convenient summary of the subject for those librarians who have developing collections of Asian and African material.

SCOPE AND CONTENT OF THE WORK

As will be explained later in greater detail the present work is concerned with books, whether written in indigenous languages or in European ones, which relate to those enormous geographical regions which are the Asian and African continents, with certain extensions into the other continents.

The word 'bibliography' is often used in a very broad sense covering a large number of more or less closely related topics. The earliest authority given in the Greek dictionaries for the use of the word *bibliographos* is the comic poet Cratinus Major, who flourished in the fifth century before Christ. As used by him the word means a writer of books (in the physical sense), or a copyist. The first recorded use of the derived form *bibliographeia*, meaning the writing of books, is given as occurring in the works of the natural scientist Dioscorides, who is thought to have been alive about the year A.D. 100. No Latin forms of either of these two words are to be found in the dictionaries of Lewis and Short or in that of Du Cange; the *Thesaurus totius latinitatis* gives a bare reference to the use of the term *bibliographicus* in a late glossary. It would seem that the first use of the word in its modern sense of 'a list of books' was made by Louis Jacot, a French book-seller, in choosing a title for his *Bibliographia gallica universalis*. It was later adopted in the French form *bibliographie* by other writers of the seventeenth century. The *Oxford English Dictionary* records the first occurrence of the word in England in the year 1678 when it still meant 'the writing of books': not until 1814 are examples attested for the word in its later usage. As employed by Dibdin and others in the early nine-teenth century, the word is given the meaning of 'the systematic des-cription and history of books, their authorship, printing, publication, editions, etc.' and is later used to signify the whole literature of a subject. In more recent times still, owing principally to the influence of the Bibliographical Society in England and other similar societies, the word conjures up in many people's minds the study of the science of books extrinsically as works of art or as objects of rarity, their contents being of lesser or no importance. This aspect of the subject may initially have been studied in the interests of textual criticism for the light that the typography of a book, its illustrations, the paper used in its manu-facture, the method in which it is bound, and the names of its former owners may throw on the history of the transmission of the text; later these topics come to be studied for their own sake. On the continent of Europe and elsewhere such studies are considered to belong to the realm of 'bibliophily' or 'love of books', a word which has never attained general currency in this country. In those languages where 'bibliophily' is of accepted usage the word 'bibliography' is restric-ted in meaning to systematic lists of books and to the techniques of compiling such lists. In the present work the word is mainly used in this restricted, continental, sense, but is extended to take in as well the study of organizations which produce the literature which constitutes the main object of our studies, such as universities, research institutes and the like, and furthermore of the establishments where this literature is housed, that is, libraries, and the methods used in storing it and making it available when required.

ARRANGEMENT OF THE WORK SYLLABUS

This work, then, is divided into three parts dealing respectively with
(i) institutions producing literature, (ii) the bibliographical apparatus
available for control and use of this literature, and (iii) libraries and
archives where the literature is stored together with the special problems affecting them.

We shall begin by studying the scope and content of Asian and
African studies, the history of these studies, and the institutions inside
and outside universities which are actively engaged in making contributions in our knowledge of the two continents. The study of the
history of Orientalism enables us to pinpoint those distinguished figures of the past whose explorations in the field and whose published
contributions to the subject have been of special significance, and whose
works are of historical importance, or even of practical current importance. A knowledge of the most recent history of these studies and of
their current organization is not only essential for recognizing which
institutions are issuing publications of value but also for discovering
the names of those persons who through their research are pushing
forward the frontiers of knowledge in these chosen fields. These persons are in possession of information on the most recent developments
which has not yet been recorded in print, or may help in the discovery
of facts hidden in such obscure places as to elude the most diligent
search.

The written record begins as a manuscript or, more usually nowadays, a typescript. A manuscript is a unique article, and however carefully it may be copied, each copy is bound to differ in some way from
all others. A typescript, or indeed a manuscript, may be made with
several carbon copies but the number of these is bound to be small,
seldom reaching double figures. A cyclostyled or mimeographed document may exist in several hundred identical copies, while the art of
printing makes it possible to produce many thousands of exact copies
of the original text.

Printed books fall into many categories according to the form which
they take and the purpose for which they are made. We may distinguish between the reference-book, at one extreme, to which one goes for
information on a specific point and dips into from time to time, and
the book which one reads from cover to cover, with an infinite number
of gradations in between. Or again, we may notice that some books are
written to provide amusement or recreation while others are intended

to instruct, whether as a learned monograph expounding new developments in a subject or as a manual or text-book intended as a convenient summary of what is known already to aid those who teach or learn. Again, there are books in the legal field, for instance, which are commentaries on other books and which in turn form the object of super-commentaries; these in their turn are glossed and super-glossed by other generations of scholars or practitioners until eventually the original substratum becomes so modified and built upon that little of the primeval text remains.

A fundamental difference exists between the book which, though it may go through several impressions and into many editions, yet retains much of its original character, and the periodical, a form of continuing publication for which no end is envisaged and which furnishes at regular or irregular intervals a means of keeping up to date with progress, including it may be, the current bibliography of a field or subject.

A knowledge of the principal bibliographies available for Asian and African studies is of fundamental importance for the librarian concerned with these areas. Retrospective bibliographies, which aim at listing works in existence at any given time, and which furnish information as to what has been published on a region or a subject in many different forms enables the librarian to examine his existing collections and to detect where the main gaps lie. They also furnish some of the sources which he may utilize in compiling his own bibliographies, whether for publication or for use within his library by staff or readers.

Current bibliographies will also receive considerable attention, as it is through the information that these provide that librarians are able to do this day-to-day selection of new books to be bought for additions to their collections.

Finally we shall turn our attention to the libraries throughout the world, but especially in Great Britain, the U.S.A. and the U.S.S.R., which pay special attention to materials relating to Asia and Africa and which have substantial collections relating to these areas. For as Humfrey Wanley, library-keeper to the Earls of Oxford in the early eighteenth century, declared, a good librarian knows as much about the contents of other people's libraries as he does about those of his own. And in these days, when it is manifestly impossible for any library concerned with anything more than the most limited of fields to be self-sufficient in meeting the demands likely to be made on it by its clientele, these words ring even more true. By observing the example of others we may improve our own methods and for this reason we shall examine the methods in use in the principal libraries in carrying out their various functions. These will include, for instance, ways in which they determine which books are to be collected, how these collections may best be organized for general use by means of catalogues and systems of classification, and schemes for inter-library cooperation in various activities.

PART ONE

PRODUCERS OF THE LITERATURE

B

[1]

Oriental, Asian and African Studies:
their scope and range

The province of the Orientalist, that is, one who pursues Oriental studies, is Asia, with, as will be explained later, certain extensions into other continents. The terms 'Oriental studies' and 'Asian studies' are, however, not exactly synonymous. Oriental studies are by popular conception concerned with philology, which entails the study of a language, written in an exotic non-Roman script, and its literature in its classical phase rather than in the modern. Departments or faculties of Oriental studies consisted until recently of those who concentrated on the language and literature of an Asian people, with some attention paid to the study of religion, law (in so far as that was of the canon rather than the civil kind) and history. Only in quite recent times have other subjects been added to the curricula of these departments. For practical purposes we may therefore distinguish between the Orientalist as one who begins his studies by learning an Asian language, and who later, it may be, turns his attention to the study of some other aspect of the classical culture of an Asian people, and the student of Asia (for whom a word needs to be coined, such as Asianist or Asiologist), who begins his career with a grounding in one of the traditional university disciplines, and who later applies himself to the study of an Asian region or country, learning the appropriate language solely in order to acquire a tool to be used in the furtherance of his studies.

For the Africanist, a comparatively recent arrival on the scene, it is not necessary to make a similar distinction. It should, however, be pointed out, that the northern, and Saharan, parts of Africa have long been regarded as falling within the province of the Orientalist. The reason for this is that at a very remote period much of Western Asia was subject to the authority of an African power (Egypt), and that in medieval times these regions formed part of a huge empire stemming from Western Asia and based on Islam.

THE MAJOR REGIONS AND COUNTRIES OF ASIA

As Asia is not a political unit, its geographical limits are not defined to everyone's satisfaction. The boundary with Europe 'is commonly accepted as following the crest of the Urals . . . and then the Ural river to the Caspian, finally along a line from the Caspian to the Black Sea which some would identify with the crest of the Caucasus, others would place further south'.[1] The Caucasus, Transcaucasia and to a lesser extent the Crimean peninsula, would by most Orientalists be regarded as falling within their sphere, but the U.S.S.R. officially regards some of these areas as constituting parts of Europe.

For the purposes of the present bibliographical study we may divide the continent of Asia into five regions, though we would not gain universal acceptance for the terms used to name these regions, nor for their constituent countries. These we propose to call the Near and Middle East, South Asia, South-East Asia, the Far East and Soviet Asia

THE NEAR AND MIDDLE EAST

This region comprises those countries where Islam is the predominant religion and those in which the people are Arabic-speaking and of Arab stock, with the non-Arab Islamic countries Persia (Iran), Afghanistan and Turkey, and Israel and Cyprus. The Arab countries have great affinities with the Arabic-speaking countries of North Africa, viz. Egypt, Sudan, Libya, Tunisia, Algeria and Morocco which are often considered to be intrinsically part of the Near and Middle East rather than of Africa. The Arabic-speaking countries, sometimes known collectively as 'Arab–Asia' are:

(i) Arabia, or the Arabian peninsula, comprising Saudi Arabia, Yemen, the Federation of South Arabia, Muscat and Oman, the Trucial sheikhdoms, Bahrain and Kuwait. Saudi Arabia is a kingdom, formed by the late 'Abd al-'Aziz ibn 'Abd al-Rahman al-Faisal Al Sa'ud in 1926. It consists of the two former territories of Hejaz and Nejd: within its borders are situated the two Holy Places of Islam, Mecca and Medina.

Yemen was ruled by an Imam until 1962, when a revolutionary government was set up by army officers, who deposed the son of the Imam and proclaimed a republic. For a brief period from 1958 to 1961 the Yemen was federated with the United Arab Republic.

The Federation of South Arabia, a dependent territory in member-

---

[1] L. D. Stamp, *Asia, a regional and economic geography*, 9th ed. (1957), p. 3.

ship of the British Commonwealth, was formed out of the State (earlier, Colony) of Aden, and several sultanates and sheikhdoms of the former Western and Eastern Aden Protectorates. The constituent states of the Federation, in order of accession to it, are Audhali, Fadhli, Lower Yafa and Upper Aulaqi (foundation members), Lahej, Lower Aulaqi, Dathina, Aden, Wahidi, Haushabi and Shaib.

The Persian Gulf states comprise Bahrain, Qatar and the seven Trucial states of Abu Dhabi, Dubai, Sharjah and Kalba, Ajman, Umm al Qaiwain, Ras al Khaimah and Fujairah. All of these are in special treaty relation with Great Britain, which has undertaken responsibility for their foreign relations.

Kuwait, Muscat and Oman are independent states, the former being ruled by a Sheikh, the latter by a Sultan.

(ii) The remaining Arab countries in the Near and Middle East (sometimes known as the Fertile Crescent) are Iraq, Jordan, Syria, Lebanon, and the former Palestine.

The former Kingdom of Iraq became a republic as a result of the revolution of 14 July, 1958. Up to the end of the First World War the country was known as Mesopotamia. It is the home of one of the world's earliest civilizations, the Sumerian and Assyro–Babylonian Empire, based on the twin rivers Tigris and Euphrates.

Jordan was formerly known as Transjordan. It was recognized by Great Britain as a sovereign independent state in 1946. The part of Palestine remaining to the Arabs under the armistice with Israel of 3 April, 1949, including part of Jerusalem, was formally incorporated in Jordan in 1950.

Syria is an independent republic which from 1958 to 1961 was united with Egypt in the United Arab Republic.

Lebanon was proclaimed an independent republic in 1941 after having been, like Syria, since the First World War, a French mandated territory under the League of Nations.

(iii) Non-Arab states. The remaining countries of the Near and Middle East, and the languages other than Arabic spoken in them are:

Israel (Hebrew). Formerly Palestine, under British mandate, Israel was proclaimed an independent sovereign republic in 1948.

Turkey (Turkish) is a sovereign independent republic, with territories in Asia (Anadolu or Anatalia) and Europe (Trakya or Turkish Thrace). It formerly possessed an empire consisting of most of the Near and Middle East, North Africa except Morocco, and large areas in the Balkans.

Cyprus (Greek and Turkish) has been an independent republic since 1960, within the British Commonwealth. See:

Directory of the Republic of Cyprus, 1962–63, including trade index and biographical section. London: Diplomatic Press and Publishing Co.; *Cyprus: a handbook on the island of Aphrodite.* Nicosia, 1964.

Iran or Persia (Persian), is a kingdom ruled by a Shah. Some territories which once belonged to Iran are now incorporated in the U.S.S.R.

Afghanistan (Pashto and Persian) is a kingdom.

These two last-named countries, Iran and Afghanistan, may be said to constitute the 'Middle' as distinct from the 'Near' East, but some would attach Afghanistan to the region next to be described. It is preferred to place Afghanistan in this section because it, with Iran, constitutes the great Iranian-speaking area of the Indo-Iranian language group. See:

The Middle East and North Africa (Europa Publications). (Formerly *The Middle East,*) 1948.

SOUTH ASIA

The term South Asia is of comparatively modern origin, used to cover the countries of the Indo-Pakistani sub-continent, with Ceylon, the Maldive Islands, Nepal, Bhutan and Sikkim.

India is a sovereign democratic republic within the British Commonwealth, a union of sixteen states and ten union territories. The states are Andhra Pradesh, Assam, Bihar, Gujarat, Jammu and Kashmir, Kerala, Madhya Pradesh, Madras, Maharashtra, Mysore, Nagaland, Orissa, Punjab, Rajasthan, Uttar Pradesh and West Bengal. The centrally-administered (union) territories comprise the Andaman and Nicobar Islands; Dadra and Nagar Haveli (formerly Portuguese territories, part of Damão), Delhi (the federal capital), Goa, Diu and Daman (these three also formerly Portuguese), Himachal Pradesh, the Laccadive, Minicoy and Amindivi Islands (nineteen islands lying off the Malabar coast of Madras), Manipur, Pondicherry (formerly the chief French settlement in India, the others being Karikal, Mahé and Yanaon), and Tripura. The North-East Frontier Agency is administered by the Governor of Assam on behalf of the Central Government.

Sikkim is a protectorate of the Government of India. See:

The Times of India directory and yearbook (including *Who's Who*).

Bombay, etc., London, 1954–55.

Bhutan is under the rule of a Maharaja. It accepts guidance as to its external affairs from the Government of India.

Nepal is an independent kingdom in the Himalayas.

Pakistan is an Islamic republic in membership of the British Commonwealth, and consists of the following former territories of British India: Baluchistan, East Bengal, North-West Frontier, West Punjab, and Sind; and those states which acceded to Pakistan on partition in 1947. It occupies between one-third and one-half of Kashmir, known as Azad Kashmir. The country is divided into the provinces of East Pakistan (capital, Dacca) and West Pakistan (capital, Lahore) with no connection between them by land. See:

West Pakistan yearbook. Directorate of Publications, Research and Films, Information Department, West Pakistan, Lahore, 1956–

Ceylon has the status of an independent nation within the British Commonwealth. The whole island was British territory from 1815 to 1948, the Coastal settlements since 1796. It was formerly under Portuguese, and then Dutch hegemony. See:

Ceylon yearbook, 1959. Department of Census and Statistics, Colombo.

The Maldive Islands are a group of some 2,000 coral islands 400 miles south-west of Ceylon, which have been under British protection since 1887, but which enjoy complete independence in their internal affairs. The inhabitants adhere to Islam.

SOUTH-EAST ASIA

The third of our regions, consists of a mainland sometimes known as the Indo-Chinese peninsula, which comprises the countries of Burma, Malaya, Thailand (Siam), Laos, Cambodia, North and South Vietnam, and the islands of the East Indian Archipelago, some of which form part of the territory of Malaysia, the remainder belonging to Indonesia and the Philippines. The whole area is sometimes regarded as forming part of the Far East.

Burma has been a sovereign independent republic since 1948, having formerly been part of the British Empire. It was at one time administered as a State of British India. It comprises the former British territories of Upper and Lower Burma, the Shan, Kachin, Karen and Kayah states and the Special Division of the Chins.

On 16 September, 1963, the Federation of Malaysia was inaugurated comprising the eleven states of Malaya (Johore, Kedah, Kelantan, Malacca, Negri Sembilan, Pahang, Penang, Perak, Perlis, Selangor, Trengganu); the Borneo states (Sabah, formerly British North Borneo, Sarawak); the State of Singapore. Brunei elected to remain outside the Federation. See:

Malaysian yearbook, 1963–64. (*The Malaya Mail*, Kuala Lumpur.)

Malaya had as its political divisions from 1 February, 1948 to 16 September, 1963 the nine states of Perak, Selangor, Negri Sembilan, Pahang, Johore, Kedah, Perlis, Kelantan and Trengganu, and the two British settlements of Penang and Malacca, with a federal capital at Kuala Lumpur. Singapore became a separate colony in 1941 and Labuan was added to North Borneo. Up to 1941 the divisions had been:

(*a*) The Straits Settlements, a British Crown Colony (Singapore, Penang, Province Wellesley, Malacca, Cocos Islands, Christmas Island, Labuan). The Cocos Islands were transferred to Australia in 1955.

(*b*) The Federated Malay States of Perak, Selangor, Negri Sembilan and Pahang.

(*c*) The Unfederated Malay States of Johore, Kedah, Perlis, Kelantan and Trengganu.

British Borneo formerly consisted of (1) the Colony of North Borneo, (2) the Protected State of Brunei, and (3) the Colony of Sarawak.

Indonesia, a sovereign independent republic, consists of the islands of Sumatra, Java and Madura, Nusa Tenggara (lesser Sundas), Maluku (Moluccas), Sulawesi (Celebes), Kalimantan (Borneo), West Irian (the western half of New Guinea), and some 3,000 smaller islands and islets. It is divided into seventeen provinces of which three are in the island of Java (West, Central and East), five in Sumatra (Atjeh, Riau, Djambi, North and South), three in Borneo, two in Celebes, two in the Lesser Sunda Islands (which include Bali, Lombok, Soembawa, Soemba, Flores and Timor), Maluku (the Moluccas or Spice Islands), and Irian (formerly Netherlands New Guinea).

The country was formerly a Dutch colonial possession (the Dutch East Indies): it gained independence in 1945.

The eastern portion of the island of Timor has been a Portuguese possession since 1586. Portuguese Timor includes also the territory of

Ambeno and the neighbouring islands of Pulo Cambing and Pulo Jako.

The Philippines consist of 7,107 islands and islets, only 462 of which are of one square mile or over in area. The largest islands are Luzon, Mindanao, Samar, Negros, Palwan, Panay, Mindoro, Leyte, Cebu, Bohol and Masbate. The republic came into existence in 1946, the islands having previously been a Spanish and later, a U.S.A. territory. The official language of the republic is Tagalog, the principal one of some seventy Malayo–Polynesian languages spoken in the islands.

Thailand, formerly known as Siam, is an independent kingdom: it is the only territory in South-East Asia which has never been subjected to a foreign colonial dominion. (It became an ally of Japan in December, 1941, and thus avoided being overrun by that power.)

France's former colonial empire in Indo-China until the Second World War consisted of the Colony of Cochin-China and the Protectorates of Annam, Tongking, Cambodia and Laos. The successor states are Cambodia and Laos, which have become independent kingdoms, North and South Vietnam, which are independent republics.

THE FAR EAST

The Far East region comprises 'Greater China', i.e. the People's Republic of China, the Republic of China (Taiwan or Formosa), Mongolia, Tibet, with the small British dependency of Hong Kong and the Portuguese overseas territory of Macao; Japan; Korea (divided as is Vietnam into a Northern Communist state and a Southern Republic).

The People's Republic of China (Mainland China) is stated to be composed of twenty-two provinces (including Taiwan), five autonomous regions of nationalities, namely Inner Mongolia, Sinkiang-Uighur, Kwangsi-Chuang, Ningsia-Hui, Tibet, and the two municipalities of Peking and Shanghai. It came under the control of the present Communist régime in 1949. Manchuria no longer exists as an administrative unit. Inner Mongolia was constituted an autonomous region in 1947. Tibet was occupied by the Chinese People's Liberation Army in October, 1950.

Taiwan (Formosa) is controlled by the remnants of the former Nationalist Government under Chiang Kai-shek. Formally incorporated into China in 1683, it was a Japanese possession from 1895 until the end of the Second World War. The area includes also the Pescadores (Penghu Islands), Kinmen (Quemoy) and Matsu. See:

China yearbook. (Formerly *The China handbook*), 1957–58. China Publishing Co., Taipei.

The Mongolian People's Republic, proclaimed in 1924, was, under the name of Outer Mongolia, a Chinese province from 1686 to 1911; since then it has been an autonomous state under Russian protection from 1912 to 1919, and a Chinese province again from 1919 to 1921.

Japan consists of the four main islands of Honshū, Kyūshyū, Hokkaidō and Shikoku. It is ruled by an Emperor. The Ryukyu Islands which lie between Kyūshyū and Formosa and were formerly part of the Japanese Empire were placed under United States control by the Japanese peace treaty of 1945. The most important of the islands is Okinawa. Other Pacific Islands under U.S. control in the area are the Daito Islands, the Bonin Islands, the Volcano Islands, and the island of Pareca Vela.

Korea was ruled by the Yi dynasty from 1392 to 1910, when it was formally annexed by Japan, having been virtually a protectorate of that country since the Russo–Japanese war of 1904–5. On the conclusion of the war against Japan in 1945, the country was divided at the 38th parallel into Russian and American spheres of influence, which later crystallized out into the Korean Republic and the Democratic People's Republic of Korea (South and North Korea).

SOVIET ASIA

'The U.S.S.R., also known as the Soviet Union, includes the eastern half of Europe and about one-third of the continent of Asia, with its entire northern portion (Siberia), the western section of Central Asia, and part of the Middle East in the region of the Caucasus.'[1]

The main administrative-territorial divisions of the U.S.S.R. are the union republics, sixteen in number. The difficulty of deciding precisely where the border of Asia lies has already been alluded to but for our purposes the following union republics may be regarded as Asian: Azerbaijani, Georgian, Armenian, Kazakh, Kirghiz, Uzbek, Tadzhik, Turkoman. Of these the first three lie in the Caucasus region, the remainder in Central Asia.

[1] T. Shabad, *Geography of the U.S.S.R.; a regional survey*, 1951, p. 3.

The Asian union republics, however, do not between them ad-
minister the whole Asian territory of the U.S.S.R. The remaining
areas, designated variously as 'Autonomous SSR, National or Autonomous Oblast or Kray, or simply Oblast or Kray, form part of the Russian
SFSR, the largest of the union republics. Among these areas may be
mentioned the regions of Eastern and Western Siberia, and the Far
East.'[1]

To make matters even more complicated some peoples of Asian
(Turkish, Iranian or Caucasian) stock inhabit regions of the Russian
SFSR in Europe. Such are the Chuvash and Tatar peoples of Turkish
stock living in the Middle Volga region, the peoples of Adyge, Cher-
kess, Kabardinian, North Ossetian and Daghestan autonomous divisions in the Northern Caucasus, and the Bashkirs (also Turks) of the
Urals.

According to this reckoning the number of territories in Asia is
fifty-two, calculated as follows:

Near and Middle East (excluding Egypt and North Africa and
counting the Trucial states as seven): 23.
Saudi Arabia, Yemen, Federation of South Arabia, Kuwait, Muscat
and Oman, Bahrain, Qatar, Trucial states (7), Iraq, Jordan, Syria,
Lebanon, Israel, Turkey, Cyprus, Iran, Afghanistan.
South Asia: 7.
India, Pakistan, Ceylon, the Maldives, Nepal, Bhutan, Sikkim.
South-East Asia: 12.
Burma, Malaysia, Brunei, Thailand, Laos, Cambodia, North Viet-
nam, South Vietnam, Indonesia, Philippines, Cocos Islands, Portu-
guese Timor.
Far East: 9.
China, Taiwan, Hong Kong, Macao, Japan, Ryukyu Islands, North
Korea, South Korea, Mongolia.
Soviet Asia: 1.

OCEANIA

A natural extension of Oriental studies is into the enormous area known
as Oceania, which is a convenient name to use for the islands and island
groups of the Pacific other than those contained in the East Indian
Archipelago, and forming part of the territories of Malaysia, Indonesia
and the Philippines. The Pacific Islands are generally divided into the

[1] Details in Shabad, *op. cit.*, pp. 503–4.

three groups Melanesia, Micronesia and Polynesia, these appelations being compounded of Greek words meaning 'Black islands', 'Small islands' and 'Many islands' respectively.

Politically speaking, the islands and their groups are administered at present as territories of the British Commonwealth, the United States, the French Community and the Republic of Indonesia (West Irian). Some were formerly German colonies or protectorates.

Western Samoa is an independent sovereign state within the British Commonwealth: Fiji, Tonga, and the territories administered by the West Pacific High Commission are 'dependent territories'. Fiji is a group of 322 islands (of which about 106 are inhabited); the largest of the islands is Viti Levu, next in size Vanua Levu. Rotuma was added to the colony in 1881. Tonga, a state under British protection which is ruled by a queen (H.M. Salote Tupou) consists of some 150 islands divided into the groups Vava'u, Ha'apai, Kotu, Nomuka, Otu Tolu and Tongatapu. The West Pacific Islands comprise the Gilbert and Ellice Islands Colony, British Solomon Islands Protectorate, and the New Hebrides Condominium, jointly held with France. The Australian Commonwealth administers the territories of Papua and New Guinea (in which there is also an Indonesian province, West Irian) and Nauru Island. Island territories coming within the jurisdiction of New Zealand are the Cook Islands, Niue Island and the Tokelau Islands.

The United States territories in Oceania include Hawaii, a state admitted to the Union in 1959, which comprises the Hawaiian Islands, formerly known as the Sandwich Islands. Among the 'outlying territories' of the United States are Guam and American Samoa. The U.S. also administers as a Trust Territory the islands forming part Micronesia, which were formerly under Japanese mandate and before that a German colony. The Trust Territory consists of the six administrative districts of Truk, Ponape, the Marshall Islands, Palau, Mariana Islands and Yap.

The French overseas territories in the region, formerly known as 'French settlements in Oceania', are French Polynesia (including Tahiti) and New Caledonia and dependencies.

AFRICA

The continent of Africa (and the adjacent islands and island groups of Madagascar, Mauritius, Seychelles, Réunion) may for our purposes be conveniently divided into six geographical-political regions:

North: Algeria, Libya, Morocco, Tunisia, Egypt.

North-East: Ethiopia, Somali Republic, French Somaliland, Sudan.

East: Kenya, Tanzania (formerly Tanganyika and Zanzibar), Uganda.

Central: Malawi (formerly Nyasaland), Zambia (formerly Northern Rhodesia), Rhodesia, Burundi, Rwanda, Congo (Léopoldville), and the former French Equatorial Africa territories of Central African Republic, Congo (Brazzaville), Chad and Gabon.

West: Gambia, Ghana, Liberia, Nigeria, St Helena, Sierra Leone, Cameroun, Dahomey, Guinea, Ivory Coast, Togo, Upper Volta, Mali, Mauritania, Niger and Senegal; the Portuguese territories Cape Verde Islands, Portuguese Guinea and São Tome e Principe; and the Spanish territories Ifni, Spanish Sahara and Spanish Guinea.

South: The High Commission territories (Basutoland, Bechuanaland, Swaziland), South-West Africa, the Republic of South Africa, the Portuguese territories Angola and Mozambique, and the islands of Madagascar, Mauritius, Seychelles, Réunion and the Comoro Archipelago.

Many of these fifty-six regions have been at some time administered by a foreign colonial power. Some remain so to this day. For the bibliography of the regions, therefore, it is necessary to have regard to that of the colonizing countries as follows:

British Commonwealth: East Africa (Kenya, Uganda, Tanzania, Sudan), West Africa (Gambia, Ghana, Nigeria, St Helena, Sierra Leone), Southern Africa (the Union, the High Commission territories, South-West Africa), Central Africa (Rhodesia and Nyasaland), Egypt, Mauritius, Seychelles.

France: West Africa and Equatorial Africa (territories listed above under *West* and *Central*), Madagascar, Réunion, French Somaliland, the Comoro Archipelago.

Portugal: Angola, Cape Verde Islands, Portuguese Guinea, São Tome e Principe, Mozambique.

Spain: Ifni, Spanish Sahara, Spanish Guinea, Morocco.

Belgium: Congo, Ruanda-Urundi.

Italy: Libya, Somalia, Ethiopia.

Germany: East, West and South-West Africa.

THE REALM OF THE ORIENTALIST

Oriental studies have, it has been said, extensions outside Asia. For instance, some of the territory of the U.S.S.R. which lies outside Asia is inhabited by peoples whose culture is the concern of the Orientalist. These include the Chuvash and Tatars in the Middle Volga region, Kabardinians, Adyge, Ossetians, Daghestanis in the Northern Caucasus, and Bashkirs in the Urals. Also in the Urals live groups of peoples who straddle the supposed borderline between Asia and Europe. These peoples speak languages such as Mordvin, Cheremiss, Votyak, Permian, Samoyedic, which are placed in the Uralian group of the Ural–Altaic family, a family which, like the Indo-European, includes Asian as well as European languages among its members.

Hebrew studies may extend outside Asia to any place in the diaspora where Jews settled and cultivated a literature in their sacred language. So, too, with Arabic studies: a quite extensive literature in their own language was nurtured by Syrian and Libyan immigrants in the countries of their adoption in North and South America.

Part of Turkish territory is inside Europe. The Ottoman Empire in Europe formerly extended over the whole of the Balkans and into Hungary and Austria and the study of these former possessions properly comes within the province of the Orientalist.

But the greatest extension outside Asia is occasioned by the requirements of the study of Islamic history in all its phases and components. In the very early years after the *hijra* Muslim conquests imposed Islamic hegemony over the whole of the North African littoral, whence it spread to other parts of Africa and across the Straits of Gibraltar into Spain and Portugal, and even across the Pyrenees into Southern France. In these countries the last remnants of the Muslim faith and the civilization it engendered were not finally expunged until 1492. Examples of Islamic influence on the architecture of those regions may still be seen today, and place-names with Arabic components occur over the whole of the Iberian peninsula.

Outside the realm of Oriental studies, though connected with Asia, are Biblical studies (except in so far as these are concerned with the text of the Old Testament in the original languages, for Hebrew and Aramaic have long been studied in Oriental departments), and Jewish studies concerned with communities outside Asia and Africa where materials outside Hebrew and other Oriental languages are used. Byzantine studies, too, may be regarded as a branch of Classical studies which relies on materials written in Greek and are hence outside the Orientalist's province, even though the city of Byzantium was situated where now lies Istanbul, in Asia Minor.

THE CONTENT OF ORIENTAL STUDIES

LANGUAGES

We have seen that the Orientalist is primarily a philologian who studies one or more of the languages of Asia and later turns his attention to the literature written in that language and possibly to the religion, law, art and history of the peoples who speak it. What are the principal languages of Asia with which he will be concerned? We attempt, in the next few paragraphs, a survey of the linguistic position in each of our Asian regions, giving the names of the main languages and the families to which they are generally ascribed.

In the Near and Middle East the Semitic family of languages holds sway. The oldest languages in the group are the Assyrian and Babylonian, written in cuneiform characters engraved on hard materials or imprinted into soft clay, and the earliest relatives of Hebrew and Aramaic, such as Canaanite, Moabite, Ugaritic, Nabatean, etc. Hebrew has three main phases, a Classical or Biblical one, the Rabbinical one used in the Mishna and other works of medieval Judaism, and the modern living language currently spoken throughout the State of Israel. Aramaic has many dialects: one of the most important is Syriac, in which an extensive Christian literature exists. Other languages in the Semitic family are Arabic, spoken all over the Fertile Crescent, the Arabian peninsula, and North Africa, and the Ethiopian languages, consisting of the ancient and sacred language of the Ethiopic Church, Geez or Ethiopic, and the modern derivatives, the spoken languages Amharic, Tigre, Tigrinya and others.

Modern Ottoman Turkish belongs to a group known as the Turkic or Turco-Tatar languages, other representatives of which are spoken in the U.S.S.R. By some scholars the Turkic languages are assigned to the Altaic family of languages which contains in addition Mongolian and Tungusic or Manchu.

Persian and Pashto with certain lesser-known languages of Central Asia constitute the Iranian side of the Indo-Iranian group of the widespread Indo-European family. Modern Persian employs the Arabic alphabet, to which certain derived letters were added to represent sounds not present in the Semitic languages: earlier forms of Persian are the various Middle Iranian languages, which include the language current at the time of the Muslim Conquest. This language employs a script based, like so many Oriental ones, on the Aramaic. The earliest form of Persian, which employed cuneiform characters, survives, together with Elamite and Assyrian versions of the same inscription, in the rock-hewn trilingual inscription at Behistun, and elsewhere.

The most widely-spread linguistic families of South Asia are the Indo-European in its Indo-Aryan branch and the Dravidian. Indo-Aryan languages are spoken all over Pakistan and Northern India as well as in Ceylon, Nepal, Bhutan and Sikkim. Fourteen of these languages are recognized as official literary languages in the Indian Constitution, viz. Assamese, Bengali, Gujarati, Hindi, Kannada (Canarese), Kashmiri, Malayalam, Marathi, Oriya, Punjabi, Sanskrit, Tamil, Telugu, Urdu.

Sanskrit with its older derivatives Pali and Prakrit may be regarded as the parent of all the modern Indo-Aryan vernaculars.

The best-known representatives of the Dravidian languages, which apart from a small pocket in Baluchistan are restricted to Southern India, are Tamil, Telugu, Kannada or Canarese, and Malayalam (not to be confused with Malay). Tamil has been carried by migrant populations into Ceylon and Malaysia. Each of these languages has its own script developed independently of the others from a common source.

Other languages of India of lesser importance are the Munda group, allied to the Mon–Khmer languages of South-East Asia, and Burushaski, which has no living relative.

South-East Asia is a linguistic complex where at least four language families mingle. One of these is the Sino–Tibetan group of the Indo-Chinese language family, in which Tibetan, Burmese, Chinese and Thai are associated, though the connections between them are extremely remote and the scripts used by them vastly dissimilar, so that a knowledge of one of the languages will be of little help in learning another. Other groups in the area are the Mon–Khmer, with the Mon language of Burma, Khmer or Cambodian and Lao as its most important representative, and the Vietnamese, formerly known as Annamese or Annamite, which formerly used Chinese characters for its writing. Since the seventeenth century, however, Vietnamese has used the Roman alphabet with a generous provision of diacritical marks serving among other things to distinguish tone, a common feature of certain Asian and African languages

Malay and Indonesian, both of which have now adopted Roman characters for writing (though the use of Arabic or 'Jawi' characters lingers on in Malaya), belong to the Indonesian group (which also includes a multitude of other languages spoken in Indonesia and the Philippine languages) of the Malayo–Polynesian family, a multi-lingual group distributed over most areas in the East Indian Archipelago as well as in Melanesia, Micronesia, Polynesia and Madagascar.

The principal languages of the Far East are Chinese with its many, and often mutually unintelligible, dialectal forms, and Japanese and Korean, none of which has any living relative. The Chinese script, derived from an ancient pictographic system of writing, has been adapted for the other two languages. This wonderful invention makes it possible for speakers of the many different Chinese dialects to recognize anything written in one of the other dialects without necessarily knowing how to pronounce or understand it when spoken.

Mongolian and Tungusic, of which the most important representative is Manchu, and which do not make use of Chinese characters, are related, and as has been said, are held by some to be connected with the Turkic languages in the Altaic group.

In Asiatic Russia there live many peoples speaking languages of Turkic and Iranian stock. For many of these an alphabet based on Cyrillic characters has been devised. In the Caucasus, Armenian or Ossetic are representatives of the Indo-European family, while Georgian is the best-known representative of the Caucasian family of languages. Both Armenian and Georgian have their own distinctive scripts. See:

Les langues du monde, par un groupe de linguistes sous la direction de A. Meillet et M. Cohen. Nouv. éd. Paris, 1952.

W. K. Matthews: *Languages of the U.S.S.R.*, 1951.

See also:

Languages of the world, C. F. and F. M. Voegelin. A publication of Archives of languages of the world, Anthropology Department, Indiana University. Published in *Anthropological linguistics*, vol. 6, no. 3 (1964).

African languages are of great diversity. In addition to the fairly cohesive and clear-cut groups of the Bantu languages (covering large tracts of the sub-Saharan region of the continent), the Semitic and Cushitic languages of Ethiopia, the Berber languages of the Northern territories, and the Bushman and Hottentot groups of Southern Africa, there are numerous languages spoken in the East, North-East and West

c

whose generic relationships have not yet been worked out to the satisfaction of all. The terms 'Hamitic', 'Nilotic', 'Nilo-Hamitic' and 'Sudanic' formerly used in the classification of these languages, have either been dropped entirely or are gradually going out of use. See:

Handbook of African languages, published by the International African Institute, 1952–60.

RELIGIONS

The principal religions of the Near and Middle East are Judaism, Christianity and Islam, the three great monotheistic religions of the world, which through missionary activity have become widely dispersed also in other continents. For Judaism, Hebrew and Aramaic are the sacred languages. Christianity, though more usually associated with continents other than Asia, has yet important communities of adherents who have developed extensive literatures of mainly theological or philosophical content in Arabic, Syriac, Coptic (the Egyptian Christians), Ethiopic, Armenian and Georgian. The languages of Islam are, in the first place Arabic, in which the holy book of Islam, the Koran, is written, Persian, Turkish and Pashto, and, outside the Near and Middle Eastern region, Urdu, Malay and Indonesian. Islam is practised as well by many millions of adherents in South Asia, South-East Asia, the Far East and Asiatic Russia.

In the non-Islamic areas of India, Hinduism in its many divergent manifestations is the predominant religion. Though the Buddha first saw the light of day in that country the religion founded by him is now almost unrepresented in his country, but is practised by millions of his followers in Ceylon, Nepal, Burma, Thailand, Cambodia, Laos, Vietnam, as well as in the Far East, where it exists side by side with Confucianism (confined to China) and Shintoism (confined to Japan). See:

The concise encyclopaedia of living faiths, edited by R. C. Zaehner, 1959.

A bibliographical essay, referring to 120 books (mostly American) which are listed at the end of the book, is afforded by:

Asian religions; an introduction to the study of Hinduism, Buddhism, Islam, Confucianism, and Taoism. By Kenneth W. Morgan. A publication of the American Historical Association's Service Center for Teachers of History. Macmillan: New York, London (1964).

HISTORY

No attempt will be made to sum up the whole course of Asian history[1] in these few following paragraphs: a mere mention will be made of the principal empires which dominated large tracts of this continent before the coming of the modern nationalistic age.

The earliest civilizations sprung up in the Ancient Near East about the beginning of the third millenium B.C. These were based on great rivers, the Nile in Egypt, the Tigris and Euphrates in Mesopotamia, and the Indus in the Indo-Pakistani sub-continent. After the decay of these civilizations had set in, the Hittites in Asia Minor, the Hebrews in the Near East, the Achaemenids in Persia dominated the scene until the conquests of Alexander the Great brought Hellenic culture as far as Persia and Northern India. The successor empires of the Seleucids in Iran and the Ptolemies in Egypt endured until each in its turn was over-whelmed by the Romans, whose empire in the Near East survived until it was finally overwhelmed by the vast outpourings from the Arabian peninsula of the followers of Muhammad.

The forces emitted by Islam speedily overran the whole of the Fertile Crescent, Egypt and North Africa. In 711 Spain was invaded and the furthest limit in Western Europe north of the Pyrenees was reached by 732. Persia and Central Asia came under Islam's sway, as did most of Northern India, and later still the Malayan peninsula and the islands which now constitute Indonesia. The outposts of Muslim civilization extended in fact to China, where many millions of those who profess Islam still live in the province of Sinkiang.

During the period of the Islamic Empire the Mongols, originating in the Far East, subdued practically the whole of Islamic Asia and made their presence felt even in Southern Russia and Eastern Europe. From the same area came the Seljuks, followed by the Ottoman Turks who caused the destruction of the Byzantine Empire by their conquest of Constantinople in 1453 and later built up a vast empire in the Balkans, Eastern Europe, the Near and Middle East and North Africa.

The history of European exploration and colonization in Asia and Africa begins with the Portuguese whose great period of expansion be-gan in the fifteenth century with the travels of Henry the Navigator.

---

[1] For this one may turn to the good succinct account provided by the distin-guished French historian, René Grousset, who died in 1954. His *Histoire de l'Asie* was first published in the series 'Que sais-je' in 1941: an English translation, *A History of Asia*, by Douglas Scott, was published in the series 'Walker Sun Books' at New York in 1963.

In the seventeenth century the Dutch ousted the Portuguese from the East Indies and laid the foundations of their empire in that region which lasted until the end of the Second World War. Also in the first year of the seventeenth century the East India Company received its charter from Queen Elizabeth I permitting it to trade to India, and this may be regarded as the beginning of British influence in South Asia, which later developed into a vast empire which included India, Ceylon, Burma, Malaya, parts of Borneo, and Hong Kong on the Chinese mainland.

The French held possessions in India until 1954, as did the Portuguese, whose possessions were taken over by the Indian Government in 1961. Denmark also owned colonies in India until 1899 when she sold her possessions to Great Britain.

The main French sphere of influence was, however, in Indo-China, where they established the Colony of Cochin-China and the Protectorates of Annam, Tongking, Cambodia and Laos.

Germany was a colonial power until she lost her overseas possessions at the end of the First World War. Belgium and Italy have held colonies in Africa, and Spain continues to do so. See:

Handbook of Oriental history . . ., edited by C. H. Philips, 1951.

OTHER SUBJECTS

The principal religions developed systems of law based on their sacred works, by which all of their adherents were bound: thus, Orientalists have to study Jewish law based on the Bible and Talmud, Islamic law based on the Koran and Hadith, Hindu law with its books derived from Vedic principles, Buddhist law, and the legal systems of the Far East.

So, too, does art transcend national boundaries and has always been promoted and fostered by religion, so that we study this subject in its Jewish, Oriental Christian, Muslim, Hindu, Buddhist and Far Eastern manifestations.

[2]

History of Oriental Studies

GENERAL

In his *A literary history of Persia*,[1] vol. 1, E. G. Browne gives a brief sketch of the development of Oriental (or rather Near and Middle Eastern) studies in Europe. The first translations from Arabic into European languages were made about the beginning of the twelfth century by Jews and Moors converted to Christianity. These were soon followed by native Christians such as Gerard of Cremona (born A.D. 1114), Albertus Magnus (born A.D. 1193) and Michael Scot, who studied Arabic at Toledo in A.D. 1217. In the thirteenth century Roger Bacon and Raymond Lull also called attention to the importance, for philosophical and scientific purposes, of a study of Oriental languages.

Pope Clement V in 1311–12 ordained that professorships of Hebrew, Chaldean (i.e. Aramaic) and Arabic should be established at the universities of Rome, Paris, Bologna, Oxford and Salamanca, for the purpose of making Latin translations and training pupils to speak these languages for missionary activities. Little, however, was done until the foundation of the Collège de France by Francis V in 1530. Armegand of Montpellier had in 1274 translated portions of the works of Avicenna and Averroes into Latin, but the first French Orientalist is declared by Browne, following Dugat, to have been Guillaume Postel, who among his other achievements was the first to cut a set of Arabic types.

In 1587 Henry III founded an Arabic chair at the Collège de France. (A Hebrew chair had been established here at the time of the college's foundation in 1530.) Chairs in Chinese and Sanskrit followed in 1814. A few years later Savary de Brèves brought to Paris excellent founts, engraved in the East, of types in Arabic, Syriac, Persian, Armenian and Ethiopic characters which with his collections of Arabic, Turkish,

---

[1] 1929 reprint, pp. 39 seq.

Persian and Syriac MSS. passed after his death into the possession of the Imprimerie Royale.

The full development of Oriental studies in Europe may, however, be said to date from the seventeenth century, since when progress has been steady and continuous. In that century Arabic chairs were founded at Cambridge, by Sir Thomas Adams in 1632, and at Oxford some four years later by Archbishop Laud. Cambridge's first professor was Abraham Wheelock, who also performed the functions of University Librarian. It is interesting to note that among his pupils was Thomas Hyde, who later became Professor of both the Hebrew and the Arabic languages, and also occupied the office of Librarian of the Bodleian.

Browne's sketch is based to a very large extent on the work of Dugat:

Histoire des orientalistes de l'Europe de XIIe au XIXe siècle, précédée d' une esquisse historique des études orientales, par Gustave Dugat, 2 vols. Paris, 1868, 1870.

Only two volumes were ever published of this work, which Dugat had intended to follow up with a long introduction on 'Orientalisme' and a kind of Oriental encyclopaedia. The two volumes are prefaced by a sketch of the history of Oriental studies from the twelfth to the nineteenth centuries, but the body of the work is taken up by a series of chapters devoted to famous Orientalists of the nineteenth century. His intention had been to go backward in time from the nineteenth to the twelfth centuries, giving biographical details of the principal Orientalists of each period with an enumeration as complete as possible of their works, the principal ones of which would be analysed. The work is, therefore, a contribution to a kind of biographical dictionary of Orientalists, the first volume arranged in no apparent order, the second alphabetically, with the lives of twenty-nine Orientalists in all being recorded.

Of much broader scope is Barthold's history of Orientalism in Europe and Russia. Originally published in Russian in 1925 under the title *Istoriya izucheniya Vostoka v Europe i Rossii*, it was translated into French and published in 1947 with the title V. V. Barthold: *La découverte de l'Asie. Histoire de l'orientalisme en Europe et en Russie*. Traduit du russe et annoté par B. Nikitine. (Bibliothèque historique.) Paris, 1947.

This fundamental work traces the whole history of European contacts with Asia, from the time of the Greeks to the early part of the twentieth century. It is in two parts, the first in twelve chapters dealing with Orientalism in Europe, the second consisting of nine chapters concerned with Russian activity in Asia and the history of Russian Orientalism. Each chapter has its own bibliography, giving chapter and verse for all the facts stated: to this Nikitine the translator has added a 'complément de bibliographie' which brings Barthold's original bibliographies up to date. A defect of the French translation is the omission of the index of names which appears in the original Russian text. Especially important for our present purpose are chapters 9, on the study of Western Asia in the sixteenth and seventeenth centuries, chapter 10, on Indian, South-East Asian and Far Eastern studies in the nineteenth century, when they may first be said properly to have got under way, and 11, on Western Asian studies in the nineteenth century.

Ein Jahrhundert Orientalistik: Lebensbilder aus der Feder von Enno Littmann und Verzeichnis seiner Schriften. Zum achtzigsten Geburtstage am 16. September 1955 zusammengestellt von Rudi Paret und Anton Schall. Wiesbaden: Harrassowitz, 1955.

Ein Jahrhundert Orientalistik is not, as might have been expected, the history of a century of Oriental studies, but an unusual type of Festschrift put together on the occasion of the eightieth birthday of the distinguished German Semitist Enno Littmann by two of his pupils. Sixteen obituary notices or speeches made in memory of Orientalists, personally known to Littmann, who died between the years 1894 and 1945, and published in various books and periodicals, are republished here, together with a catalogue of 525 writings by Littmann or works edited by him.

FRANCE

The story of Oriental studies in the various countries of Europe has been told by many scholars. First in the field was Paul Colomiès (Colomesius) whose *Gallia Orientalis*, published in 1665, gives biographies of Frenchmen who studied Hebrew and other Oriental languages up to that date.

A series of jubilee volumes published by societies and other institutions tells a good deal about the more recent history of Oriental studies in France.

Société asiatique: *Le livre du centenaire* (1822–1922). Paris, 1922.

(1. Historique de la société, par L. Finot. 2. Cent ans d'orientalisme en France.)

Livre jubilaire composé à l'occasion du 4e centenaire du Collège de France. Paris, 1933.

Cinq-cinquantenaire de l'École des langues orientales. Histoire, organisation et enseignements de l'École nationale des langues orientales vivantes. Paris, 1948.

Société des études indochinoises: *Cinquante ans d'orientalisme français.* (*Bulletin de la S.E.I.*, nouvelle série, tome XXVI, no. 4, 4e trimestre, 1951, pp. 406–578.)

'Aperçu d'un demi-siècle de travaux scientifiques à l'École Française d'Extrême-Orient, par Louis Malleret.' *France-Asie*, 125–27, October–December, 1956, pp. 271–306. [The triple issue of *France-Asie* in which this article appears is dedicated to a discussion of French institutions in Asia under the general title of 'Présence de la France en Asie'.]

ITALY

The history of Oriental studies in Italy from the earliest times may be read in a series of works of which the titles are listed below:

Origine e progresso dello studio delle lingue orientali in Italia. F. Predari. Milano, 1842.

Matériaux pour servir à l'histoire des études orientales en Italie, par Angelo De Gubernatis. Paris, 1876.

Bibliografia degli studi orientalistici in Italia dal 1912 al 1934. G. Gabrieli. Roma, 1935.

Francesco Gabrieli. *Gli studi orientali.* (Estratto dal Vol. II. Cinquant'anni di vita intellettuale italiana 1896–1946 [Scritti in onore di B. Croce].) Napoli, 1950.

De Gubernatis, who was Professor of Sanskrit at the Institute of Oriental Studies at Florence brought up to date and extended the work of his predecessor Predari in a volume presented to the Third International Congress of Orientalists held at St Petersburg in 1876, the first to be attended by delegates from Italy. In this work the history of the study of the various Oriental languages in Italy is delineated in chapters devoted to Semitic, African, Turanian, Armenian and Iranian, Indian, and Monosyllabic and Altaic languages. An index of authors mentioned in the work makes it easy to find biographical and bibliographical details of every Italian Orientalist since these studies were first established in that country. The work of Gabrieli senior contains a brief account of the history of Oriental studies in Italy for the period 1912 to 1934. Francesco Gabrieli's contribution to the Croce Festschrift is described by him as a quick sketch of the main currents of Oriental studies during the fifty-year period rather than a bibliographical bulletin, aiming to provide a framework for those studies within the general panorama of Italian culture and scholarship of the period. He also seeks to describe the main currents and methodology of these studies within the orbit of the general outlook and intellectual climate of the nation at the time. The prominent personalities of the period are recalled and their principal works mentioned, in the whole range of Oriental studies – African, Semitic, Islamic, Indian and Chinese.

U.S.S.R.

The U.S.S.R. has always demonstrated a great interest in the history of Oriental studies, as is exemplified by Barthold's monumental works and the histories of Arabic studies by Krachkovskiy and Islamic studies by Smirnov. Between the years 1953 and 1960, the Academy of Sciences, through the Institute of Oriental Studies (now known as the Institute of the Peoples of Asia) published a series of five volumes of essays (sborniki) on various aspects of the subject. The titles of the individual essays, all of which are written in the Russian language, are given below in English translation.

Akademiya Nauk SSSR. Institut Vostokovedeniya. *Ocherki po istorii russkogo vostokovedeniya.* [Essays on the history of Russian Orientalism. 5 vols. Moskva, 1953–60.

1. 1953
I. Yu. Krachkovskiy. Oriental studies in the letters of P. Ya. Petrov to V. G. Belinskiy.
I. Yu. Krachkovskiy. One of the first studies on the Eastern elements in the 'Lay of Igor's campaign'.
A. Yu. Yakubovskiy. On the history of research on the Mongols in the XIth to the XIIIth centuries.
E. I. Gnevusheva. The journey of P. I. Pashino through Persia and India.
G. D. Tyagay. Works of Russian scholarship as a source for the modern history of Korea.

V. A. Romodin. On the history of the study of the Afghans and Afghanistan in Russia.

B. M. Dantzig. On the history of Russian travels to the Near East and the study of this region before the time of Peter the Great.

2. 1956

A. L. Gal'perin. Russian historical scholarship on the non-Russian Far East from the 17th to the mid-19th century.

V. S. Vorob'ev-Desyatovskiy. The Russian Indianist Gerasim Stepanovich Lebedev (1749–1817).

L. S. Gamayunov. On the history of Indian studies in Russia: the contribution of G. S. Lebedev.

G. F. Shamov. The scientific work of O. M. Kovalevsky in the University of Kazan.

N. P. Shastina. The importance of the work of N. Ya. Bichurina for Russian Mongol studies.

P. E. Skachkov. The literary remains of N. Ya. Bichurina preserved in the Saltykov-Shchedrin Public Library.

I. S. Katznel'son. Materials for the history of Egyptology in Russia.

Z. I. Gorbacheva, N. A. Petrov, G. F. Smykalov, B. I. Pankratov. The Russian Sinologist Academician Vasiliy Pavlovich Vasil'ev (1818–1900).

R. R. Orbeli. Academician P. K. Kokovtzov and his manuscript literary remains.

K. K. Kurdoev. Khachatur Abovyan as a Kurdologist.

B. M. Dantzig. On the history of Near Eastern studies in Russia in the first quarter of the eighteenth century.

A. S. Shofman, G. F. Shamov. The Eastern Faculty of Kazan University.

D. I. Tikhonov. History of the Asiatic Museum.

O. E. Livotova. Important writings on the Asiatic Museum and the Institute of Oriental Studies of the Academy of Sciences (1776–1954).

3. 1960

V. V. Struve. The contribution of V. S. Golenishchev to Egyptology.

D. G. Rader. Scholarly and popular writings of M. V. Nikol'sky.

M. A. Korostovtzev, S. I. Khodzhash. Adrian Viktorovich Prakhov (1846–1916).

M. A. Korostovtzev, S. I. Khodzhash. Vladimir Georgevich Bok (1850–99).

A. S. Shofman. The Russian Sanskritist P. Ya. Petrov.

A. A. Starikov. Oriental philology at Moscow University; A. V. Boldyrev and P. Ya. Petrov.

L. S. Puchkovskiy. Aleksandr Vasilevich Igumnov (1761–1834).

O. E. Livotova. Bibliography of the publications of the Asiatic Museum and the Institute of Oriental Studies of the Academy of Sciences of the U.S.S.R. (1917–58).

4. 1959
B. M. Dantzig. On the history of Near Eastern studies in Russia during the second quarter of the eighteenth century.

K. K. Kurdoev. The works of P. I. Lerkh on Kurdish studies.

I. M. Smilyanskaya. K. M. Bazili – Russian diplomat and historian of Syria.

A. G. Perikhanyan. Karl Germanovich Zaleman.

P. P. Bushev. Life and works of V. A. Zhukovskiy.

I. M. Oranskiy. The study of the history of the Tajik and Persian languages at the St Petersburg University.

5. 1960
This volume is a memorial volume devoted to the Iranist V. A. Zhukovskiy (1858–1918), containing ten essays on his life and works and his literary remains.

Other examples of works in this genre are:

A. E. Krymskiy i V. F. Minorskiy. *Ocherki iz istorii orientalistiki v XVI i XVII veke.* (Iz II t., III vyp. 'Drevnostey vostochnykh' Imp. Moskovsk. Arkheol. Obshch.) Moskva, 1903. 27 pp. [On the history of Oriental studies in the sixteenth and seventeenth centuries.]

1872–1902. *Tridtzatiletie spetzial'nykh klassov Lazarevskago Instituta Vostnochnykh Yazykov.* Pamyatnaya knizhka, izdannaya na sredstva Pochetnago pochitelya Lazarevskago Instituta Knyazya S.S. Abame-lek-Lazareva. Moskva, 1903. [Thirty years of the special classes of the Lazarevsky Institute of Oriental languages. Memorial volume. This institute was formerly an Armenian school, but from 1828 it provided instruction in Oriental languages. After the Revolution its name was changed several times until finally, as the Moscow Institute of Oriental Studies, it was liquidated in 1955 because of its inability to provide sufficient numbers of specialists with adequate linguistic training. The memorial volume includes lists of the works of teachers prominent during the period.]

Materialy dlya istorii Fakul'teta Vostochnykh Yazykov. Tom 4. Obzor deyatel'nosti Fakul'teta 1855–1905, sostavlennyy prof. V. V. Bartol'dom. S prilozheniem obzora istorii vostokovedeniya v Rossii do 1855 g. S.–Peterburg, 1909. [Materials for the history of the Faculty of Oriental Languages in the University of St Petersburg, vol. 4: A survey of the work of the Faculty from 1855 to 1905, with a preface on the history of Oriental studies in Russia up to 1855.]

A. V. Marakuev. *Desyat' let vostokovedeniya na sovetskom Dal'nem Vostoke* (1922–32). Vladivostok, 1932. 12 pp. (Reprinted from 'The Bulletin of the Far Eastern Branch of the Academy of Sciences of the USSR', no. 1–2, 1932.) [Ten years of Oriental studies in the Soviet Far East.]

Vostokovedenie v Leningradskom Universitete. (Uchenye zapiski Leningradskogo ordena Lenina Gosudarstvennogo Universiteta imeni A. A. Zhdanova, no. 296. Vostochnyy Fakul'tet, seriya vostoko-vedcheskikh nauk, vyp. 13.) Leningrad, 1960. [Oriental studies in Leningrad University. A series of articles by several scholars on the departments of Chinese, Korean, Japanese, Mongolian, Turkish, Indian, Iranian philogies, African studies, history of the Far East and history of the Near East, with an introductory chapter on the Oriental Faculty. Other chapters treat of Arabic and Semitic studies in the Faculty, Egyptology and Assyriology in the University and the Faculty Library. In appendices are given (1) the names of teachers in the various departments as at 15 October, 1959; (2) courses of lectures and seminars held during the sessions 1954–55 to 1959–60; (3) works of members of the Faculty published during the years 1957–59 (up to October 1), and (4) a basic bibliography for the history of the Faculty.]

OTHER EUROPEAN COUNTRIES

For the history of Oriental studies in other countries the works named below provide information:

EIRE

Oriental studies in Ireland and Irish Orientalists, by M. Mansoor. Reprinted (with additional notes) from Hermathena, vol. LXII, November, 1943. Dublin (1943). [Mostly at Trinity College, Dublin. The author intended to publish a more adequate treatment of the subject, with a bibliography and a biographical index of Irish Orientalists.]

GERMANY

'Ein Jahrhundert morgenländischer Studien an der Münchener Uni-versität. Von Franz Babinger.' ZDMG 107, 2 (N.F. 22, 1957), pp.

241–69. [A hundred years of Oriental studies at Munich University from 1826–1926.]

HOLLAND

Quatre esquisses détachées relatives aux études orientalistes à Leiden. Leiden, 1932.
Le Legatum Warnerianum: (1) Les manuscrits sémitiques, par M. van Arendonk, (2) Les manuscrits indonésiens, par M. van Ronkel.
L'Institut Kern, par M. Vogel.
Les études hollando-chinoises au XVIIième et au XVIIIiéme siécles par M. Duyvendak.
The contribution of the University of Leiden to Oriental research, by J. Ph. Vogel. Leiden, 1951. [Also published in *Indian art and letters,* 23, 2, 1949, pp. 45–59.]

POLAND

'Dix ans d'études orientales en Pologne populaire [1945–54]. (Rapport présenté par la délégation de l'Académie Polonaise des Sciences au XXIIIe Congrès International des Orientalistes à Cambridge, le 27. VIII, 1954.)' Warszawa, 1956. [Reprint from *Rocznik orientalistyczny.*]

Szkice z dziejów polskiej orientalistyki, 1957. [Sketches of the history of Oriental studies in Poland, edited by Stefan Strelcyn. The contents, all of which are in Polish, are: 1. Marian Lewicki:Władysław Kotwicz (20. iii. 1872–3. x. 1944). 2. Ananiasz Zajączkowski: Tadeusz Kowalski and his writings on Oriental subjects (21. vi. 1889–5. v. 1948). 3. Ananiasz Zajączkowski: Stanisław Schayer – organizer of the Warsaw Oriental Centre. 4. Jan Reychman: Oriental studies in Silesia and Pomerania from the XVIth to the XVIIIth centuries. 5. Jan Reychman: Interest evinced in Oriental studies in the circle of Mickiewicz in Vilna and Petersburg. 6. Ananiasz Zajączkowski: Pages from the history of Polish Orientalism at the time of Mickiewicz. 7. Jan Reychman: Karol Zatuski and the first translations of Polish literature into Oriental languages. 8. Stefan Przeworki: Polish research on Western Asia. 9. Kazimierz Michaławski: Polish excavations at Edfu. 10. Hela Willman-Gradbowska: Indian and related studies in Poland.]

PORTUGAL

Moses Bensabat Amzalak. *The Oriental studies in Portugal.* Address presented at the General Meeting of the XVIIth International

Congress of Orientalists. Lisbon, 1928. [History of the East, Arabic, Hebrew, Assyrian (*sic;* a professor of theology from Goa who travelled in Persia in 1602), Ethiopian, Indian, Ceylon, Chinese, Japanese, Egyptian.]

SWITZERLAND

Les études orientales à la Société d' Histoire et d'Archéologie de Genève 1838–94. (Édouard Favre.) Genève, 1894.

U.S.A.

University of California. *Asiatic and Slavic studies on the Berkeley campus,* 1896–1947. University of California Press (1947). [A brief history of Oriental studies at Berkeley, with the names of teachers of the subjects represented, courses provided, a short note on library and museum resources, and a list of the sixty doctorates granted in the Asiatic and Slavic fields, 1920–47.]

Other references may be found in my *Index Islamicus,* 1906–55 and *Index Islamicus Supplement,* 1956–60 (section I, b 1) which, in addition to articles on Islamic studies in particular, notices many concerned with Oriental studies in general.

UNITED KINGDOM

The British Council sponsored the publication of a series of pamphlets during the Second World War which relate the story of British contributions to several branches of Oriental studies. These may be read with profit by all requiring an introduction to the subject. Their titles are:

British contributions to Arabic studies, by Bernard Lewis. London, 1941.
British contributions to Persian studies, by Arthur J. Arberry. London, 1942.
British contributions to Turkish studies, by Harold Bowen. London, 1945.
British contributions to Indian studies, by Sir Atul Chatterjee and Sir Richard Burn. London, 1943.

The other branches of Orientalism, and especially Far Eastern studies, are significant omissions from this list. But for Chinese studies a useful contribution, which aims at listing the most prominent British

Sinologists of the nineteenth century and provides details of their works, whether these be printed in the form of monographs or periodical articles, or indeed remain only in typescript state, and which also lists works about these scholars, was compiled by Joseph C. Ting while in receipt of a British Council grant in 1951. This work, entitled *British contributions to Chinese studies*, is in the library of S.O.A.S. (shelf-mark R.2.f.3). For the thirty-five outstanding British Sinologists he has provided a bibliographical outline, list of works: manuscripts, books and periodical literature, biography and criticism, all set out in tabular form. At the end of the book are listed all other British Sinologists of the period. In all, 1824 titles of their publications are listed. Thus a very useful collection of source materials is put together for the use of some future historian to sketch the development of studies of China in this country during the nineteenth century.

Professor A. J. Arberry was also the author of a pamphlet published in 1943 in the 'Britain in pictures' series, entitled *British Orientalists*, which gives a good readable general account of those who contributed to the knowledge of Asia in this country from the translators of the twelfth century. From this we may gather what has been achieved in all fields of Oriental studies, including Malayan studies, in the development of which the founder of Singapore, Sir Stamford Raffles, played a prominent part.

African studies are a comparatively recent growth in this country as elsewhere. No comprehensive account has so far been published and only the briefest sketch is available in the 'Scarbrough Report' (p. 11) of which we shall hear more later.

Incoming professors often make a practice of outlining the history of the teaching of their subject in the inaugural lecture customarily delivered soon after taking up office. Examples of this are the three lectures listed below:

Japanese studies in the University of London and elsewhere. An inaugural lecture delivered on 7 November, 1962, by F. J. Daniels. London: S.O.A.S., 1963.

Land tenure and the social order in T'ang and Sung China. An inaugural lecture delivered on 28 November, 1961, by Denis Twitchett. London: S.O.A.S., 1962. [The first few pages of this pamphlet contain a sketch of the history of the teaching of Chinese in London.]

The Cambridge School of Arabic. An inaugural lecture delivered on 30 October, 1947, by Arthur J. Arberry. Cambridge U.P., 1948. [On the best-known incumbents of the two Arabic chairs in Cambridge, the Sir Thomas Adams, founded in 1632, and the Lord Almoner's. The latter chair was founded, with its twin at Oxford, in 1715, but became extinct on the death of its last holder, A. A. Bevan, in 1933.]

BRANCHES OF ORIENTAL STUDIES

The individual branches of Oriental studies have also had their historians. Johann Fück recounted the historical development of Arabic studies from the twelfth century to the War of 1914 in his:

Die arabischen Studien in Europa bis in den Anfang des 20 Jahrhunderts. Leipzig, 1955.

The early chapters of this work, describing the early history of Arabic studies, had also been published previously in the volume edited by Richard Hartmann and Helmuth Scheel and entitled *Beiträge zur Arabistik, Semitistik und Islamwissenschaft* (1944). The remaining chapters provide thumb-nail sketches of most of the prominent Arabic scholars of the period covered by the book, as well as chapters on the early collectors of Arabic manuscripts, on travellers to Arabia, on the bibliographers and on the study of Arabic philology and science in Germany. Here again we have a series of biographies of Arabic scholars, similar in style to Dugat's work, but this time presented in a more connected form.

A similar work by Windisch traces the history of Sanskrit philology and Indian antiquities down to the First World War. The compiler had intended to complete the two published volumes by means of a third which would relate the story of Indian contributions to Sanskrit philology, as well as the study of Buddhism in the Southern countries and the most recent period of Indological research. Unfortunately he died before the work could be completed, but three chapters of the third volume were published posthumously, as noted below:

E. Windisch: *Geschichte der Sanskrit-Philologie und indischen Altertumskunde.* (Grundriss der indo-arischen Philologie und Altertumskunde, I. Band, 1, Heft B.) 2 vols. Berlin und Leipzig, 1917, 1920.

Philologie und Altertumskunde in Indien. Drei nachgelassene Kapitel des III. Teils der Geschichte der Sanskrit-Philologie und Indischen Altertumskunde von Ernst Windisch. (Abhandlungen für die Kunde des Morgenlandes, XV. Band, no. 3.) Leipzig, 1921.

Herbert Franke, writing in 1953, declared that up to then a comprehensive history of Sinology had not been written, but he nevertheless provides many references to the history of these studies and various aspects of them in his *Sinologie*. (Wissenschaftliche Forschungsberichte, geisteswissenschaftliche Reihe, Band 19. Orientalistik, 1 Teil.) Bern, 1953, which covers the period since 1935.

Recent developments in Oriental Studies in the United Kingdom

Many men of distinction, and, indeed, some few women also, made their mark on the world of scholarship and literary appreciation by their contributions during the earlier period in the history of British Orientalism. Some of them, like Raffles and Warren Hastings were Government servants but yet found time to make some study of the languages and cultures with which they came into contact. Many were engaged in commercial pursuits as officers of the East India Company and spent their leisure time and their years of retirement in these studies. Others occupied the few existing university chairs and though some of these eminent scholars never travelled further East than Vienna, for all that they interpreted the treasures of Eastern literature to the cultured English-speaking general public with understanding. As a result of their efforts few now would agree with Macaulay's dictum[1] that the whole of Oriental literature was not worth a single shelf of the classics of Europe. This ill-advised opinion, however, had a far-reaching effect and was to a large extent responsible for the neglect from which these studies suffered for many years. The twentieth century is marked by a series of committee reports which changed the whole outlook of Oriental studies in this country. First of these was that of the Reay Committee[2] of 1908, followed by the Scarbrough Commis-

[1] Contained in a Minute written by Macaulay as a Member of the Council of India on 2 Feb. 1835 and published on pp. 107–17 of Bureau of Education, India: *Selections from educational records*, part 1, 1781–1839. H. Sharp. Calcutta, 1920.
'I have never found one among them [sc. Orientalists] who could deny that a single shelf of a good European library was worth the whole native literature of India and Arabia.' (P. 109).
[2] Treasury Committee on the Organization of Oriental Studies in London: *Report of the Committee appointed by the Lords Commissioners of His Majesty's Treasury to consider the organisation of Oriental studies in London, with copy of minute and letter appointing the Committee and appendices.* (Cd. 4560.) London: H.M.S.O., 1909.
Minutes of evidence . . . with list of witnesses examined and index. (Cd. 4561.) Ib., 1909.

sion[1] in 1946 and more recently by that of the Hayter Sub-Committee[2] of the University Grants Committee, which was published in 1961. The reports form the basis of the study of the recent history of Oriental studies in Great Britain which follows.

The Reay Committee produced its report at the end of the year 1908. It had been set up largely as a result of representations made by the Royal Asiatic Society which in common with other learned societies and individual persons felt the provision made for teaching and research in Oriental studies in London to be hopelessly inadequate, comparing unfavourably with the provision made in France, Germany and other countries. The Committee stressed the urgent need for suitable training in London for those about to take up administrative and commercial posts in Asia and Africa: to meet this need it recommended that a School of Oriental Studies should be set up in London and that this School should become a School of the University of London. These proposals proving acceptable to the Government of the day and the University authorities, a site was found in Finsbury Circus where the premises of the London Institution were taken over for the newly-formed establishment, the University agreed to admit the School as a college of the University in December of 1916, and the small number of existing students and teachers of Oriental languages already working in University and King's Colleges joined the School, which opened its doors in January, 1917. By July of the same year the number of students had increased from the nine taken over at the time of opening to 125. The first Director of the new institution was Sir Edward Denison Ross. Of him it has been said that he 'sought but just missed the universalism of Sir William Jones' but he nevertheless had some acquaintance at least with no fewer than forty-one languages. He presided over the affairs of the School until 1937 with aplomb and urbanity. The Royal Charter bestowed by King George V in 1916 set out the purposes of the School to be 'to further research in, and to extend the study and knowledge of the languages of Eastern and African peoples, Ancient and Modern, and the Literature, History, Religion, Law, Customs and Art of those peoples . . .' and required that 'such knowledge [should be] disseminated by publications, lectures and courses of study including courses suitable to the needs of persons about to proceed to

---

[1] Foreign Office: *Report of the Interdepartmental Commission of Enquiry on Oriental, Slavonic, East European and African studies*. London: H.M.S.O., 1947.

[2] University Grants Committee: *Report of the Sub-Committee on Oriental, Slavonic, East European and African studies*. London: H.M.S.O., 1961.

the East or to Africa for study and research, for the public service or commerce, or for the pursuit of a profession or other calling'. . . . This dichotomy of function clearly indicates the School's dual role as a university institution and a provider of information and instruction to persons interested in Asia and Africa outside the University: this explains much of the School's subsequent history, including the development of its library into a national lending library for Asian and African studies. Sir Denison Ross was succeeded in 1937 by Professor (afterward Sir Ralph) Turner, who steered the School through the difficult times of the Second World War, when the School made an important contribution to the war effort predominantly by the provision of 'crash' courses in Japanese and other languages, and through the years of vast expansion in the post-war period. In 1957 he in turn was succeeded by Professor C. H. Philips, who had formerly been Head of the Department of History. In 1938 the Charter was amended to change the title of the School to School of Oriental and African Studies and it has been familiarly known as 'S.O.A.S.' ever since.

Largely as a result of the School's initiative, in 1944 the Foreign Secretary (Sir Anthony Eden, as he then was) set up an Interdepartmental Commission of Enquiry on Oriental, Slavonic, East European and African Studies, under the chairmanship of the Earl of Scarbrough, who later, appropriately enough, became chairman of the School's Governing Body and who later still was called to the important traditional office of Lord Chamberlain. He is distinguished in many walks of life but his fame for posterity will rest the more secure for his report, presented in 1946, which has been described as 'a new charter for Oriental studies'. For a time, too, he added a new word to the English language, for Treasury studentships in these fields, awarded as a result of the Commission's recommendations were popularly known as 'Scarbroughs'.

The Scarbrough Commission emphasized the importance to the country of maintaining contacts with the countries of Asia and Africa and of making good deficiencies which existed in the number of people possessing expert knowledge about these parts of their world, their languages, sciences, political institutions and cultures. To improve the unsatisfactory position which it found to exist at the end of the war the Commission declared that the most important objective was to build up 'an academic tradition comparable in quality and in continuity with those of the major humanities and sciences' and proposed as measures to bring about this desirable state of affairs the building-up of strong departments concentrated in the major universities and the making available of a number of Post-Graduate Studentships (the 'Scar-broughs') of which one hundred were to be allocated to Oriental studies. It recommended, too, the development of non-linguistic studies and the establishment of a balance between these studies and language studies and between classical and modern period studies. Earmarked grants for the development of these studies were awarded for a period of five years to seven universities (Cambridge, Durham, London, Manchester and Oxford in England; Edinburgh and Glasgow in Scotland), and an additional annual expenditure from public funds of from £25,000 to £30,000 a year was proposed to enable university teachers to visit periodically the countries where the languages and cultures they taught were to be met with.

So for the first quinquennium of what we might call the post-Scarbrough era Oriental departments in British universities had 'never had it so good'. Total grants of nearly £750,000 were made to the seven privileged universities, and as a result of this beneficence the number of staff employed in them rose from 95 in 1946–47 to 220 in 1951–52, and the numbers of students awarded honours degrees showed a modest increase from 16 to 26 over the same period, but the figures for post-graduate students rose from 67 to 158.

But these years of plenty were followed by the customary years of famine. For the quinquennium 1952–57 it was decided to 'un-earmark' the grants and merge the special grant with the general grant to the universities – a very painful operation, as most of the universities found. It arrested further development in the Oriental departments in most universities and many of the plans put forward in 1947 remained uncompleted, many of the universities having incorrectly assumed, as it subsequently turned out, that the earmarked grants would continue for ten years.

The facts and figures in the two preceding paragraphs are taken from the third and most recent report, this time produced by a Sub-Committee set up by the University Grants Committee to examine the situation in Oriental, Slavonic, East European and African studies. This Sub-Committee began work in January, 1960 and presented its report in May, 1961. Its chairman was Sir William Hayter, formerly ambassador to Moscow and now Warden of New College, Oxford. He presided over a working group consisting of three university professors, a diplomat and a business man. This report puts forward recommendations which must inevitably determine the whole direction taken by Oriental studies in this country in the future.

But before considering these recommendations it may be useful to look for a moment at the position in Oriental studies in the U.K. as it was at the time of the publication of the Hayter Committee's report. Facilities for Near Eastern studies (if we except Hebrew, Biblical and Ancient Near Eastern studies from this appellative) were available at eight universities in England and Scotland; for Indian and Far Eastern studies in Cambridge, London and Oxford and for S.E. Asian studies only in London. London (S.O.A.S.) participated in studies of all areas of Asia and Africa and tried to maintain the equitable balance between classical and modern studies and between languages and other subjects postulated by the Scarbrough Commission, as will be shown later. The other universities, with the possible exception of Durham were rather heavily weighted on the side of the classical and the philological, though there were significant evidences of change at Cambridge (where a Middle East Institute financed out of funds supplied by oil companies had been set up in recent years), and at Oxford, where St Anthony's College had laid the main emphasis since its foundation in 1950 on modern history and international affairs, as evidenced by published volumes of papers emanating from seminars and lectures held in Oxford relating to all fields of modern Asian studies.

S.O.A.S. had become a veritable Oriental and African University. It had a teaching staff of more than 150 and the student population numbered 755 in the session 1960–61, of which 247 came from the Commonwealth and 193 from foreign countries. It possessed a library with a quarter of a million volumes in some 2,500 languages to support these studies. Teaching could be and was provided regularly in some 130 languages and dialects, ancient, medieval and modern, ranging from Acholi to Zulu and including besides the more familiar tongues of Asia such more exotic variants as Khwarezmian and Old Mon. Teaching was available as well in other cultural or non-linguistic subjects. The work of the School was organized in ten teaching departments, of which five were on a regional basis and taught such subjects as languages, philosophy, religion and art of the various regions of Asia and Africa, whereas five were concerned with the academic disciplines of phonetics and general linguistics, history, law, anthropology and sociology, and economic and political studies. A further department, geography, was contemplated for establishment in the near future. Thus, for example, Far Eastern studies had their exponents not only in the Department of the Far East, but also in each of the academic discipline departments, and inter-departmental seminars were held regularly to bring together for discussion those who cultivated all the fields of study taught in the School.

All of these activities have been strengthened with the aid of funds provided on the Hayter Sub-Committee's recommendation by the U.G.C.

As has already been stated, under the terms of its Charter, the School is not only a university department training students for first and advanced degrees, but also supplies teaching to persons not members of the University who may, if they wish, work for certificates and diplomas awarded by the School itself. Its extra-mural activities include the stimulation of an interest in Asia and Africa by holding conferences and lectures for schools and training colleges, and the holding in vacations of advanced courses for Government officials, business executives, school-teachers and other interested persons which provide up-to-date assessments of political, economic and social developments in the various countries of Asia and Africa. In the session 1964–65, fellowships were awarded to a small number of practising school-teachers who spent a sabbatical term at S.O.A.S.

To return now to the Hayter Report, its terms of reference were 'to review developments in the universities in the fields of Oriental, Slavonic, East European and African studies, consequent upon the recommendations made in 1947 by the Inter-departmental commission of enquiry presided over by Lord Scarbrough; and to consider, and advise on, proposals for future developments'. The Sub-Committee attempted to ascertain the progress made in these studies in universities and the direction in which they should be aiming. It found that whereas a new impetus was given to Oriental studies through the acceptance by the Government of the day of the main recommendations of the Scarbrough Report in so far as they affected the universities, and rapid expansion ensued as a consequence, this expansion came to an abrupt halt in 1952 with the ending of the earmarked grants. After 1957 some improvement was recorded and an increasing increase of student members, especially in Arabic and Chinese, was noted, though numbers remained small. It regarded the overall pattern of the development of Oriental studies as disappointing. Interest in modern studies in the language departments of universities was small and in the non-language departments little attention was paid to the countries of Asia and Africa as living societies. In spite of great changes in the world since 1939 and the increasing importance of the part played in world affairs by newly-emerging countries in Asia and Africa, the British educational system was still preoccupied with Western Europe, little attention being paid to the remaining parts of the world. It came to the conclusion, therefore, that the main expansion of these studies should take place not in the language departments but in the departments of history, geography, law, economics and other social science departments and declared that its aims were threefold: to expand the total amount of research being carried out on Asia and on the Asian and on the other areas included in its brief, to increase the number of students taking Asian and African subjects, and to achieve a better balance between linguistic and other studies and between classical and modern studies.

To further these aims the Sub-Committee made the following main recommendations:

First, the creation of a fund to serve as a pool on which universities could draw over a period of the years for making appointments to posts in non-language departments of persons trained in the various disciplines who were prepared to concentrate on studies on these less-popular areas, and who would be expected to visit the area of their choice and learn the appropriate language. In all 125 such posts were contemplated. Second, the creation of a hundred post-graduate awards over ten years to encourage students again in the non-language departments to specialize in an area, travel in it and learn the language. Third, the setting up of six or eight new centres of 'area studies' similar to those which exist in many American universities. In these centres scholars representing many disciplines are enabled to come together to take part in seminars and similar gatherings, and to discuss one another's work from their several points of view. On the basis of the wide range of topics in which it has an interest, S.O.A.S. may be regarded as a congeries of such area centres, and the main developments in these lectures were expected to take place in universities which have not hitherto contributed toward advances in Asian studies, including some of the new ones now being established in England.

The difficulty of bringing students up to a graduate level of knowledge of languages not taught in, or studied insufficiently in schools, is recognized in the fourth recommendation, which proposes intensive courses in the more difficult languages to be held either before entry to, or in the first year of, the university course. An experiment of this kind in the teaching of Chinese has been tried out at S.O.A.S. and has proved markedly successful.

The remaining two recommendations encourage universities to include in their estimates sums for travel grants for lecturers to enable them to visit the area of their studies at least once in every five to seven years, and for increased amounts to be spent on libraries. A special study should be made of the possibilities of co-operative action in both buying and cataloguing of books.

The work of the Sub-Committee received a good deal of highly critical appraisal in the various universities. It was claimed, not entirely without justification, that conclusions were based on insufficient evidence, collected by the Sub-Committee in the course of rather hurried visitations of the centres where Oriental studies are carried on. The drafting of the Report also received unfavourable comment: in one much-quoted passage the centre of gravity of the world was stated in the last fifteen years to have moved outward, east, west and south, which gives the impression of a very wobbly world, which may perhaps have been the subliminal intention. But the most voluble and outspoken critics were the members of linguistic departments, especially those concerned with classical languages who felt left out in the cold by the Hayter recommendations. Some of these scholars declared that a sound knowledge of a language, the achievement of which might entail concentration for as much as ten years, was essential before any useful appreciation even of modern trends and events can be made. The opposition party maintained that even with a difficult language like Chinese, it is possible within a year for, say, an economist, to acquire sufficient of the language to be able to consult primary source materials and secondary comments in journals and monographs and to make a useful evaluation of the problem based on these sources. The truth, as always, lies somewhere in between these two extremes. But in their appeal for a better balance between classical and modern studies on the one hand, and between philological and social studies on the other, the Committee is only following a movement which began with the Reay Committee and the foundation of S.O.A.S. in the early part of this century, and which has gained momentum in recent years in America, in Japan, and in other parts of the free world and, indeed, the communist world as well, and which is gaining ground even in that last stronghold of classico-philological studies, continental Western Europe. This is exemplified by the recent foundation of the South Asia Institute of Heidelberg University.

The Hayter Committee was the first of the three to include in its purview a survey of libraries and its recommendations in respect of these institutions will be examined in some detail later. That the Sub-Committee was working along the right lines in view of modern tendencies seems obvious and any deficiencies of style and presentation in the Report should not blind us to this fact. It is a matter of regret, however, that the Sub-Committee's scope was perforce restricted to consideration of the needs of universities and that it was not able to consider certain broader issues of provision for Oriental studies as did its predecessors. No suggestions were made on the subject of exchanges of university teaching staffs from different countries from which great advantages are derived, and it could not bring up again the proposal made by the Scarbrough Committee, but not accepted by the Government, for an Oriental Centre in London, to provide lectures, exhibitions and information on the East for the benefit of the general public.

As a direct result of the Hayter recommendations the universities of Leeds, Sheffield and Hull have been enabled to set up centres of Chinese, Japanese and South-East Asian studies respectively. The new University of Sussex has established a School of African and Asian studies (reversing the usual order) which initially, at least, will concentrate on modern, extra-linguistic studies on Central and Southern Africa, and on India. Funds were provided for centres of African studies in Edinburgh and Birmingham (the latter restricted to West Africa). Oxford University received a grant enabling it, among other things, to appoint a Middle Eastern bibliographer to select books for a half-dozen libraries in the University other than the Bodleian. S.O.A.S. and Durham received increases to their annual library grant and in due course a bibliographical centre will be set up in S.O.A.S. which will compile and keep up to date a union catalogue of books published in Asia. The same Library has made a study of the publishing output of Asian and African countries, and of the publications relating to these countries which are issued outside Asia and Africa. A centre for South Asian studies has been set up recently in Cambridge.

[4]

Organizations interested in Oriental,
Asian and African Studies

Oriental, Asian and African studies may be pursued at the present time and the resulting publications issued by a great many types of associations: international organizations, governments and government-sponsored bodies, non-official bodies such as universities and research institutes (which may or may not be attached to universities), academies and learned societies, libraries and museums, and individuals. A universal list of all of these would be of colossal dimensions and is not available: the information has to be extracted from a large number of sources.

INTERNATIONAL ORGANIZATIONS AND
WORLD-WIDE DIRECTORIES

The *World of learning* gives the names of the principal institutions of all types interested in these studies, with sometimes brief particulars of their history, organization, function and policy, but the details have to be dug out from among a vast array of facts relating to all subjects, while for universities only the title of the chair and name of the incumbent is as a rule given. *The Commonwealth Universities yearbook* gives much more information within the limits of its scope and it is to be noticed that in addition to universities in Commonwealth countries, the yearbook gives information on those in the Union of South Africa and the Republic of Ireland. In its pages will normally be found the names of all teachers (whether professor, reader, lecturer or holder of a post of any other designation) in the individual departments, as well as particulars of all research institutes and some information on library collections.

Among the organizations affiliated to the International Council for Philosophy and Humanistic Studies (Conseil International de la Philosophie et des Sciences Humaines – C.I.P.S.H.) are the International Union of Orientalists and the International Congress of Africanists. The former organization has taken on a programme of publication which includes the *Philologiae Turcicae fundamenta*, collections for Sumerian lexicography, a Sanskrit thesaurus, *the Corpus inscriptionum Iranicarum*, *Wörterbuch der klassischen arabischen Sprache*, *Materialien zur mongolischen Literaturgeschichte*, a new critical edition of the *Mahābhārata*, and a linguistic atlas of Iran: it is also responsible for the publication of the *Annual Egyptological bibliography* and the *Bibliographie bouddhique*. Among projects being undertaken by the International Congress of Africanists, which met for the first time in Accra in December, 1961, are the publication of sources for African history, to be entitled *Fontes Africae historiae* and a directory of African and Malagasy studies.

Other publications of Oriental interest being issued by, or under consideration by, other constituent members of C.I.P.S.H. are:

Concordance and indexes of Moslem tradition.
Pali dictionary.
Historical documents relating to Japan in foreign countries.
A new edition of Brockelmann's *Geschichte der arabischen Literatur*.
(*All the above by the International Academic Union.*)
Encyclopaedia of Buddhism (International Association for the History of Religions).

The *Yearbook of international organizations, 1962–63* lists the following inter-governmental and non-governmental organizations with Asian interests:

Inter-governmental Organizations

No.
254 Asian African Legal Consultative Committee
255 Asian Productivity Organization
264 Colombo Plan Council for Technical Co-operation in South and South-East Asia
298 Indo-Pacific Fisheries Council
332 International North Pacific Fisheries Commission
360 North Pacific Fur Seal Commission
371 Permanent Commission for the Conservation of the Maritime Resources of the South Pacific
375 Plant Protection Committee for the South-East Asia and Pacific Region

377   South Pacific Commission
378   South-East Asia Treaty Organization
380   Unesco Research Centre on Social and Economic Development in Southern Asia

International non-governmental Organizations

No.

387   Asian Federation of Library Associations
426   Organization of Asian News Agencies
428   Agudas Israel World Organization
440   East Asia Christian Conference
502   World Fellowship of Buddhists
592   East India Association
599   Federation of Asian Women's Associations
622   Jewish Agency for Israel, World Zionist Organization
630   Pan-Pacific and South-East Asia Women's Association
667   World Muslim Conference
670   Asian People's Anti-Communist League
671   Asian Socialist Conference
869   Asian Regional Organization
951   Afro-Asian Organization for Economic Co-operation
1013   General Union of Chambers of Commerce, Industry and Agriculture for Arab countries
1037   International Chamber of Commerce Commission on Asian and Far Eastern Affairs
1168   Arab Association of Tourism and Travel Agents
1227   East Asian Regional Organization for Planning and Housing
1380   Asia-Pacific Academy of Ophthalmology
1381   Asian Pacific Dental Federation
1498   Pan-Pacific Surgical Association
1582   Asian Broadcasters' Conference
1645   Ikebana International

National Organizations in consultative status with the United Nations

1711   All India Women's Conference
1712   All Pakistan Women's Association
1720   Indian Council of World Affairs

The Institut International des Civilisations Différentes (International Institute of Differing Civilizations) in Brussels published in 1955.

Répertoire international des centres d'étude des civilisations et de leurs publications.

International guide to study centers on civilizations and their publications. Bruxelles, 1955.

It lists 275 institutions concerned with the study of civilizations as a whole, and not those concerned only with one aspect of culture, or purely educational institutions. There are chapters for Arab or Islamic civilizations, Africa in general and its major regions, Asia in general and its regions, and the Pacific. Currently published periodicals are noted, and post-1945 non-periodical publications. Incidentally, it may be noted that Cyprus is regarded as forming part of Europe, and the Azores as part of Africa.

A recent (1962) publication covers institutions concerned with the Middle East:

An international directory of institutes and societies interested in the Middle East. Edited by Florence Ljunggren and Charles L. Geddes. Amsterdam, Djambatan (1962).

Containing 353 entries, the directory 'is an attempt to provide the names, addresses and other basic information of all societies, sub-sections of societies, institutes, university seminars, departments, programs and the like, which primarily have as their aim advanced instruction, research, publication of, or the promotion of interest in, any subject pertaining to the Middle East, from prehistory to the present'.

(Government ministries and their departments have been excluded, as well as museums of Near Eastern art and the India Office Library.)

Though by title apparently restricted in scope to the Middle East, the directory in fact covers studies relating to the whole of our Near and Middle East region, with the addition of North Africa, the Sudan, Pakistan and 'Muslim (Northern) India'. Because, too, of the fact that studies of these regions are often conducted in institutions concerned with the whole of Asian and/or African studies, a good deal of information is incidentally available on these.

The work was compiled on the basis of questionnaires sent to all known institutions interested in the region. Inevitably, many of these were never returned, though in some cases six reminders were sent. The work would have been improved if published sources of information could have been used as well.

It is arranged by country, and thereafter by town where the institutions are situated. It has indexes of serial publications (with some surprising omissions and inclusions, of which 'Divers' and 'Hors série' may be given as examples) and 'Institutes, etc.' where those included in the body of the work are arranged by their names in alphabetical order.

The Centre for East Asian Cultural Studies, inaugurated in July, 1961, at the suggestion of UNESCO and housed at the Toyo Bunko, the celebrated Oriental Library in Tokyo, included in its programme for the fiscal year 1962–63 a project for the compilation of directories of research institutes in Japan and elsewhere. (See *East Asian cultural studies* II, 1–2, June, 1962, p. 6.) The Centre's first three published directories (which embrace South-East as well as East Asian studies) for Japan and Korea will be mentioned later.

The first volume of *East Asian cultural studies* (1962), contains a series of reports on Far Eastern and South-East Asian studies in Cambodia, Hawaii, Czechoslovakia and East Europe, Germany, Scandinavia, France, India, Japan (where the numbers of universities giving lectures on East Asian and South-East Asian topics are given, p. 91, as well as the 'nineteen representative research institutes for humanistic and social sciences in Japan, selected from more than seventy'), the Philippines and Thailand.

NATIONAL DIRECTORIES

U.S.A.

Several countries have produced guides to institutions interested in Asia within their territory. Pride of place must be granted to the U.S.A. for the two publications here listed:

American institutions and organizations interested in Asia. A reference directory. 2nd ed. Compiled by the Asian Society, Inc. Editor: Ward Morehouse. Assistant editor: Edith Ehrman. New York, 1961.

A Survey of American interests in the Middle East, covering business, philanthropic, welfare, educational and cultural, governmental and international organizations with major interests in the Middle East. Edited by Frances C. Mattison. Washington, D.C., The Middle East Institute (1953).

Morehouse lists in his second edition almost a thousand programmes of universities, religious and educational organizations, foundations, museums and libraries, scientific professional and philanthropic societies and other groups, in fact all non-profit-making organizations with an interest in Asia, which is here interpreted to mean, as is often the case in the U.S.A., those countries between Afghanistan in the West and Japan in the East. The Middle East was omitted because it was dealt with by Mattison in her survey. A detailed indexing apparatus provides co-ordinates for institutions engaged in any particular type of activity and the area in which they operate.

Mattison's is an entirely different type of publication from that of Morehouse. The former author covers the Near East and North Africa, Afghanistan, India, Pakistan and Ceylon, but does not extend farther eastwards, and begins with a 'name index of organizations' as Part I. The second part contains listings of business firms (arranged by category, including press and publications); philanthropic, religious, welfare, educational and cultural organizations; and U.S. government agencies and international organizations in which the United States participates. In this work the emphasis is on commercial organizations and government and international agencies, which are specifically omitted from Morehouse, who normally supplies much more information on libraries and publications. Although the second section provides some information on university activities in the U.S.A., there are significant omissions, among them being Harvard and Yale.

Area studies programmes in the U.S.A. have increased fourfold in the last decade. Two reports issued recently by different government organizations divulge the magnitude of the provisions now being made for these studies in the U.S.A.:

Language and area study programs in American universities. (Department of State, Bureau of Intelligence and Research, External Research Division). Compiled by Larry Moses, 1964.

Resources for language and area studies. A report on an inventory of the language and area centers supported by the National Defence Education Act of 1958. Joseph Axelbrod and Donald L. Bigelow. Washington, D.C.: American Council on Education (1962).

The first-named survey is a revision of *Area study programs in American universities*, previously published in 1954, 1956 and 1959, and in 1962 under the present title. It describes 153[1] distinct programmes in foreign language and area study being offered for graduate degrees in 64 universities and colleges (Africa 16, Asia in general 11, East Asia 19, South and South-East Asia 15, Near East 17). Also included are Latin America, the Soviet Union and Eastern Europe, and Western Europe. Reference is made to previous directories in the introduction.

Language and area study programmes have been defined as 'studies unlimited by historical or disciplinary boundaries but concerned with

[1] Seventeen more than in 1962.

a single world region and its social, economic, political and cultural life'. They draw together scholars from various university departments to form a team of specialists possessing a broad, general knowledge of the area, high ranking in their own discipline, with field experience in, and a knowledge of the language or languages of, the area. To qualify for inclusion in the present report the following criteria are demanded: award of graduate degrees in inter-disciplinary language and area study, or in academic disciplines; insistence on the study of languages or the subject of linguistics; ability to attract federal, foundation, or corporation grants; and the maintenance of adequate specialized library collections. See also:

Area studies reconsidered, by Sir Hamilton Gibb. London: S.O.A.S., 1963.

The most frequently-taught languages at present are Chinese and Japanese. Near Eastern programmes are frequently orientated toward history and archaeology and tend to place more stress on the study of the fine arts and the humanities than do the other programmes. African courses have doubled in number since the 1959 edition.

For each course described the following information is given: title, name of director and number of staff (faculty); degrees awarded; language and area courses provided and library facilities; the extent of outside financial support (in most cases of breath-catching volume by European standards); and the number of national fellowships available n each programme.

The inventory of N.D.E.A. language and area centres gives particulars of 34 organizations enjoying funds derived from this source (Oriental studies 2, South Asia 6, Africa 4, Far Eastern 11, Ural-Altaic 1, South-East Asia 3, Middle Eastern 7, as well as East European 10, and Portuguese 2). For each centre is stated the languages in which instruction was given in Autumn, 1960, and the amount of federal support in funds granted for the academic year 1960–61. All of these centres are named ' . . . Language and Area Center' or ' . . . Studies Center'. Overall policy in respect of them is administered by the Committee on anguage and area centres of the American Council of Education, the members of which are named on a fly-leaf.

Much information on resources for South Asian studies may be gleaned from the published reports of two conferences held in 1960 and 1961:

Resources for South Asian language studies in the United States. Report

E

of a Conference convened by the University of Pennsylvania for the United States Office of Education, 15–16 January, 1960. W. Norman Brown. Philadelphia, University of Pennsylvania Press (1960). [Gives a list of languages taught or soon to be taught in the United States, mostly Indo-Aryan and Dravidian, but including also Persian and Tibetan.]

Resources for South Asian area studies in the United States. Report of a Conference convened by the Committee on South Asia of the Association for Asian Studies for the United States Office of Education, 23–25 February, 1961. Edited by Richard D. Lambert. Philadelphia, University of Pennsylvania Press (1962). [Contains the text of working papers submitted to the Conference, with some additions. Librarians should note especially the contribution by Horace I. Poleman, 'American research library resources and needs for support of studies of South Asia.']

CANADA

The Contribution of Canadian universities to an understanding of Asia and Africa (A bibliographical directory of scholars. Edited by W. A. C. H. Dobson. Ottawa, 1964.) Contribution des universités canadiennes à la connaissance de l'Asie et de l'Afrique. Répertoire bibliographique des universitaires.

The Canadian National Commission for UNESCO published the above-named directory, in which Professor Dobson has listed 102 scholars working in Canada on Asian and African studies, with the titles of books, articles and reviews compiled by them. An index gives the areas of interest of the scholars: Africa (24 names); Ancient Near East (9); The Islamic World (including Turkey, Iran and Pakistan) (17); India and Ceylon (12); South-East Asia (5); China, Japan and Central Asia (23); The Pacific Region (including Indonesia, the Philippines) (5); and General (7). In a short preface Professor Dobson mentions other publications of the National Commission: *Book list on Asia for Canadians,* edited by G. M. Wickens; *Book list on Africa for Canadians,* edited by L. Gray Cowan; and *Asian studies and the Canadian universities,* by W. A. C. H. Dobson and G. M. Wickens. The East–West Committee of the National Commission was also responsible for a survey of Asian and African studies in the universities of Canada, on which a report entitled *International studies* was published by the Canadian Universities Foundation.

UNITED KINGDOM

Compared with the wealth of information available for the U.S.A., for Great Britain only a minimum amount of information is available in the meagre summary given in the statement of courses available in British universities given in the Association of British Orientalists' *A select list of books on the civilizations of the Orient* (Oxford, 1955). This is now greatly out of date, and a new survey is urgently required, especially since the adoption of many of the Hayter recommendations and the formation of area study centres in many universities. For more up-to-date information see the calendars of the relevant universities.

JAPAN

Survey of humanistic studies in Japan, 1960. Compiled by Japanese National Commission for UNESCO and High Education and Science Bureau, Ministry of Education. Published by Science Council of Japan, 1961. Tokyo.

The main part of this unique survey lists the titles of all the courses in the humanities offered at 135 out of the 141 universities in the country which have faculties concerned with 'humanistic studies', and the names of those who deliver the lectures or conduct the courses.

There are eighty topics of instruction included, comprised in four groups, Literature (and language), Thought (including Religion and Education), History and Arts. The topics with an Oriental or Asian content are: Japanese literature A – D, Chinese literature A – C, Indian literature, Hebraic literature; Chinese philosophy A – C, Indian philosophy A – C, Japanese ethics, Oriental ethics, Buddhism, Shintoism; Japanese history A – E, Oriental history A – D, Japanese archaeology, Oriental archaeology; History of Japanese fine arts, History of Oriental fine arts, Japanese and Oriental musicology. Other Asian and African topics, especially those relating to the Middle East and Africa, may be found recorded under 'general' sections in each of the four divisions.

Chapter II records the 'Activities of research institutes, member societies of the Union of Japanese Associations, learned Societies and Associations and others', providing details of the directorate, research staff, history, purpose, research activities, library and publications of these organizations.

Research institutes for Asian studies in Japan. Directories, no. 1. The Centre for East Asian Cultural Studies, Toyo Bunko, Tokyo (1962). Editor: Kazuo Enoki.

This lists 96 research institutes engaged in the study of Eastern and South-East Asia only, arranged by subject, with an appendix giving a selected list (50 names) of learned societies and associations in Japan, also arranged subject-wise.

Japanese researchers in Asian studies. Directories, no. 2. The Centre for East Asian Cultural Studies, Tokyo (1963). Editor: Kazuo Enoki.

This directory lists some four thousand Japanese scholars engaged in research in Asian studies in the fields of the humanities and the social sciences, i.e. philosophy, religious studies, prehistory and archaeology, history, geography, law and politics, economy [*sic*], sociology, education, anthropology and ethnology, fine arts, language and literature. For each scholar named details are given of date of birth, present post held, establishment where his degree was obtained, address and subject in which he works. At the end is given a list of the English names of academic institutions mentioned in the book (universities and colleges and research institutes).

Other works giving information on the structure of Asian studies in Japan include the following titles:

'Trends of Asian studies in postwar Japan.' *The Developing Economies*, Preliminary issue no. 1, March–August, 1962, pp. 75–105. [*The Developing Economies* is the English language journal of the Institute of Asian Economic Affairs in Tokyo. The Institute's monthly journal in Japanese, *Ajia Keizai*, began in 1960. This particular article supplies notes on 'Trends of research activities on Asian areas in Japan; Trend of theories on the development of less-developed countries in Japan; Studies of the Indian economy in Japan; and Post-war researches in Japan on the economies of South-East Asian countries other than India.']

Soviet–Asian relations conference. Conference report no. 7. Japanese studies of contemporary China, by Yuji Muramatsu. (With a supplement: 'A Soviet view of Chinese studies in Japan', by S. L. Tikhvinskiy.) School of International Relations, University of Southern California, Los Angeles, 8, 9 and 10 June, 1959. [One of fifteen conference papers, most of which deal with Russian and Asian studies in various parts of the world, but which have not been available to me. This paper deals with the origin and background of Japanese interest in China and Chinese communism, and provides details of training, library resources, research organizations, publications and personnel resources. A chapter on 'conclusions' estimates the needs of Japanese studies of contemporary China. Two appendices give a 'Who's who in the modern Chinese field in Japan' and 'selected bio-bibliographies of Japanese specialists on modern China.'

Japanese science review: economic sciences, no. 8 (1962) contains in addition to the customary bibliography and abstracts of economic sciences, two short review articles on money and banking, and the history of social and economic thought (1956–60), as well as reports on the activities of two societies, the Japan Society of Political Economy and the Society for Asian Political and Economic Studies. Two addenda list (1) major projects of research supported by government grants, and (2) a directory of universities, national, local-prefectural or city (Koritsu) and private (Shintsu), with full details of faculties and graduate schools of economics, commerce or business administration.

Asian studies in Japan. Aziya Seikei Gakkai (The Society for Asian Political and Economic Studies), 1964. [A pamphlet containing seven essays on studies of the economics and politics of China, India and South-East Asia. The Society operates from the Research Room, Library of Tokyo University.]

Japanese universities and colleges 1963, with major research institutes. Published by Japan Overseas Advertiser Co., Ltd., Tokyo, Japan.

This work provides information in English on all of the universities, junior colleges and technical colleges, arranged by administrative district. The major research institutes also mentioned are mainly controlled by government departments. For each university is normally given General information, and details of Undergraduate schools and departments, Graduate school, and 'Attached facilities', under which heading are included libraries, publications and foreign students.

From the above paragraphs it will be seen that we have for Japan, thanks especially to the unremitting labours of all those connected with the Centre for East Asian Studies, and especially its assistant director, Kazuo Enoki, a documentation unrivalled by any other country. We have lists of four thousand scholars engaged in Asian research, their spheres of activity, the institutes in which they work, the universities with all their research institutes, libraries and publications, and even (in the Survey of humanistic studies), a detailed inventory of all the courses of lectures and seminars held in these universities.

TAIWAN

Directory of the cultural organizations of the Republic of China. National Central Library, Taipei, Taiwan, China, 1961.

This work provides details of learned societies; research institutes; libraries, museums and social education centres; universities and colleges; and research departments in public and private enterprises. There is no index, although the contents list indicates that it had been intended to provide one.

KOREA

The third in the series of directories issued by the Centre for East Asian Cultural Studies is devoted to:

Research institutes and researchers of Asian studies in the Republic of Korea. Directories, no. 3. The Centre for East Asian Cultural Studies, Tokyo (1963). Editor: Kazuo Enoki.

It includes information on the major activities, publications and 'researchers' of seventy organizations interested in general studies, psychology, religious studies, the humanities and social studies, and adds to these a list of 'researchers' giving brief details of thirty-eight Korean scholars, their names arranged in alphabetical order, and indexes to the research institutes names in the book, and names of scholars mentioned in the body of the work as well as in the list of 'researchers'.

INDIA

Oriental studies in India; edited by R. N. Dandekar, V. Raghavan. Organizing Committee, 26th International Congress of Orientalists, New Delhi, 1964.

The first part of this work, presented to all delegates attending the 26th International Congress of Orientalists, gives a series of surveys of achievements in Indian Oriental studies since 1947 (the date of the country's achievement of independence). Special attention is given to books, treatises, editions of texts and studies published in the years under review. Though primarily (and naturally) Indological in inclination, with some excursions into what were once called 'Greater Indian studies' (South-East Asia, Tibet, China, Central Asia and the Middle East), Oriental studies in India are paying increased attention to other regions of Asia and Africa.

In the second part, Dr Raghavan has edited a directory of centres of Oriental studies in India. Research institutes, universities and their several departments, libraries, publication agencies, and in fact all organizations with a stake in the Oriental world are recorded, with a great deal of very useful information on the scope and purpose, publications, library collections and historical details of each. Of these institutions 369 are named, arranged under states and the union territories of Delhi, Goa, Himachal Pradesh, Pondicherry, and including five All-India bodies, i.e. congresses and learned societies.

CZECHOSLOVAKIA, EASTERN EUROPE

Dušan Zbavitel: *Oriental studies in Czechoslovakia.* (Translated from the Czech by Iris Urwin.) Prague; Orbis, 1959.

Zbavitel has given us a short history of the development of Oriental studies in Czechoslovakia, as well as information as to the present situation in respect of Near Eastern, Indian and Chinese studies in his country. Names of prominent scholars of the past are given, with their principal works as well as names of present-day workers in the field with details of the work on which they are currently engaged. Details are also given of Oriental studies outside Prague, of studies at universities, the Oriental Institute, periodicals, societies and museums.

A brief account of the situation in East Asian and South-East Asian studies in Czechoslovakia and Eastern Europe was made by Jaroslaw Prusek to the International Meeting of Experts and Representatives of Research Institutes in East Asia in 1961, and is reported in *East Asian cultural studies* I, 1–4, March, 1962, pp. 38–42. A more detailed article on Czechoslovakia alone was published in the same journal, vol. III, nos. 1–2, June, 1962, pp. 52–56. In the former article brief notes only are given on Poland, Hungary, Rumania and Yugoslavia in addition to Czechoslovakia. In Eastern European countries research is undertaken not only in the universities, but also in a large variety of research institutes forming part of the network of the Academy of Sciences. In the U.S.S.R., for example, there are two institutes of Oriental studies (each now called Institute of the Peoples of Asia), of which the Leningrad one is concerned mainly with philological and the Moscow one with modern studies, as well as similar institutes attached to the academies of the various Asiatic republics. The two main institutes are said to employ about one thousand research workers.

FRANCE

Paul Demiéville: 'Organization of East Asian studies in France.' *J. Asian studies,* 18 (1958), pp. 163–81.

Demiéville provides particulars of work done and courses provided at the principal universities, libraries, museums and other institutions in Paris and the provinces, as well as in institutions overseas under French control, in the fields of Indian and Far Eastern studies, with names of the holders of chairs and lectureships in the various institutions, and much information about libraries and their collections. The article includes a list of theses concerning East Asia completed in France during the period 1946–58.

WEST GERMANY

Denkschrift zur Lage der Orientalistik. Im Auftrage der Deutschen Forschungsgemeinschaft und im Zusammenarbeit mit zahlreichen Fachvertretern herausgegeben von Prof. Dr Adam Falkenstein. Wiesbaden, Steiner, 1960.

The *Denkschrift* is the West German equivalent of the Scarbrough Report. Compiled at the behest of the German Research Commission (Deutsche Forschungsgemeinschaft), it is one of a series of such surveys made in many branches of science in order to bring to the notice of education officials, parliaments and ministries the needs of the various disciplines for future development. A whole section is given up to a statement of the present situation in Oriental studies, beginning with a delineation of the scope and range of the individual branches of these studies – Egyptology; Ancient Near East; Semitic and Islamic studies; Iranian studies, Indology and Tibetan studies; Sinology, Japanology, Mongol and Central Asiatic Turkish studies, South-East Asian studies; Languages and cultures of Austronesia; Languages and cultures of Africa – each of which is represented at one or more of the West German universities. This is followed by a description of the present facilities provided at the Oriental institutes and seminars in the universities, at the Seminar für orientalische Sprachen at the University of Bonn (an establishment for teaching modern Oriental languages for practical purposes), at technical universities and polytechnics (Hochschulen), in libraries and museums, and in academies, societies and research institutes of various kinds. The section on publication opportunities indicates the periodicals and monograph series at present providing these facilities. Proposals are put forward for the amelioration of all existing services.

After a general analysis of the situation, a series of tables, in the form of folding charts, gives information on the position in respect of chairs, departments, established posts and those occupied at the time of writing, the state of the Seminar library (number of books and catalogues available) and the state of the Oriental section of the University

Library, for the seven fields of study at the universities of Berlin (Freie Universität), Bonn, Erlangen, Frankfurt, Freiburg, Göttingen, Heidelberg, Kiel, Köln, Mainz, Marburg, München, Münster, Saarbrücken, Tübingen and Würzburg. It seems that the only West German university making no provision for Oriental studies is Giessen.

ITALY

Commissione nazionale italiana per l'UNESCO. *Contributo italiano alla conoscenza dell'Oriente: repertorio bibliografico dal 1935 al 1948.* Firenze, Le Monnier (1962).

This work, a bibliography of works on Oriental and African studies published in Italy or by Italians from 1935 to 1958, contains an introductory section providing a summary list of institutions, that is university institutions where Oriental and African languages are taught, cultural institutes and museums with collections of Oriental objects.

TYPES OF ORGANIZATION

I. UNIVERSITIES

Oriental and African studies in universities are fostered by means of the teaching of students for first and higher degrees and by research. The first of these functions may be carried out centrally or in individual colleges: research may be undertaken in centres, institutes, seminars, departments, and carried out by working parties and other groups which may or may not be based on a building which provides facilities including a library. All universities publish calendars which give names and posts held by academic staff, details of courses provided, facilities for research and the like: they, or their component parts may sponsor or issue their own publications proclaiming the results of research carried out under their auspices. The knowledge that a person holds a teaching post in a university normally guarantees that a work bearing his name as author may be regarded as scientific, authoritative, based on original materials and thought, and reliable.

Senior scholars in universities train graduate students for research by supervising a particular piece of work on a chosen topic which, if successfully carried to completion, leads to the compilation of a thesis and the award of a higher degree. These theses, which are sometimes printed and issued for sale on the Continent, are deposited in university libraries. They represent a young scholar's first essay in research and are compiled principally in order that he may be trained in the techniques of research. Nevertheless they must contain original material by requirement of the university's regulations, and they may in certain cases represent the only available information on some topic of abstruse interest or limited scope. Hence these are often listed by librarians and others either as successful higher degree exercises as in the following works, or sometimes while in progress. Examples for the U.S.A., Germany, Great Britain and Taiwan are given below:

Columbia University members' essays and doctoral dissertations on Asia 1875–1956. Compiled by the East Asiatic Library . . . New York, 1957.

C. W. Stucki: *American doctoral dissertations on Asia, 1933–58, including appendix of master's theses at Cornell University.* Ithaca, 1959.

University of Chicago. Committee on Far Eastern Civilizations and Committee on Southern Asian Studies. *The University of Chicago doctoral dissertations and master's theses on Asia 1894–1962.* Compiled by the Far Eastern Library, University of Chicago Library. Chicago, 1962. [455 masters' and 175 doctoral dissertations on the Far East (including Siberia), South-East Asia, South Asia and Pacific Islands, submitted during the years 1891–1962.

Verzeichnis indienkundlicher Hochschulschriften; Deutschland-Österreich-Schweiz, von Klaus Ludwig Janert. Wiesbaden: Harrassowitz, 1961. [Dissertations on Indological subjects submitted to universities in Germany, Austria and Switzerland.]

Preliminary list of Ph.D. dissertations on South Asia, 1933–60 (unedited), compiled by Earl R. Schmidt. (University of Wisconsin, Madison, n.d.) [American dissertations only, arranged in one alphabetical sequence by name of author.]

Deutsche Dissertationen über Afrika; ein Verzeichnis für die Jahre 1918–59, zusammengestellt von Jochen Köhler. Bonn, 1962. [German dissertations on Africa submitted during the years 1918–59.]

Library of Congress. *A list of American doctoral dissertations on Africa.* Compiled by the African Section. Washington, 1962.

Standing Conference of Libraries with Materials on Africa. *Theses on Africa.* Cambridge, 1964.

Handbook of current research projects in the Republic of China. National Central Library, Taipeh, Taiwan, 1962. [Brief account of 366 research projects currently being undertaken by the Academia Sinica, in universities and other research establishments in Taiwan, arranged in systematic order by subject. All branches of learning are included, but the bulk of the entries are for the natural and applied sciences – 277 (139 on agriculture) out of 366.]

Under the title of *External research*, the External Research Staff of the Bureau of Intelligence and Research of the Department of State, Washington 25, D.C., publishes lists of work in progress in the U.S.A. on the regions of the world, including Asia, Middle East and Africa. The lists are compiled from entries incorporated into the 'Research catalog on foreign areas and international affairs' which had been sent in by American scholars. An estimated date of completion for each item of work is given and a forecast of the form that the completed work will take, Ph.D. dissertation, paper, book, etc. Completed work is included in lists published twice a year in Spring and Fall which are entitled *External research: a list of recently completed studies*, which cover the same regions.

II. PROFESSIONAL ASSOCIATIONS

In some countries persons engaged professionally in research or teaching have banded together to form associations. These are not trade unions but exist to provide a forum where members of academic staffs of universities as well as librarians and museum officials can get together to discuss matters of common interest affecting their work. Meetings may be held at regular intervals where papers are read and discussions held, and newsletters may be published with the function of providing information on current developments in the profession. In the U.K. the two organizations of this kind are the Association of British Orientalists (ABO) and the African Studies Association of the United Kingdom (ASA).

The ABO owes its inception to a Conference held to mark the bicentenary of the birth of Sir William Jones at University College, Oxford, on 2–6 September, 1946, which recommended that the Conference should be put on a permanent footing. The Constitution of the Association was approved on 21 August, 1947 at the second Conference held at Pembroke College, Cambridge. Proceedings of the first two Conferences were published as separate pamphlets by the Royal India (and Pakistan) Society, those of the third to the sixth in the journal of that society (*Indian*) *Art and letters*. No printed records exist of the eleventh Conference but reports on the twelfth (Durham), thirteenth (Oxford) and fourteenth (Edinburgh) were published in the *Bulletin of the Association of British Orientalists*.

Proceedings of the Sir William Jones bicentenary conference, held at University College, Oxford, 2–6 September, 1946. London: Royal India Society [1946?]

Conference of British Orientalists held at Pembroke College, Cambridge, 20–22 August, 1947. London: The Royal India and Pakistan Society [1947?]

'Association of British Orientalists: Third Conference, Durham, 18–21 July, 1949.' *Indian art and letters* N.S. 23, 2, 1949, pp. 76–82.

'—Fourth Conference, Oxford, 11–14 September, 1950.' *Art and letters* N.S. 25, 2, 1951, pp. 33–44.

'—Fifth Conference, Cambridge, 23–26 July, 1951.' *Art and letters* N.S. 26, 2, 1952, pp. 74–87.

'—Sixth Conference, Edinburgh, 15–20 July, 1953.' *Art and letters* N.S. 27, 2, 1953, pp. 51–58.

'—Seventh Conference, Oxford, 18–21 July, 1955.' *Art and letters* N.S. 30, 1, 1956, pp. 33–34.

'—Eighth Conference, Cambridge, 17–20 September, 1956.' *Art and letters* N.S. 31, 1, 1957, pp. 23–26.

'—Ninth Conference, Manchester, 15–18 September, 1958.' *Art and letters* N.S. 32, 1, 1959, pp. 23–25.

'—Tenth Conference, Bangor, 6–9 July, 1959.' *Art and letters* N.S. 33, 1, 1960, pp. 22–23.

'Twelfth Conference of British Orientalists [Durham, 3–6 September 1962].' *Bull. Assoc. Brit. Or.* N.S. 1, 1 March, 1963, pp. 3–4.

'Thirteenth Conference of British Orientalists [Oxford, 25–28 March, 1963].' *Bull. Assoc. Brit. Or.* N.S. 1, 2 October, 1963, pp. 2–5.

'Fourteenth Conference of British Orientalists [Edinburgh, 6–9 April, 1964]'. *Bull. Assoc. Brit. Or.* N.S. 2, 1–2 December, 1964, pp. 2–4.

The ABO has published a *Bulletin of Oriental Studies* from 1951 to 1962, which included titles of theses and books already submitted or published, or which had reached an advanced stage of preparation as well as additions to manuscript collections. In 1963 the *Bulletin* appeared in a new form as the *Bulletin of the Association of British Orientalists* and now contains reports of conferences, notes on library accessions and publications, news of the profession, a list of all books relating to Asia and Oriental studies published in the U.K. during the previous few months, and an article of a general bibliographical character. A list of theses submitted recently to the universities has been distributed with each issue in the new series.

The ASA was founded only in 1963, and also publishes a newsletter.
ABO has a libraries group which has set up a joint committee with
SCONUL to discuss library co-operation along the lines recommended
in the Hayter Report. ASA will not set up a similar committee but will
work in close association with SCOLMA, an organization of libraries
with collections of materials on Africa which was founded in 1962 and
which publishes a newsletter three times a year entitled *Library materials
on Africa*.

The African Studies Association of the U.S.A. likewise has an active
library committee which publishes useful articles of a bibliographical
character in the Association's *Bulletin*.

The Association for Asian Studies plays a dual role in the United
States: it publishes a learned journal (*Journal of Asian Studies*) and a
Newsletter giving news of interest to members of the profession.

III. LEARNED SOCIETIES

The International Union of Orientalists formed in 1951 by the 22nd
International Congress of Orientalists has as its object 'to promote con-
tacts between orientalists throughout the world, and to organize con-
gresses, research and publications'. It sponsors the publication of
Orientalist bibliographies on Egyptology, the Ancient Near East and
Buddhism.[1]

Most countries in Europe have a national Oriental society in addition, it may be, to a professional organization for Orientalists. Membership of the society is normally open to amateurs as well as professionals,
persons who may have spent some years in the service of their country
overseas, or members of the general public with an interest in these
areas. These societies meet regularly to hear papers delivered by members or guests and may possess their own premises where a substantial
library may have been built up. They often in addition publish a journal
which may rank as one of the foremost periodical publications in the
field.

The principal Orientalist societies of Europe and America are:

Royal Asiatic Society of Great Britain and Ireland.
　　See *Centenary volume* ... 1923.
Société asiatique (France).
　　See *Société asiatique: le livre du centenaire (1822–1922)*. Paris, 1922.
Deutsche morgenländische Gesellschaft (Germany).

---

[1] For other international societies, see pp. 44–5.

Società asiatica italiana.
Polskie Towarzystwo Orientalistyczne (Poland).
American Oriental Society.

The International African Institute, with its seat in London, is a information centre for African ethnology, linguistics and social studies: it conducts research programmes and stimulates production of literature in African languages, as well as publishing two important journals, *Africa* and *African abstracts*, the *Africa bibliography series*, and monographs on ethnographical and linguistic subjects.

IV. CONGRESSES

National Orientalist societies are usually responsible for making arrangements in connection with the International Congress of Orientalists. First held in Paris, 1873, the Congress now meets every three years, the last one being held in New Delhi early in 1964. The published proceedings of these Congresses are useful not only for the complete texts or summaries of papers delivered before sessions of the Congress which are normally included in them, but also for the lists of delegates which indicate the principal institutions interested in Oriental studies, and the names and addresses of those who attended the Congress.

Here is a list of the conferences held up to 1964, with details of their published proceedings:

1. Paris, 1873. *Compte-rendu.* 3 vols. 1874–76.
2. London, 1874. *Transactions.* 1876.
3. St Petersburg, 1876. *Travaux.* 2 vols. 1879–80.
4. Florence, 1878. *Atti.* 2 vols. 1880–81.
5. Berlin, 1881. *Verhandlungen.* 2 vols. in 3. 1881–82.
6. Leiden, 1883. *Actes.* 4 vols. 1884–85.
7. Vienna, 1886. *Berichte (Verhandlungen).* 5 vols. 1888–89.
8. Stockholm and Christiania, 1889. *Actes.* 5 vols. Leide, 1891–
9. London, 1892. *Transactions.* 2 vols. 1893.
10. Geneva, 1894. *Actes.* 3 vols. Leide, 1895–97.
11. Paris, 1897. *Actes.* 5 vols. 1898–99.
12. Rome, 1899. *Actes.* 3 vols. Florence, 1901–2.
13. Hamburg, 1902. *Verhandlungen.* Leiden, 1904.
14. Algiers, 1905. *Actes.* 3 vols. in 4. Paris, 1906–8.
15. Copenhagen, 1908. *Actes.* 1909.
16. Athens, 1912. *Actes.* 1912.
17. Oxford, 1928. *Proceedings.* 1929.
18. Leiden, 1931. *Actes.* 1932.

19. Rome, 1935. *Atti.* 1938.
20. Brussels, 1938. *Actes.* Louvain, 1940.
21. Paris, 1948. *Actes.* 1949.
22. Istanbul, 1951. *Proceedings.* Istanbul, 1953; Leiden, 1957.
23. Cambridge, 1954. *Proceedings.* London, n.d.
24. Munich, 1957. *Akten.* (1959.)
25. Moscow, 1960. *Trudy.* 4 vols. 1962–63.
26. New Delhi, 1964.

From the XXIII Congress onwards the delegation attending from the U.S.S.R. has provided copies of papers read by its members in separate pamphlet form. English translations were supplied of the original Russian texts of the papers, submitted to the XXIII Congress, which may or may not have been printed in summary form in the published proceedings of the Congress. The individual papers were collected into groups corresponding to the sections of the Congress: each group has title-pages in Russian and English:

Doklady Sovetskoy delegatzii na XXIII Mezhdunarodnom Kongresse Vostokovedov—Papers presented by the Soviet delegation at the XXIII International Congress of Orientalists. Moskva, 1954.

The papers presented to the XXV Congress were published as separate pamphlets, the majority in Russian, with some in English, French and German. They carry the imprint 'Moskva, 1960'.

For the XXVI Congress all but a very few of the papers were published in English. They are dated Moscow, 1963.

These international conferences may nowadays be attended by upwards of a thousand Orientalists representing the disciplines of Egyptology; Ancient Near Eastern studies; Biblical, Hebrew and Jewish studies; the Christian East; Semitics; Islamic studies; Turcology; Iranian and Caucasian studies; Indology; Central Asian and Altaic studies; the Far East; South-East Asia and African studies.

International conferences on a rather smaller scale have been held annually in Japan since 1956. Foreign scholars 'of upper graduate level and above' are invited to attend to meet representative Japanese scholars for the 'exchange of knowledge'. The papers and proceedings of the conferences are published in English and other European languages under the title:

Transactions of the International Conference of Orientalists in Japan. The Tōhō Gakkai (The Institute of Eastern Culture). 1956.

National Orientalists' Congresses have also been held on occasion, especially in France, Germany and India.

The French held conferences in the 1870's, for which volumes (*Compte-rendu*) were published as follows:

Paris–Levallois, 1874.   Paris, 1875.
Saint-Étienne, 1875. 2 vols.   Paris, 1878.
Marseilles, 1876.   Marseilles, 1876.
Lyons, 1878.   Lyon, 1880.

The German conferences have been held since 1849; their proceedings are published in the *Zeitschrift des Deutschen Morgenländischen Gesellschaft.*

The proceedings of the first two Belgian Orientalist congresses were announced in 1965 as being in the press.

Actes des deux premières rencontres des orientalistes belges sous le titre 'Journée des orientalistes belges' 1963 et 1964.

I am indebted to Col. Geoffrey Wheeler of the Central Asian Research Centre in London for the following information in respect of conferences held in the Soviet Union:

'The first All-Union Conference was held in Tashkent in June, 1957. The Conference of 22–26 May, 1962 was held in Baku and not in Tashkent as stated in *Central Asian Review*, 10, 3, p. 265. It was not described as an All-Union Conference but as an All-Union Scientific Session of Orientalists devoted to the history and economy of Afghanistan, Iran and Turkey. A brief account of this was published in *C.A.R.* 11, 1, pp. 98–102. A volume containing the text of all the papers was published in 1963 (*Kratkiye Soobshcheniya Instituta Narodov Azii,* no. 73).

'There were detailed accounts of the 1957 Tashkent Conference in the daily press and a summary of them was published in *C.A.R.* 5, 1957, pp. 258–70. The titles of papers read in plenary and departmental sessions were given in *East Turkic R.* 1, 1958, pp. 113–18. *Sovetskoye Vostokovedeniya,* 1957, no. 3, pp. 7–16, contained the opening speech by B. G. Gafurov and some other information. No. 4 of *Sov. Vost.* gave an account of the Conference and the concluding speech. There was also a report of the proceedings in *Izv. A.N. Uz. SSR,* 1957, no. 2. It appears that the full text of all the papers has never been published.

'In addition to the above there have been two All-Union Conferences on Oriental Textology, the first held in Moscow in March, 1962 and the second in Tashkent in June, 1963. There have also been various

other conferences on such subjects as Turcology and Iranology. These
are called inter-republican conferences, possibly because they are only
attended by the republics concerned.

'It appears that there has so far been only one All-Union Conference
of Orientalists under that name, the one held in Tashkent in 1957.'

The All-India Oriental Conference has been held at intervals of a few
years since its first meeting at Poona in 1959. A brief historical sketch
(1919–49), together with author and title catalogues of papers submitted
to the first twelve sessions, and published in the *Proceedings (and
Transactions)* is given in the publication:

*Index of papers submitted to the All-India Oriental Conference sessions
I–XII (1919–44).* Compiled by K. Venkateswara Sarma. Poona,
1949.

Sessions of the Conference have been held at, and the proceedings
published at, the places given in the following titles:

Date and place	Date published
1. Poona, 1919	2 vols. 1920.
2. Calcutta, 1922	1923
3. Madras, 1924	1925
4. Allahabad, 1926	2 vols. 1927–28
5. Lahore, 1928	2 vols. 1930
6. Patna, 1930	1933
7. Baroda, 1933	1935
8. Mysore, 1935	Bangalore, 1937
9. Trivandrum, 1937	1940
10. Tirupati, 1940	Madras, 1941
11. Hyderabad-Deccan, 1941	2 vols. 1943
12. Benares, 1943–44	4 vols. 1946–48
13. Nagpur, 1946	1951
14. Darbhanga (Mithila), 1948	2 vols. 1949–52
15. Bombay, 1949	n.d.
16. Lucknow, 1951	2 vols. 1953–55
17. Ahmedabad, 1953	n.d.
18. Annamalainagar, 1955	1958
19. Delhi, 1957	2 vols. 1959–61
20. Bhubaneshwar, 1959	Vol. 2, pt. 2, 1961
21. Ahmedabad, 1961	

The first International Congress of Africanists was held at Accra,
Ghana, in December, 1962.

F

INDIVIDUAL SCHOLARS

There is no current directory of Orientalists or Africanists, on an international scale, though the British associations are working on the compilation of directories of scholars in these fields in this country. As has already been mentioned, the directories of the Centre for East Asian Cultural Studies contain lists of scholars prominent in the area falling within the Centre's range of interests. Prior to the First World War there was published in Germany the *Internationales Taschenbuch für Orientalisten*, ed. R. Haupt (2nd ed. 1910), which gave the names and addresses of Orientalists and the various specialities to which each was addicted, as well as details of institutes and learned societies, the titles of the principal Orientalist periodicals, and the names of heads of state of Oriental countries. Each issue contained copies of photographs of Oriental scholars, who had died during the previous year. Another source for Oriental iconography is the rather quaintly titled *Picturesque Orientalia*, by R. N. Sardesai (Poona, 1938), which contains reproductions of 103 photographs of eminent Indologists. Pictures of a hundred German Indologists, born between 1682 and 1899, are given in the work:

> *Bilder hundert deutscher Indologen*, von Wilhelm Rau. (Verzeichnis der orientalischen Handschriften in Deutschland, Supplementband 4.) Wiesbaden, 1965.

> Some of these are taken from a collection of photographs of eminent Orientalists in possession of the Deutsche Morgenländische Gesellschaft.

The names of about one thousand Orientalists, including many alive at the time, are listed in alphabetical order, with dates and places of births and – where applicable – deaths, are given in:

> *Orientalistisches Datenbuch. Eine Sammlung von Geburts- und Todesdaten von Orientalisten seit den Anfängen der orientalischen Sprachwissenschaft bis auf die Gegenwart in alphabetischer Anordnung*. Herausgegeben von Arthur Heyne. Leipzig, 1912.

PART TWO

THE LITERATURE AND
ITS CONTROLS

[5]

Manuscripts

Although the art of printing with movable types was invented in the Far East in the eleventh century A.D., many centuries before its introduction into Europe, the manuscript book continues to be used in other parts of Asia right up to the present day. Printing was used for Hebrew books and Arabic books in Hebrew characters soon after its 'invention' by Gutenberg in the second half of the fifteenth century, but it was not until the eighteenth century that it came to be used for the reduplication of books in languages using the Arabic script in the Middle East, and not until the end of that century was it used in India. This reason, coupled with the fact that Orientalists have always been fewer in number than philologists of other persuasions, accounts for the extraordinary importance that the manuscript still plays in Oriental studies. An acquaintance with the manuscript situation, therefore, is of vital concern to the Asian librarian and bibliographer.

For an account of all types of manuscript books in the East, the materials used for writing and other features of Oriental manuscripts, see:
  The hand-produced book, by David Diringer London (1953).

EUROPEAN MSS. RELATING TO ASIA

Before turning to a consideration of manuscripts in Oriental languages, it is necessary to recognize that vast numbers of unpublished documents in European languages relating to Asia are to be found in all the principal repositories in Europe and America. These documents may be archives, in the sense of official records of business transactions of all kinds, or manuscripts, in the sense of compositions of imaginative writing or connected accounts relating to all subjects.

The principal collections of archives in Great Britain are to be found in the Public Record Office and the India Office Library, in either case consisting of the official records of government departments, the India

Office Library being restricted to those of the India Office and its predecessor, the East India Company. The India Office is the only department whose records are housed outside the Public Record Office. The records of all other departments are eventually transferred to the P.R.O., which has recently published a guide to its collections:

> *Guide to the contents of the Public Record Office. Vol. I. Legal records etc. Vol. II. State papers and departmental records.* London, H.M.S.O., 1963. Revised and extended (to 1960) from the *Guide* by the late M. S. Giuseppi.

The P.R.O. is also publishing a series of 'Public Record Office handbooks'. The scope of this series, originally called 'Sectional Guides', embraces not only guides to specific categories of records but also 'works of other kinds serving to elucidate the public records or to facilitate research in them'. Those so far published which are especially relevant to studies of Asia and Africa are:

3. *The records of the Colonial and Dominions Offices.* 1964.

4. *List of Cabinet papers 1880–1914.* 1964. (To be continued in a later handbook to December, 1916, when the Cabinet Secretariat was formed.)

6. *List of papers of the Committee of Imperial Defence to 1914.* 1964.

The India Office Records at the Commonwealth Relations Office are closely linked with the Library, the librarian being also Keeper of the Records. They consist of the records of the East India Company (1600–1858), Board of Control (1784–1858), India Office (1858–1947) and Burma Office (1937–47). Also included are a comprehensive collection of maps of the Indian sub-continent, and a collection amounting to some 100,000 volumes of official publications. These include virtually complete sets of British Parliamentary publications relating to undivided India, and the publications (to 1947) of the Central and Provincial Governments of India and the Indian States.

A brief introduction to the records is being compiled for publication, and the new guide to the Library will also contain a section on the records. For information as to guides and lists already published see the pamphlet:

> *The India Office Library; its function, scope and resources.* Commonwealth Relations Office, May, 1962. (pp. 7–8, The India Office Records.)

Other collections of archives, official or national, exist in many depositories, including the county record offices, where they may be found interspersed among the manuscript collections. The India Office Library is also noted for its manuscripts, both in European and Oriental languages, which are described in a series of catalogues listed in:

Commonwealth Relations Office, *A Guide to the India Office Library*, by S. C. Sutton. London, H.M.S.O., 1952. [New edition in preparation.] (European MSS. pp. 22–26; Oriental MSS. pp. 26–39).

It should be remembered that the East India Company operated at various periods in its long history in many countries of Asia, and indeed Africa, too, outside its main sphere in the Indo-Pakistan sub-continent. For this reason there will be found also among the collections made by the Company's servants many documents relating to the Far East, South-East Asia, the Near and Middle East, and Africa.

Next in order of importance comes the British Museum, which possesses among its foundation collections and its additional manuscripts much material relating to Asia and Africa. A list of the manuscript catalogues in the Museum was compiled by the present Keeper of the Western Manuscripts:

The Catalogues of the manuscript collections in the British Museum, by T. C. Skeat. Rev. ed. London, British Museum, 1962. (Originally published in the *Journal of Documentation*, vol. 7, March, 1951, no. 1.)

In addition to these two prime sources for manuscripts in European languages, examples are to be found in very many of the governmental, university, special and public libraries, business houses, county record offices, museums, and in private ownership throughout the United Kingdom. For nearly a hundred years the Historical Manuscripts Commission has been publishing detailed reports on manuscript collections in Great Britain, mostly of the eighteenth century or earlier. Two indexes, of persons and places, have been published: these facilitate the discovery of single items and whole collections relating to Asia and Africa existing in a wide variety of libraries, but especially in private hands. An introduction to the Commission's work, for the use of students, was compiled by R. A. Roberts, and these list indexes to places and persons mentioned in the collections:

Guide to reports on collections of MSS. of private families, corporations and institutions in Great Britain and Ireland (1870–1911). Part 1, Topographical. Part 2, Index of persons. 3 vols. London, 1914–38.

The Reports of the Historical MSS. Commission, by R. A. Roberts. (Helps for students no. 22). London, 1920.

Reports of the Royal Commission on Historical Manuscripts, revised to 31 August, 1956. (Government publications, sectional list no. 17), H.M.S.O.

The National Register of Archives, a branch of the Historical Manuscripts Commission, maintains a collection of typescript reports on privately-owned manuscript collections throughout the country. Indexes of names and subjects are being compiled and are available for consultation by scholars and research workers. The Register is held at the Public Record Office.

For information on other organizations interested in European archives and manuscripts see the introduction to:

A Guide to manuscripts relating to America in Great Britain and Ireland. Ed. by B. R. Crick and Miriam Alman, under the general supervision of H. L. Beales. Oxford U.P., 1961.

The work just mentioned is the latest in a series of guides, or union catalogues, to manuscript collections relating to America which began in 1912. A similar series for manuscripts in European languages relating to Asia and Africa is being compiled in the School of Oriental and African Studies. The first volume, dealing with South and South-East Asia was published in 1965 by the Oxford University Press. Similar guides, covering the remaining parts of Asia and Africa are in process of compilation.

A Guide to manuscripts and documents in the British Isles relating to South and South-East Asia; compiled by M. D. Wainwright and Noel Matthews, under the general supervision of J. D. Pearson. Oxford U.P., 1965.

A similar guide to source materials available for the study of modern Indian history in Indian archives is being undertaken by V. C. Joshi of the National Archives of India. A description of the scheme was given in the first issue of *South Asia microform newsletter* (February, 1964) and in a pamphlet entitled:

Guide to sources of modern Indian history project. The Indian Institute of Public Administration [1963?].

The Institute of Historical Research in the University of London has embarked upon a scheme for the production of a series of guides to materials for the history of West Africa to be found in European archive collections and libraries. The first volume has already been published:

Materials for West African history in the archives of Belgium and Holland, by Patricia Carson. London, Athlone Press, 1962. (Guides to materials for West African history in European archives, 1.)

Others listing materials in France, Italy and the Vatican, Portugal and Scandinavia are in process of compilation. The United Kingdom materials collected by S.O.A.S. in the course of its larger project will be used for the compilation of this country's volume.

Examples of other union catalogues of specific groups of documents are given below:

Sources for the history of British India in the seventeenth century, by Shafaat Ahmad Khan. (Allahabad University Studies in History, 4.) Oxford U.P., 1926.

This work indicates the contents of documents in the British Museum, Public Record Office; manuscripts relating to the East Indies in the Bodleian Library and All Souls' College, Oxford; Privy Council registers; India Office records; MSS. relating to British India in the Guildhall Library, London, and Lambeth Palace Library; and records in Indian record offices.

The English Factories in India, 1618–69, a calendar of documents in the India Office, British Museum, and Public Record Office, by Sir William Foster. 13 vols. Oxford, 1906–27.

— New series, vols. 1–3, (1670–84), by Sir Charles Fawcett. Oxford, 1936–54.

Materials preserved in libraries of the U.S.A. are listed in the following works:

The National Union catalog of manuscript collections 1959–61, based on reports from American repositories of manuscripts. Compiled by the Library of Congress with the advice of the Advisory Committee on the National Union Catalog of Manuscript Collections under a grant from the Council on Library Resources, Inc. (The Library of Congress catalogs.) Ann Arbor, Mich.: J. W. Edwards, 1962.
— *1962.* Hamden, Conn.: Shoe String Press, 1964.
— *Index 1959–62.* Ib., 1964.

A Guide to archives and manuscripts in the United States. Compiled for the National Historical Publications Commission. Philip M. Hamer, Editor. New Haven: Yale U.P., 1961.

Guide to photocopied historical materials in the United States and Canada; edited by Richard W. Hale, Jr. Cornell U.P., Ithaca, N.Y., for American Historical Association (1961).

The National Union catalog of manuscripts is kept in card form in the Library of Congress. Cards are sent in from repositories all over the country, having been drafted by the curators of the collections in accordance with a code for the cataloguing of manuscript collections devised specially by the Library of Congress for the purpose. These cards were then printed by the Library's Card Division, where they are available for purchase, and were then reproduced in the volumes listed above. By the end of 1962 cards had been printed for 12,324 manuscript collections in 398 repositories.

The National Historical Publications Commission's guide contains information on collections in some 1,300 depositories.

Not a great deal of material relating to Asia is included in these publications, which cover all subjects and regions, but what there is can be detected from the indexes.

THE CATALOGUING OF ORIENTAL MANUSCRIPTS

Because a manuscript is a unique object, even if copied in a single scriptorium by many persons at the same time of dictation, greater attention to detail is required in its description than with printed books, which in recent times at any rate come out in editions of multiple identical copies.

In addition to the usual details of author, title, language, number of leaves (foliation) and date, full accounts of the material used, the measurements of the actual leaves and the areas covered with writing, the number of columns and lines to a page, the way in which the leaves were put together to make up the book (collation), the form of handwriting used and the name of the scribe when given, the binding, and the marks of former ownership need to be given. All these details may help to establish the date at which the manuscript was written and hence its place in the hierarchy of copies made from the original text, information which is vital to the editor of work seeking to get back as closely as possible to the author's actual words, for in few cases is the author's own handwritten copy (the holograph) still extant. In the course of time, too, manuscripts often get broken up into two or more parts, and these parts come to ground in libraries many miles apart or even in different countries, and the details referred to may assist in re-uniting dispersed parts of the same manuscript.

PALAEOGRAPHY

As the date of writing a manuscript is so frequently omitted, or the colophon, giving the circumstances under which the manuscript was written, lost because of its very vulnerable position on the last page, a whole science of palaeography, or the study of the history of hand-writing, has grown up. This knowledge enables one to date a manu-script often with a high degree of accuracy, and though it is highly developed in the study of Greek, Latin and modern European manu-scripts, much remains to be done in the field of Oriental palaeography. The following works may, however, be mentioned for the information they give on this science and on the whole subject of manuscripts generally.

HEBREW

Carlo Bernheimer. *Paleografia ebraica.* Firenze, 1924.
The Hebrew scripts, by Solomon A. Birnbaum. Part two: the plates. London: Palaeographia, 1954–57.

COPTIC

Koptische Paläographie: 25 Tafeln: Mit einen Versuch einer Stilgeschichte der koptischen Schrift, bearbeitet von Viktor Stegemann, Heidelberg: Bilabel, 1936.

Koptische Paläographie, von Maria Cramer. Wiesbaden: Harrasso-witz, 1964.

ARABIC

Arabic palaeography; a collection of Arabic texts from the first century of the Hidjra till the year 1000. Edited by B. Moritz. (Publications of the Khedivial Library, Cairo, no. 16.) Cairo, 1905.

India Office Library: *Specimens of Arabic and Persian palaeography*, selected and annotated by A. J. Arberry. London, 1939.

Album de paléographie arabe, par Georges Vajda. Paris: Adrien-Maisonneuve, 1958.

INDIAN

Indische Palaeographie von circa 350 a. Chr. – circa 1300 p. Chr., von G. Bühler. (Grundriss der indo-arischen Philologie und Altertumskunde, 1 Band, 11 Heft.) Strassburg, 1896.

Translated into English as:
Indian palaeography, by Johann Georg Bühler. Edited as an Appendix to the *Indian Antiquary*, vol. XXXIII, 1904, by John Faithfull Fleet. Bombay, 1904.

Reprinted in:
Indian studies past and present, vol. 1, October, 1959 – July, 1960, pp. 9–138, plates and transliteration tables I–IX. (With the obituary notice of Bühler by Max Müller, originally published in J.R.A.S., 1898, pp. 695–707.

Indian palaeography, by Ahmad Hasan Dani. Oxford, 1963.

The contents of manuscripts must be fully and analytically inventoried, for many handwritten volumes contain several different compositions, often of highly dissimilar subject content. When dealing with works not yet edited and published it is desirable to give the title headings of parts, sections, chapters or any other divisions of the work, and for this reason the great manuscript catalogues of the part are often worth resorting to for a complete listing of the contents of a work. With anonymous works it is useful to give the opening (*incipit*) and closing (*explicit*) words of the manuscript: this may help later in identifying its authorship.

In these days it is becoming increasingly difficult for the libraries with collections of manuscripts to produce catalogues with detailed descriptions (catalogues raisonnés) as they did in the past. The high cost of printing in this country, especially of Oriental characters, is primarily responsible for this, but another factor is the ever-increasing amount of administration that librarians in common with other professional men are called upon to do. This leaves them an appreciably smaller amount of time to acquire techniques enabling them to undertake works of scholarship, such as the cataloguing of manuscripts. In fact, some well-known libraries have not been able to publish catalogues of manuscripts in certain languages for over a hundred years. For these reasons some libraries have taken to publishing brief descriptive lists or short-title catalogues of their collections, cut down to the minimum of detail. These at least provide information as to which manuscripts exist in their collections, and make it possible for other libraries or individual scholars to order photographic copies. Such are the British Museum catalogues:

Descriptive list of the Hebrew and Samaritan MSS. in the British Museum. Edited by G. Margoliouth. London, 1893.

Descriptive list of Syriac and Karshuni MSS. in the British Museum acquired since 1873. By G. Margoliouth. London, 1899.

A Descriptive list of the Arabic manuscripts acquired by the Trustees of the British Museum since 1894. Compiled by A. G. Ellis and Edward Edwards. London, 1912.

and the most recent catalogue of Arabic and Persian manuscripts in Cambridge University Library:

A Second supplementary hand-list of the Muhammadan manuscripts in the University & colleges of Cambridge, by A. J. Arberry. Cambridge U.P., 1952.

A short article in Dutch on the cataloguing of Oriental manuscripts represents the publication of a talk given by Dr P. Voorhoeve (well known for his catalogues of Arabic manuscripts in Holland and of Indonesian manuscripts in Holland and elsewhere) to the Research Libraries section of the 27th Congress of Librarians held at Arnhem in 1956.

'Het Beschrijven van oostersche handschriften, door P. Voorhoeve.' *Bibliotheekleven*, 41, no. 11, November, 1956, pp. 321–34.

A short summary in English gives the gist of Dr Voorhoeve's article. From this it appears that the principal European collections of Oriental manuscripts originated at the time of the Renaissance. Elaborate descriptive catalogues first appeared in the eighteenth century, but most of them were produced in the nineteenth. Though modern conditions favour the production of short hand-lists rather than detailed descriptive catalogues, it is to be hoped that the latter will not be entirely supplanted by the former. The cataloguer of Oriental manuscripts has much to learn from his colleague in the Western field. The question of arrangement is discussed: whether the catalogue should list the items in simple numerical order or in a subject arrangement is a debatable point. The lack for many languages of a definitive history of literature may make a subject arrangement more pertinent in these instances.

LISTS OF COLLECTIONS AND CATALOGUES

Enrique Sparn. *Las mayores colecciones de manuscritos orientales existentes en las bibliotecas del mundo.* Cordoba (Rep. Arg.), 1935.

How many manuscripts in Oriental languages exist in the world to-day? Sparn, who was obviously of a statistical turn of mind, decided to enumerate and consider briefly the libraries possessing more than 2,000 Oriental manuscripts, papyri not included, and published his book in the improbable place of Cordoba in the Argentine Republic. To these statistical data he has added a list of a number of small but important collections with fewer than 2,000 manuscripts. His data were taken mainly from *Minerva* and the *India generalis*. At the time of writing, he estimated that there were forty-nine libraries in the world, which possessed more than 2,000 Oriental MSS.: of these, 25 (with 253,348 MSS. between them) were in Asia, 19 (with 161,425 MSS.) in Europe, 4 (with 42,048 MSS.) in Africa, and one (more than 2,000 MSS.) in America. The total held in these forty-nine libraries was computed to be 458,821. The individual country with the largest number of manuscripts is said to be India, followed by China, Great Britain, Egypt, France, Turkey in Europe, Germany, Italy and America.

Here, for what it is worth, is his order for the 'first division', i.e. those libraries with more than 10,000 Oriental MSS.:

National Library, Peking	46,300
Bibliothèque Nationale, Paris	35,000
Maharaja Sarfoji Saraswati Public Library, Tanjore	27,000
National Library of Egypt, Cairo	23,000
Asiatic Society of Bengal, Calcutta	20,000
Preussische Staatsbibliothek, Berlin	19,720
Adyar Library, Madras	17,584
Dacca University Library	17,000
British Museum	16,000
India Office Library	15,000
Public Library, Istanbul ⎫ Library of al-Azhar, Cairo ⎭	*c.* 15,000
Oriental Institute, Baroda	13,726
Government Oriental Library, Mysore	10,506
University of Mysore	10,294
Government Oriental MSS. Library, Madras	10,000 +

In a brochure distributed to all delegates to the XXIII International Congress of Orientalists in 1954, J. D Pearson listed the available catalogues for Oriental manuscripts in all languages in libraries in Great Britain and Ireland and, in addition, estimated the numbers of those manuscripts for which only unpublished catalogues existed and those which had not yet been catalogued.

Oriental manuscript collections in the libraries of Great Britain and Ireland, by J. D. Pearson. London: Royal Asiatic Society, 1954.

The catalogues of Oriental manuscripts in the British Museum were listed by F. C. (now Sir Frank) Francis in an article published in the *Journal of Documentation* for 1951 and reprinted in 1959.

The Catalogues of the British Museum. 3. Oriental printed books and manuscripts, by F. C. Francis. 1951.

More up-to-date information, so far as Southern Asia and Eastern Asia are concerned, is contained in:

'The Department of Oriental Printed Books and Manuscripts of the British Museum. Contributed by K. B. Gardner, E. D. Grinstead and G. M. Meredith-Owens.' *Journal of Asian Studies*, 18, 1959, pp. 310–18.

The catalogues of the India Office Library will be found enumerated in the Library's guide by S. C. Sutton. See also:
'The India Office Library. Contributed by S. C. Sutton.' *Journal of Asian Studies*, 18, 1959, pp. 425–28.

For the Bodleian see:

'The Oriental manuscript collections of the Bodleian Library, by A. F. L. Beeston.' Reprinted from the *Bodleian Library Record*, 5, no. 2 (October, 1954).

The Bibliothèque Nationale in Paris published a list of its catalogues still in print in 1953. This includes printed books, prints, medals and exhibitions as well as manuscripts.

Les Catalogues imprimés de la Bibliothèque Nationale. Liste établie en 1943 suivi d'un supplément (1944–52). Paris, 1953.

Manuscripts in Italy are listed in the following works:

Giuseppi Gabrieli. *Manoscritti e carte orientali nelle biblioteche e negli archivi d'Italia*. Dati statistici e bibliografici delle collezioni, loro storia e catalogazione. (Bibliotheca di bibliografia italiana, diretta da Carlo Frati. Supplementi periodici a *La Bibliofilia*, diretta da Leo. S. Olschki, X.) Firenze, 1930.

Gabrieli's work lists collections of Oriental (with three African and five Mexican manuscripts and papers existing in a large number of libraries in Italian cities, the Vatican, Cheren (in Eritrea) and Tripoli. The collections are arranged by town and then by library: every catalogue produced and every reference to manuscripts in the collections have been enumerated. At the end of the book there is an index by language and a list of papers, letters, etc., of Orientalists. This is followed by six appendices giving lists of:

I.   Arabic MSS. in the Bibl. Riccardiana in Florence.
II. Raineri-Biscia papers in the Bibl. Com. dell'Archiginnasio di Bologna.
III. Oriental MSS. in the Bibl. Vittorio Emmanuele in Rome, not included in the various printed catalogues.
IV. Arabic MSS. in the Lanzone collection in the Bibl. Nazionale di Torino.
V.   Letters to G.B. de Rossi in the Palatina di Parma.
VI. Georgian MSS. and printed books belonging to P. Bernardo Cioffi of Naples, preserved in the offices of the Presidente dell' Orfanotrofio (formerly Convent of the Cappuccini) in Torre del Greco.

Gabrieli had intended this work to be the first part of a 'Museografia orientale italica' which was to include indications and brief descriptions of all Oriental collections in Italy, such as monuments, documents (inscriptions and coins, everything other than manuscripts and maps), works of art, arms and armour, scientific instruments, etc.

Cataloghi dei codici orientali di alcune biblioteche d'Italia stampati a spese del Ministero della Pubblica Istruzione, Firenze, 1878–1904. 7 pts.

Between 1878 and 1904 the Italian Ministry of Education published a series in seven parts of catalogues of Oriental manuscripts in certain Italian libraries. The catalogues, which contain descriptions of manuscripts in Hebrew, Arabic, Persian, Turkish, Syriac, Coptic, Ethiopic and Samaritan, were compiled by the most prominent Orientalists of the day, as the following list will show:

Rome, Bibl. Vittorio Emmanuele (I. Guidi – Syriac, Arabic, Turkish, Persian; A. di Capua – Hebrew), pp. 1–53.
Rome, Bibl. Angelica (I. Guidi – Syriac, Arabic, Ethiopic, Turkish; A. di Capua – Hebrew), pp. 55–103.
Rome, Bibl. Alessandrina (I. Guidi – various), pp. 105–8.

Parma, Bibl. Nazionale (P. Perreau – Hebrew MSS. not described by De Rossi), pp. 109–97.

Naples, Bibl. Nazionale (L. Buonazia – Arabic), pp. 199–241.

Venice, Bibl. Marciana (M. Lattes – Hebrew), pp. 243–53.

Florence, Bibl. Nazionale (L. Buonazia – Arabic), pp. 255–97.

Florence, Bibl. Medicea Laurenziana (I. Pizzi – Persian), pp. 299–320.

Bologna, Bibl. della R. Universita (L. Modona – Hebrew), pp. 321–72.

Palermo, Bibl. Nazionale (B. Lagumina – Oriental), pp. 373–402.

Rome, Bibl. Casanatense (L. Bonelli – Arabic, Persian, Turkish; G. Sacerdote – Hebrew, Samaritan), pp. 403–665.

General Index (by language), pp. 667–741.

Information on manuscript collections in some important libraries of the U.S.S.R. may be found in:

Akademiya Nauk SSSR. Institut narodov Azii. *Vostokovednye fondy krupneyshikh bibliotek Sovetskogo Soyuza: stat'i i soobshcheniya.* Moskva, 1963. (Oriental collections in the most important libraries of the Soviet Union.)

This gives details of the manuscript collections in the Leningrad sector of the Institute of the Peoples of Asia, the Uzbek Academy in Tashkent, the Matenadaran in Erivan, the Buryat Institute of the Siberian Academy, the Saltykov–Shchedrin Public Library and the libraries of the Universities of Moscow, Leningrad and Kazan.

An inventory of catalogues of Arabic manuscripts in libraries all over the world was compiled by G. Vajda:

Répertoire des catalogues et inventaires de manuscrits arabes, par G. Vajda avec la collaboration de Madeleine Durantet. (Centre National de la Recherche Scientifique. Institut de Recherche et d'Histoire des Textes, II.) Paris, 1949.

A similar list for Persian manuscripts was compiled by Iraj Afshar:

Bibliographie des catalogues des manuscrits persans, par Iraj Afshar. (Publications de l'Université de Tehran, no. 485.) Tehran, 1958. (Also with title-page in Persian.)

Dr K. L. Janert published the first part of a list of catalogues of Indian manuscripts in 1965:

An Annotated bibliography of catalogues of Indian manuscripts. By Klaus Ludwig Janert. Wiesbaden: Steiner, 1965.

G

UNION CATALOGUES

These lists are essential preliminaries for the compilation of catalogues which describe all the manuscripts in a particular language which exist in a single country or indeed, throughout the world. An interesting undertaking of the former kind is the plan for the publication of a series of catalogues of Oriental manuscripts in Germany under the title of *Verzeichnis der orientalischen Handschriften* in Deutschland, edited in consultation with the German Oriental Society by Dr Wolfgang Voigt. It is estimated that in all there are over 60,000 Oriental manuscripts in libraries, museums, archives and private possession in Germany, of which about half are already described in printed catalogues. This new series will consist of some twenty-five to thirty volumes, of which the following had appeared by Spring, 1965.

1. Mongolian MSS., block prints and maps. W. Heissig, 1961.
2. Indian MSS., Part I. W. Schubring, ed. K. J. Janert, 1962.
3. Georgian MSS., J. Assfalg, 1962.
4. Armenian MSS., J. Assfalg and J. Molitor, 1962.
5. Syriac MSS., J. Assfalg, 1963.
6. Hebrew MSS., Part II. E. Roth and H. Striedl, 1964.
8. Saray albums. Diez paste-in volumes (Klebebände) from the Berlin collections, 1964.
9. Thai MSS., K. Wenk, 1964.
10. Turfan Sanskrit MSS., Part I. E. Waldschmidt, 1964.

Under preparation are catalogues of the Hebrew, Na-khi (Mo-so), Chinese, Manchurian and Japanese, Indian part 2, Turkish and Persian MSS., and Tibetan MSS., block prints and maps. Two supplementary volumes have been published and two others are planned:

1. *An annotated bibliography of the catalogues of Indian manuscripts.* Part I. By Klaus Ludwig Janert, 1965.
2. *Life and culture of the Na-khi.* J. F. Rock.
3. *Mongolian place-names.* M. M. Haltod and W. Heissig.
4. *Bilder lundert deutscher Indologen.* von Wilhelm Rau, 1965.

One volume will be devoted to African manuscripts.

A similar series is being produced by the Polish Academy of Sciences (Oriental Section) for collections in Polish libraries,

Katalog rękopisow orientalnych ze zbiorow polskich; Catalogue des manuscrits orientaux des collections polonaises; sous la direction de

Stefan Strelcyn, avec la collaboration de Marian Lewicki et Ananiasz Zajączkowski.

Three volumes appeared in 1959 and 1960 for Turkish documents; Armenian and Georgian; and Egyptian, Coptic and Ethiopic.

I. 1. Katalog dokumentow tureckich; dokumenty do dziejow polski i krajow osciennych w latach 1455–1672. Catalogue des documents turcs; documents concernant la Pologne et les pays voisins de 1455 a 1672, par Zygmunt Abrahamowicz, sous la direction de Ananiasz Zajączkowski. Ire partie. Warszawa, 1959. (Intended to be in four parts, the second to contain documents concerning Poland and neighbouring countries from 1455 to 1792, the third documents concerning Poland and Polish emigration to Turkey during the nineteenth century, and the fourth, miscellaneous documents relating to countries other than Poland.)

III. Katalog rękopisow ormianskich i gruzinskich. Catalogue des manuscrits arméniens et georgiens. Manuscrits arméniens décrits par Kazimierz Roszko sous la direction de Eugeniusz Słuszkiewicz; manuscrits georgiens décrits par Jan Brun. Warszawa, 1958.

IV. Katalog rękopisow egipskich, koptijskich i etiopskich. Catalogue des manuscrits égyptiens, coptes et éthiopiens. Manuscrits égyptiens décrits par Tadeusz Andrzejewski; manuscrits coptes décrits par Stefan Jakobielski; manuscrits éthiopiens décrits par Stefan Strelcyn. Warszawa, 1960.

V. 1. Katalog rękopisow arabskich. Catalogue des manuscrits arabes par Wojciech Dembski sons la direction de Ananiasz Zajączkowski. Warszawa, 1964.

The series was planned to consist of eight volumes in all: the ones not so far published were to be:

II. Tatar and Persian documents.
V. Persian and Turkish MSS.
VI. Hebrew, Aramaic and Samaritan MSS.
VII. Indian MSS.
VIII. Varia et addenda.

The value of these catalogues is diminished by the fact that they are all drafted in the Polish language.

Already in 1938 H. I. Poleman, the present Chief of the Oriental Division of the Reference Department had published his union catalogue of 'Indic' manuscripts in the United States and Canada:

A Census of Indic manuscripts in the United States and Canada. Compiled by H. I. Poleman. (American Oriental series, vol. 12.) New Haven, Conn., 1938.

This is a brief-title catalogue, classified by subject where desirable, of 7,273 manuscripts which were contained in sixty-nine public and thirty-eight private libraries in these countries. In addition, there is listed in an Appendix a number of uncatalogued and special collections, including two Mongolian manuscripts (a language not represented in the main body of the work). 5,485 of the titles are for manuscripts in Sanskrit, the remainder being designated as 'Vernacular texts' and including titles in the languages of India, neighbouring countries and South-East Asia (Bengali, Bugis, Burmese, Gujarati, Hindi, Hindustani and Urdu, Javanese, Kanarese, Kashmiri, Malay, Marathi, Nepali, Oriya, Pali, Panjabi, Prakrit, Bhāsā, Pushtu, Rajasthani, Siamese, Sinhalese, Tamil, Telugu, Tibetan), as well as a few 'miscellaneous and unidentified manuscripts'.

The first part of a catalogue of ola leaf manuscripts in the Temple libraries of Ceylon, was published in Sinhalese in 1959 by K. D. Somadasa. It contains a list of about 2,000 manuscripts in Sanskrit, Pali and Sinhalese, preserved in the libraries of 913 temples.

Dr D. N. Mackenzie has compiled a union catalogue of manuscripts in Pushtu preserved in the libraries of Great Britain and in that of Trinity College, Dublin; it is hoped to publish this shortly.

Examples of universal union catalogues are the following:

Catalogus catalogorum: an alphabetical register of Sanskrit works and authors, by Theodor Aufrecht. 3 vols. Leipzig, 1891–1903. (Photographic reprint, Wiesbaden: Steiner, 1962.)

This represents an 'attempt . . . to give an account of the whole of Sanskrit literature as contained in manuscripts deposited in India as well as in Europe'. The entries under author and title are presented in Devanagari script and are arranged in the Sanskrit alphabetical order. For the first volume, the compiler extracted titles from fifty-six catalogues published up to the year 1888: the second and third volumes list as sources twenty and twenty-two titles of printed catalogues and collections – these may be regarded as supplements to the first volume, being arranged in the same manner as that is.

New catalogus catalogorm: an alphabetical register of Sanskrit and allied works and authors, prepared by V. Raghavan. (Madras University

Sanskrit series 18.) Madras, 1949. Volume 1. [No more published as yet, Spring, 1965.]

This comprises the first letter of the Devanagari syllabary only. All the entries in Aufrecht's Catalogues were checked, and all entries added from subsequently acquired lists by the compiler, Dr Raghavan, who 'also read through a large number of Sanskrit works both in print and in manuscripts, collected citations (went) through various books and articles relating to bibliography and chronology and made many investigations himself to make the entries as informative as possible'. Among changes introduced are the inclusion of Buddhist, Prakrit and Jain works and authors: references are given to one or more printed editions, if the work has been published, and to critical notices of works and authors in research journals. Works and authors known through citations only are included. Over 400 sources are listed, consisting of published catalogues and unprinted hand-lists.

What may be described as Union catalogues on an even more elaborate scale exist for Arabic and Persian literature, wherein the lists of manuscripts are arranged in such a way so that with the addition of information of a bibliographical and historical character, the final result is a history of literature, packed with bibliographical detail. These are:

Geschichte der arabischen litteratur, von Carl Brockelmann.

2 vols. Weimar, 1898; Berlin, 1902.

— 1. Supplementband. Leiden, 1937.

— 2. Supplementband. ib., 1938.

— 3. Supplementband. ib., 1942.

— Zweite, den Supplementbänden angepasste Auflage. 2 vols. Leiden, 1943, 1949.

(Three volumes of an Arabic translation have appeared, published at Cairo, 1960–)

Persian literature, a bio-bibliographical survey. By C. A. Storey. Vol. I (in two sections, 1 + 3 fascicules), Quranic literature; History and biography. London, 1927–53.

Vol. II, Part 1: A. Mathematics, B. Weights and measures, C. Astronomy and astrology. D. Geography. Ib., 1958.

A similar publication for Turkish literature has been compiled by H. Hofman and will be published shortly.

[6]

Reference Books

A reference book is a book to which one has recourse in order to obtain information on specific questions as distinct from a book which is intended to be read from beginning to end. Some types of reference book will be dealt with in later chapters: these include bibliographies, catalogues, periodicals and their indexes, and works about libraries. The present chapter is concerned solely with lists of reference books, encyclopaedias (alphabetical or otherwise), and handbooks covering the whole of Asia or Africa.

LISTS OF REFERENCE BOOKS

Guide to reference books, by Constance M. Winchell. Based on the *Guide to reference books*, sixth edition, by Isadore Gilbert Mudge. 7th ed. Chicago: American Library Association, 1951.

— Supplement, 1950–52, by Constance M. Winchell and Olive A. Johnson. Ib., 1954.

— Second supplement, 1953–55, by Constance M. Winchell, Ib., 1956.

— Third supplement, 1956–58, by Constance M. Winchell, assisted by John Neal Waddell and Eleanor Buist. Ib., 1960.

— Fourth supplement, 1959–June 1962, by Constance M. Winchell, assisted by John Neal Waddell, Eleanor Buist, Eugene P. Sheehy. Ib., 1963.

Guide to reference material, edited by A. J. Walford, with the assistance of L. M. Payne. London: The Library Association, 1959.

— Supplement, edited by A. J. Walford, with the assistance of L. M. Payne and C. A. Toase. Ib., 1963.

The two principal guides to reference books compiled for English-speaking peoples are Mudge–Winchell (American, 7th ed. 1951, with four supplements each covering three year periods to 1962; an eighth edition is under preparation); and Walford (British, 1959; supplement, 1963). Mudge–Winchell is intended to serve (1) as a selection aid for the librarian, (2) as a reference manual for the library assistant, research worker, or other user of library resources, and (3) as a textbook for the student. It contains a total of 8,135 entries, and these are arranged in accordance with the subject sequence used in the Dewey Decimal classification, the notation numbers being replaced by the letters A–V. In each section, the titles of books are arranged in the following sequence of categories when applicable: Guides and manuals; Bibliographies; Indexes and abstracts; Encyclopaedias; Handbooks; Dictionaries of special terms; Annuals and directories; Histories; Biographical works; Atlases and collections of illustrations; Serial publications. The main work contains 339 entries relating to Asia and Africa, with 91, 118, 101 and 122, respectively, in the supplements.

Walford is designed along similar lines and is intended for use by roughly the same clientèle, but it places an emphasis on current material and on material published in Britain. It does not make a feature of listing general bibliographies as do its main competitors, and omits maps, anthologies and most source books, as well as the majority of periodicals. There are 3,782 main entries (other titles are included in the annotations) as compared with the 8,135 in Mudge–Winchell and its supplements. Walford proffers 233 titles (including those listed in the annotations) relating to Asia and Africa in the original volume, and 226 in the supplement. The annotations to these are sometimes inaccurate, incomplete and, frankly, misleading.

Undoubtedly the best of the general guides to reference books so far as Asian and African studies are concerned, though somewhat defective in the fields of social sciences, statistics and biography, which are better covered by both Mudge–Winchell and Walford, is:

L.-N. Malclès: *Les Sources du travail bibliographique.* 3 vols. in 4. Genève: Droz, Lille: Giard, 1950–58.
Tome 1: Bibliographies générales. 1950.
Tome 2 (in 2): Bibliographies spécialisées. 1952.
Tome 3: Bibliographies spécialiséea (sciences exactes et techniques), avec la collaboration de G. Garnier, P. M. Guelpa, G. Koest, M. G. Madier, J. Miet. 1958.

The sections concerned with Asia and Africa are:

Vol. 1, pp. 296–97: Les pays slaves et balkaniques: Turquie.

Vol. 1, pp. 333–36: Russie–U.R.S.S.: Républiques non-russes de l'Union Soviétique.

Vol. 2, ch. vi (in part), pp. 201–21; Bibliographie des territoires d'Outre-Mer.

Vol. 2, ch. xviii (in part), pp. 800–8; Pays slaves et balkaniques; langue, littérature et histoire (Turquie).

Vol. 2, ch. xix, pp. 810–69; L'Orient: Proche-, Moyen- et Extrême-Orient (in collaboration with B. Kasme).

The author's original intention had been to produce a text-book to accompany courses in bibliography delivered to candidates for the 'Diplôme technique de bibliothécaire' since 1933, but this proved in the event too limiting and the author got carried away into compiling a magnificent work in four large volumes, covering general bibliographies and special bibliographies in the humanities and natural sciences. The work is devised in such a way as to provide a list of 23,514 sources to be used in information work, or in the compilation of bibliographies which is an activity closely related to it. A prominent place is occupied by lists of bibliographies, retrospective and current, but the work is by no means restricted to these. To a large extent it supplies for each subject a 'guide to the literature' listing, with annotations where necessary, the encyclopaedias, dictionaries, general surveys of the 'Handbuch' or 'Reallexikon' variety, elaborate expositions of the subject in series form, introductions to the subject, treatises, manuals and monographs. Finally, it provides a service not to be had in Mudge–Winchell or Walford, lists of the more important periodicals.

The sections of most interest to Orientalist and Africanist libraries are indicated above: the parts of the first volume concerned with national bibliographies of the Asiatic republics of the U.S.S.R. and the rest of Asia and Africa, and three chapters in the second. The first section in volume 2 (chapter vi) is concerned with bibliographies of European overseas territories and is included in the chapter which also covers the history of Europe and America: it comprises sections on colonial bibliographies and history generally, French and British overseas territories, Africa and Oceania (including the Pacific region generally, Polynesia and Micronesia, as well as Indonesia, Malaya and Borneo and Philippines, territories which others would assign to Asia, with Indonesia as the sole representative of Asia. Chapter xviii (Slav and Balkan countries: language, literature and history) includes a section on Turkey. The fullest treatment of Asian studies occurs in chapter xix: The

Orient; Near, Middle and Far East. This chapter is written with the purpose of 'assisting non-specializing libraries with advice on Eastern subjects, directing them toward basic works'. It is not designed for specialist Orientalists and is limited almost exclusively to works in Western languages. Its main divisions are: the Orient in general and Orientalism (including works on Oriental studies, their teaching and history, terminology, Festschriften, general bibliographies, booksellers' catalogues, printed catalogues of libraries and general Orientalist periodicals), Semitic languages, the Ancient Near East, Islam, Near and Middle East, countries of the Arab East, the Christian Orient, Armenia, Judaism, Far East, India and Pakistan. Each section lists the principal periodicals of the subject, those for East and South Asia occurring in a final section beginning on page 868.

If one includes the periodical titles, 1,277 works in all are listed for Asia and Africa, as compared with about 750 in Mudge–Winchell and about 500 in Walford.

An interesting study of the comparative strengths and weaknesses of each of the three guides to reference books which was made in 1964, tabulates the main differences between them:

'Winchell, Walford, or Malclès?' By Frances Seaholm. *College and research libraries*, 25, no. 1, January, 1964, pp. 21–26.

The main criticism levelled against Walford is that he provides no introductions to his sections. Winchell is said to emphasize the 'practical, library-oriented point of view', Malclès the scholarly. 'Top billing' is accorded in Walford to languages and literatures, in Winchell to 'generalities', in Malclès to mathematics and natural sciences.

The poor representation given to books published in Asia and Africa is demonstrated in a table which shows the 'top ten' countries of origin of books. Walford lists six titles published in 'other' countries, Winchell and Malclès none at all. This defect is to some extent rectified by the UNESCO publication:

Directory of reference works published in Asia. Répertoire des ouvrages de référence publiés en Asie. By/par P. K. Garde. (UNESCO bibliographical handbooks.) UNESCO (1956).

By 'reference books' is meant 'ready-reference books', we are told, the most common categories of which are: atlases and map collections; bibliographies, indexes and subject catalogues; biographical dictionaries like *Who's Who;* dictionaries – linguistic and subject; directories and/or yearbooks; encyclopaedias – general as well as of specific subjects; gazetteers and statistical yearbooks. 'Asia' includes the countries from Afghanistan going in an easterly direction to Japan, viz. Afghanistan, Burma, Cambodia, Ceylon, China, Hong Kong, India, Indonesia, Japan, Laos, Malaya, Pakistan, Philippines, Singapore, Thailand and Vietnam. We may note the omission of Korea, Mongolia and Nepal from this list. (But there are in fact no entries under Afghanistan and Singapore, and several under Korea, as the following list of entries given under each country shows:)

Burma	9	Japan	882
Cambodia	1	Korea	25
Ceylon	8	Laos	1
China	148	Malaya	17
China (Formosa)	29	Pakistan	108
Hong Kong	9	Philippines	12
India	242	Thailand	22
Indonesia	71	Vietnam	23

(The total of these figures is 1607 which indicates that twelve titles have been lost somewhere along the line, the entries being numbered 1–1,619.)

There are but two entries under 'Asia' in the index, a work on Asian labour laws published by the International Labour Office, Indian Branch, in 1951, and three bibliographies (two published in Japan and one in India).

This is the first attempt to list reference books and bibliographies of all kinds published at all periods in sixteen countries of Asia. 1,619 titles in all are arranged initially by subject in U.D.C. order, and within each subject group according to country of publication. Titles in Asian languages are transliterated and provided with translations into English. There are indexes of authors (referring to running numbers), subjects (referring to U.D.C. numbers) and language dictionaries.

The work was compiled on the basis of a carefully-drafted questionnaire sent to 75 libraries and 5 national bibliographical working groups: replies were received from only 21 of these. This indicates the disadvantages of the questionnaire method and accounts for the large number of omissions. If other reference books had been used, many more titles could have been added. For instance, a more thorough consultation of Ssu-yu Teng and Biggerstaff, *An annotated bibliography of selected Chinese reference works* would have yielded many more titles of catalogues of periodical articles, not to mention other categories of reference book.

There are also guides to reference books published in a single Asian country:

A guide to works of reference published in Pakistan, by Khwaja Nur Elahi, A. Moid and Akhtar H. Siddiqui. (Pakistan Bibliographical Working Group publication no. 1.) Karachi, 1953.

This publication lists some 400 reference books, the titles being arranged in the order of the Dewey Decimal Classification, preceded by an alphabetical index of contents. It includes works published in what is now Pakistan before that country became an established political unit in 1947. Works in the press and in process of publication are included, but there is no author index. For our present purpose we may note the sections on atlases and maps, bibliographies (including catalogues), biography, census, dictionaries, directories, encyclopaedias, gazetteers, guide books, journalism, newspapers, vocabularies and year-books. The supplement on pp. 35–36 should not be overlooked.

'Buku² panduan (reference) dalam bahasa Melayu. Oleh Syed Ahmed bin Ali.' *Malayan library J.*, 1, iv, 1961, pp. 17–21.
[Reference books in the Malay language, containing 100 titles in one alphabetical author sequence.]
A similar list for India was published by the Madras Library Association:

S. R. Ranganathan and K. M. Sivaraman: *Bibliography of reference books and bibliographies*. (Madras Library Association publication series, 10.) Madras, 1941.[1]

A guide to basic Japanese reference works, entirely in Japanese, containing 2,900 entries for books and serials published up to October, 1961, and intended for the use of the general reader, was published in 1962:

Nihon no sankyō tosho henshū iinkai. Nihon no sankō tosho. Tokyo, 1962.

The following two items were compiled for the benefit of Western scholars working in special fields:

An Annotated bibliography of selected Chinese reference works. Rev. ed. Compiled by Ssŭ-yü Têng and Knight Biggerstaff. Harvard U.P., 1950.

[1] I have not been able to locate a copy of this work. The title was taken from Garde, *Directory of reference works published in Asia*, 1956, p. 91.

A list with detailed annotations of the principal reference books in Chinese 'compiled with the intention of providing Western students in the field of Sinology with an elementary guide to the most important reference works' and classified to meet the needs of the student seeking general information rather than those of the specialist. The reference books are listed in eight categories: Bibliographies (including catalogues of rare editions and of ts'ung shu, and indexes to periodicals and newspapers); Encyclopaedias; Dictionaries; Geographical works (dictionaries, atlases, tables and indexes); Biographical works (including works on the identification of Japanese names); Tables (including Concordances with the Western Calendar); Yearbooks and Sinological indexes. The first two sections especially have useful notes prefixed on the nature and history of bibliographies and encyclopaedias.

Garde refers to two other lists in Chinese (nos. 63 and 65).

K.B.S. bibliography of standard reference books for Japanese studies with descriptive notes. Tokyo: Kokusai Bunka Shinkokai, 1959–

The Society for International Cultural Relations (K.B.S.) is compiling a 'classified and annotated bibliography of standard works and source materials' in Japanese for the benefit of research workers in the field of Japanese studies, the annotations being in English. The complete series will comprise ten parts: Generalia; Geography and travel; History and biography; Religion; Philosophy, science and education; Language and literature; Arts and crafts, music, dance and drama; Manners and customs; Politics and law; and Economy and finance; making some dozen volumes in all. So far published are:

Vol. I.   Generalia. 1959. 110 pp.
Vol. II.   Geography and travel. 1962. 164 pp.
Vol. III. History and biography. Part I. 1963. 197 pp.
Vol. IV.   Religion. 1963. 181 pp.
Vol. VI (A).   Language. 1961. 155 pp.
Vol. VI (B).   Literature. Part I. 1962. 122 pp.
Vol. VII (A).   Arts and crafts. 1959. 170 pp.
Vol. VII (B).   Theatre, dance and music. 1960. 182 pp.
Vol. VIII. Manners and customs, and folklore. 1961. 101 pp.

The Generalia volume lists general reference books in fifteen sections, with detailed notes for each of the 157 titles: Bibliographies of bibliographies (3); National bibliographies (6); Catalogues of libraries (24); History of books and Miscellaneous notes on books (35); Lists and indices of books on series (6); Catalogues and indices of periodical publications (6); Libraries, their history and directories (10); Owner's seals

(2); Cataloguing codes and classification codes (5); Encyclopaedias (14); Statistics and yearbooks (5); Books in series (21); Newspapers (8); Booksellers and Price of books (5); Learned institutions (7).

Three other lists in Japanese are noted by Garde (nos. 66–68).

Guide to South African reference books. 3rd rev. ed. Compiled by Reuben Musiker. Grahamstown, Rhodes U.L., 1963.

The aim was to include the most important reference books on South African topics published (with few exceptions) in the Republic of South Africa. Many handbooks have been included where reference books of the traditional type were not available. Some classes of reference book have been omitted, viz. South African annuals and subject bibliographies (listed in Grey bibliographies 4 and 11), textbooks, periodicals, publishers' catalogues, official departmental guides and brochures, and university calendars. More than 500 titles are included in this edition listed in sections on bibliography, libraries, encyclopaedias, periodicals and newspapers and then by subject. It is not comprehensive for publications in Afrikaans. A paragraph on 'desiderata' indicates that a new edition of Mendelssohn's South African bibliography is in preparation, as are a general encyclopaedia and a dictionary of South African biography.

A work which, though intended for historians, will be of great value to all students, librarians and bibliographers is:

The American Historical Association's Guide to historical literature. Board of editors: G. F. Howe, Chairman; G. C. Boyce, T. R. S. Broughton, H. F. Cline, S. B. Fay, M. Kraus, E. H. Pritchard, B. C. Shafer, *ex officio.* Assisted by section editors, a central editor and others. New York: Macmillan, 1961.

The chapters relevant to Asian and African studies are:

Part I. Introduction and general history.
      Section D. History of religions.

Part II. Historical beginnings.
      Section E. Regions, peoples and cultures: general and prehistoric.
      Section F. The Ancient Orient.
      Section G. Early history of Asiatic peoples.

Part III. The middle period in Eurasia and Northern Africa.
      Section J. General: Eurasia and Northern Africa (ca. A.D. 476–1453).
      Section M. The Muslim World (to 1453).

Part IV.   Asia since early times.
     Section N. Asia: General (ca. 200 B.C. to the present)
     (includes Korea, Mongolia, Central Asia, Tibet).
     Section O. China.
     Section P. Japan.
     Section Q. South-East Asia.
     Section R. South Asia (includes Afghanistan).
     Section S. The Middle East since 1450.

Part V.   Modern Europe.
     Section X. Russian and the Soviet Union (including the
     Russian Empire in Asia).

Part VII. Africa.
     Section AC. Africa.

Part VIII. Australasia and Oceania.
     Section AE. Oceania.

Though fairly comprehensive, the *Guide* is deficient in some sections in respect of works written in foreign languages and it seems not to mention catalogues of manuscripts. It was designed to be 'a valuable aid to students, teachers, librarians and others who seek the most satisfactory works for historical studies'. The *Guide* is in a sense 'a bibliographic panorama as well as an inventory of the best historical literature extant at the time of compilation. Its purpose is to furnish directions to the best means of gaining a broader knowledge of history. Although it is not designed for the specialist, it may serve to help him establish a good foundation for his later, more concentrated, research'.

Items published in 1957–60 were not systematically covered. The 'standard pattern of organization within the sections (which) has been closely approximated rather than rigidly imposed', consists of:

Bibliographies, libraries and special musuem collections
Encyclopaedias and works of reference
Geographies, gazetteers and atlases
Anthropologic, demographic and linguistic works
Printed collections of sources
Shorter and longer general histories
Histories of periods, areas and topics
Biographies
Government publications
Publications of academies, universities and learned societies
Periodicals.

ENCYCLOPAEDIAS

The function of an encyclopaedia, which may be arranged as a dictionary in accordance with an alphabetical list of subjects, or may attempt
a systematic conspectus of all available knowledge on one or more or
all subjects, is to provide for rapid reference a summary of the latest
information on all the subjects dealt with, with indications as to where
the subjects are more fully treated and where more information on
individual aspects may be found. They go back to a respectable antiquity, especially among the Chinese and the Muslim peoples. Originally
arranged in the form of a systematic survey of all knowledge, the
alphabetical arrangement is in most places preferred today, though the
older form is still used extensively in the German-speaking world.[1]

The most important alphabetical encyclopaedias giving information
on Asia and Africa are:

*The Jewish encyclopaedia. A descriptive record of the history, religion,
literature, and customs of the Jewish people from the earliest times to the
present day.* Ed. by Cyrus A. E. Singer and others. New ed. 12 vols.
New York and London, 1901–6. (Reprints, 1916, 1925.)

Encyclopaedia Judaica: das Judentum in Geschichte und Gegenwart. 10
vols. Berlin, 1928–34. [This was completed only to the end of letter
'L', being discontinued at the time of Hitler's purge of the Jews.]

*The Encyclopaedia of Islam. A dictionary of the geography, ethnography
and biography of the Muhammedan peoples.* Prepared by a number of
leading Orientalists. 4 vols. (issued in fascicles). Leiden, London,
(1908–) 1913–36.
— Supplement, (1934–) 1938.
— New edition, (1954–) 1960–

The work is not provided with a preface, but the outside cover of
Fasc. 1 gives a few details about the compilation. It is published because
the eighteenth-century *Bibliothèque Orientale* of d'Herbelot, once so
useful in spite of the lack of method in its compilation and its number-
less defects, had become totally antiquated. It was intended that the
encyclopaedia should contain (1) the name of every person, no matter
in what way celebrated, in pre-Islamic times and the thirteen centuries
following them; (2) that of all nations where Islam is or has been the
predominating religion, of important towns and places famous by

[1] For a general history of encyclopaedias see now: *Encyclopaedias: their history
throughout the ages. A bibliographical guide with extensive historical notes to the general
encyclopaedias issued throughout the world from 350 B.C. to the present day.* Robert
Collison, New York and London: Hafner, 1964.

reason of events for which they provided a theatre and (3) everything concerning the religion and civilization of the different nations which profess Islam.

It was issued simultaneously in three versions, in English, French and German.

The supplement contains additions and corrections, with, on occasions, substantial revisions of part or even the whole of an article. It also gives a list of abbreviations. It is to be noted that the covers of the individual fascicles (both of the original edition and the supplement) often contain further brief additions and corrections and should be carefully preserved for this reason.

A new edition, published this time in two versions, English and French,[1] began publication in 1954. The general plan of the first edition was retained, together with the antiquated transliteration system, but more space is given to economic and social topics and to artistic production. Many more cross-references in English or French have been introduced in their alphabetical places. (As most of the entries for topics appear under their names in Arabic, it is difficult for those not knowing this language to use the original edition.) Each fascicle gives a list of the authors of the articles included. An asterisk following the name of the authors of an article indicates that the text has been revised by the editors. Names of authors in square brackets are those of the authors of articles reprinted or revised from the first edition.

Two selections of the articles on Islam as a religion have been published under the auspices of the Royal Netherlands Academy, a German edition with the title *Handwörterbuch des Islam*, edited by A. J. Wensinck and J. H. Kramers in 1941, and an English one with the title *Shorter Encyclopaedia of Islam*, edited by H. A. R. Gibb and J. H. Kramers, in 1953. The German version states that a small number of articles have received additions from the author or editors or has been shortened or otherwise changed in some way. A few articles have been newly added. In the English versions additions have been made to most of the bibliographies accompanying the texts of the articles. The German version provides a list of articles giving the authors' names and showing what changes, if any, have been made in them, a feature absent from the English edition. Both editions contain a subject index to the articles included.

---

[1] Because translation is an inexact science, sometimes undertaken by hacks for financial advantage, libraries specializing in Islamic or other Oriental studies will do well to carry both the English and the French editions.

There are also Turkish and Urdu encyclopaedias of Islam:

Islam ansiklopedisi. Islam âlemi coğrafya, etnoğrafya ve bioğrafya lugatī. Istanbul, 1941–
Urdu encyclopaedia of Islam. Under the auspices of the University of the Panjab, Lahore. 1959–

The Turkish encyclopaedia was compiled on the basis of the Encyclopaedia of Islam, its supplement, and the *Handwörterbuch des Islam.* The majority of the articles have been corrected, revised, and brought up to date in the process of compilation. Those articles which concern Turkey and Turkish peoples have been specially drafted for this edition.

According to Walford a UNESCO plan for an encyclopaedia of non-Islamic Asia has been adopted (see *Manchester Guardian,* 19 January, 1957), which will cover Asian thought and culture, secular history and art, anthropology, geography and economics.

An encyclopaedia of Buddhism is being published in Ceylon:

Encyclopaedia of Buddhism. Edited by G. P. Malalasekera. Government of Ceylon, 1961–

Two rather antiquated encyclopaedias cover the major part of the rest of Asia:

The Encyclopaedia Sinica, by Samuel Couling. Shanghai, 1917.

This is said to be valuable for Western personalities and activities rather than for those of the Chinese.

E. G. Balfour: *The Cyclopaedia of India and of Eastern and Southern Asia, commercial, industrial, and scientific; products of the mineral, vegetable, and animal kingdom; useful arts and manufactures.* By Edward Balfour. 3rd ed. 3 vols. London, 1885. (First published in 1858, 2nd ed. 1873.)

This is said to be still useful since a more up-to-date work is not available. It placed the major emphasis on India.

Some modern Asian general encyclopaedias are described in:

Encyclopaedias: their history throughout the ages. A bibliographical guide with extensive historical notes to the general encyclopaedias issued throughout the world from 350 B.C. to the present day. Robert Collison. New York and London: Hafner, 1964.

H

A proposed encyclopaedia of Africa was discussed at the First International Congress of Africanists held in Ghana in December, 1962. The Académie des Sciences d'Outre-Mer is contemplating the production of a 'Dictionnaire encyclopédique d'Outre-Mer'. See: *Comptes-rendus mensuels des séances.* 24 (1964), pp. 470–72.

'HANDBÜCHER'

German scholars are addicted to the systematic encyclopaedia, which is usually published with the title of 'Real-Lexikon', 'Handwörterbuch', or 'Handbuch'. These have been compiled for the history of Egyptian religion, Assyriology and the Bible. Of especial importance is the *Handbuch der Orientalistik* which was originally intended to cover only Near and Middle Eastern studies and which since 1952 has published several volumes in this field. In 1957 the decision was taken to extend its scope into the other branches of Orientalist learning by devoting additional divisions (Abteilungen) to India, South-East Asia, China and Japan. In fact, the five Abteilungen announced in a prospectus issued in 1959 cover, in addition to the Near and Middle East, India, China, Japan and Art and Archaeology. By 1965, however, nothing had been published in any section other than the first.

Handbuch der Orientalistik. Hrsg. von B. Spuler unter Mitarbeit von H. Franke, J. Gonda, H. Hammitzsch, W. Helck, H. Kees, J. E. van Lohuizen – de Leeuw (und F. Vos). Leiden (Köln): Brill, 1952–
Already published (from list in 1 Abt., 5 Bd., 1 Abschnitt – Turkologie, publ. 1963).
Abt. 1: Der Nahe und der Mittlere Osten, hrsg. von. B. Spuler.

    I. Band: ÄGYPTOLOGIE, hrsg. von. H. Kees.
        1. Abschnitt, *Ägyptische Schrift und Sprache*, mit Beiträgen von H. Kees, S. Schott, H. Brunner, E. Otto, S. Morenz. 1959.
        2. Abschnitt. *Literatur*, mit Beiträgen von Hellmut Brunner, Hermann Grapow, Hermann Kees, Siegfried Morenz, Eberhard Otto, Siegfried Schott, Joachim Spiegel. 1952.

    II. Band: KEILSCHRIFTFORSCHUNG UND ALTE GESCHICHTE VORDERASIENS.
        1. u. 2. Abschnitt. Geschichte der Forschung, Sprache und Literatur. Lieferung 1. *Das Sumerische*, von A. Falkenstein. 1959 (photographical reprint, 1964). Lieferung 2. *Hurrisch (Churritisch) und Urartäisch*, von J. Friedrich; *The Elamite language*, by E.

Reiner; *Altkleinasiatische Sprachen.* Beiträge von A. Kammen-
huber (Hethitisch, Paläisch, Luwisch und Hieroglyphenluwisch),
G. Neumann (Lykisch), A. Heubeck (Lydisch), A. Heubeck
(Hattisch). [*In preparation,* 1965.] Lieferung 3. *Akkadische Gram-
matik,* von D. O. Edzard. [*In preparation,* 1965.]
3. Abschnitt. *Geschichte des Alten Vorderasiens,* von Hartmut
Schmökel. 1957.
4. Abschnitt. *Orientalische Geschichte von Kyros bis Mohammed.*
Lieferung 1. Beiträge von G. Widengren (Geschichte Irans bis
zum Einbruch der Araber), E. Visser (Ägypten), H. Volkmann
(Ägypten unter römischer Herschaft). [*In preparation,* 1965.]
Lieferung 2. Beiträge von A. Dietrich (Geschichte Arabiens vor
dem Islam), F. M. Heichelheim (Kleinasien; Syrien und Paläs-
tina), G. M. Widengren (Mesopotamien in achämenidischer
Zeit). [*In the press,* 1965.]

III. Band: SEMITISTIK.
1. Abschnitt. (*Kananäisch und Ugaritisch, Hebräisch.* Mit Beiträgen von Carl Brockelmann, Ernst Ludwig Dietrich, Johann
Fück, Bertold Spuler. 1953.
2. u. 3. Abschnitt. *Aramäisch und Syrisch, Arabisch, Äthiopisch.*
Mit Beiträgen von Anton Baumstark, Carl Brockelmann, Johann Fück, Maria Höfner, Enno Littmann, Adolf Rücker,
Bertold Spuler. 1954. (Photographical reprint of both Abschnitte, 1964.

IV. Band: IRANISTIK:
1. Abschnitt. *Linguistik.* Mit Beiträgen von Karl Hoffmann,
W. B. Henning, H. W. Bailey, G. Morgenstierne, W. Lentz.
1958.
2. Abschnitt. *Literatur.* Beiträge von I. Gershevitch (Old-Iranian
literature), M. Boyce (The Manichaean literature in Iranian/
Middle-Persian literature), A. von Gabain (Buddhistisch und
Christlich), O. Hansen (Die christliche Literatur), P. Avery (History of Persian literature, from the beginning of the Islamic
period to the present day), B. Spuler (Die historische und geo-
graphische Literatur in persischer Sprache), M. J. Dresden (Survey of the history of Iranian studies). [*In preparation,* 1965.]
3. Abschnitt. *Tocharisch,* von Wolfgang Krause. 1955.

V. Band: ALTÄISTIK.
1. Abschnitt. *Turkologie,* mit Beiträgen von Annemarie von
Gabain, Omeljan Pritsak, Nikolaus Poppe, J. Benzing, Karl H.
Menges, Ahmet Temir, Zeki Velidi Togan, Franz Taeschner,
O. Spies, Ahmed Caferoglu, Abdullah Battal-Taymas. 1963.

2. Abschnitt. *Mongolistik*, mit Beiträgen von N. Poppe, U. Posch, G. Doerfer, P. Aalto, D. Schröder, O. Pritsak, W. Heissig. 1964. [Not seen.]

3. Abschnitt. *Tungusologie*. Beiträge von W. Fuchs (Die mandjurische Literatur), I. Lopatin (Tungusische Volksdichtung), K. H. Menges (Die tungusischen Sprachen; das Evenki, das Lamutische, Udehe, Nanai (Goldisch), Zûrčen. D. Sinor (La langue mandjoue). [*In preparation*, 1965.]

4. Abschnitt. *Rudimentär überlieferte Sprachen* (*Sprachreste der Hunnen, Awaren, Chasaren, Petschenegen und Bolgaren*), von O. Pritsak. [*In preparation*, 1965.]

5. Abschnitt. *Geschichte Mittelasiens*. Beiträge von K. Jettmar (Mittelasien und Sibirien in vortürkischen Zeit), H. W. Haussig (Awaren, Shuan-Shuan, Hephtaliten), B. Spuler (Geschichte Mittelasiens seit dem Auftreten der Türken, 552), I. Petech (Tibet). Vorwort und Literaturverzeichnis von B. Spuler. 1965. [*In the press.*]

VI. Band: GESCHICHTE DER ISLAMISCHEN LÄNDER.
   1. Abschnitt. *Die Chalifenzeit*. Entstehung und Zerfall der islamischen Weltreichs, von Bertold Spuler. 1952.
   2. Abschnitt. *Die Mongolenzeit*, von Bertold Spuler. 1953.
   3. Abschnitt. *Neuzeit*, mit Beiträgen von H. J. Kissling, H. Scheel, G. Jäschke, H. Braun, E. Klingmüller, H. Härtel. 1959.

VII. Band: ARMENISCHE UND KAUKASISCHE SPRACHEN, mit Beiträgen von G. Deeters, G. R. Solta, Vahan Inglisian. 1963.

VIII. Band: RELIGION.
   1. Abschnitt. *Religionsgeschichte des Alten Orients*. Lieferung 1. Mit Beiträgen von Otto Eissfeldt, Johannes Hempel, Heinrich Otten, Eberhard Otto. 1964. Lieferung 2. Beiträge von W. G. Lambert [and a further unknown person]. [*In preparation*, 1965.]
   2. Abschnitt. *Religionsgeschichte des Orients in der Zeit der Weltreligionen*, mit Beiträgen von Johannes Leipoldt, Geo. Widengren, Alfred Adam, Bertold Spuler, Ernst Ludwig Dietrich, Johannes W. Fück, A. J. Arberry, R. Strothmann, Annemarie von Gabain. 1961.

Ergänzungsband 1, Heft 1. *Islamische Masse und Gewichte umgerechnet ins metrische System*, von Walther Hinz. 1955.
Ergänzungsband 2. Herausgegehen von A. Grohmann.
   1. Halbband. *Arabische Chronologie und Papyrus-Kunde*, von A. Grohmann. 1964. [*In the press.*]

2. Halbband. *Arabic paleography. A history of the origin and development of Arabic writing till the year 1000 A.H.*, by A. Grohmann; *Numismatics*, von P. Balog. [*In preparation*, 1965.]

Ergänzungsband 3. *Orientalisches Recht*, mit Beiträgen von E. Seidel, V. Korošec, E. Pritsch, O. Spies, E. Tyan, J. Baz, Ch. Chehata, Ch. Samaran, J. Roussier, J. Lapanne-Joinville, S. S. Ansay. 1964.

Ergänzungsband 4. *Orientalische Musik*. Beiträge von H. Hickman, W. Stander. [*In preparation*, 1965.]

Ergänzungsband 5. *Keilschrifturkunden*.

1. Abschnitt. *Einleitung in die assyrischen Königsinschriften.* 1 Teil. Das zweite Jahrtausend v. Chr., von Riekele Borger. 1961.

Ergänzungsband 6. *Natur- und Geheimwissenschaften, Mathematik sowie Medizin im Islam*, von. M. Ullmann; *Islamische historische Geographie*, von H. Braun; *Islamische Philosophie*, von R. Walzer. [*In preparation*, 1965.]

Abschnitte one and two of the sixth Band have appeared in an English translation:

The Muslim World, a historical survey, by Bertold Spuler. Translated from the German by F. R. C. Bagley. 2 vols. Leiden: Brill, 1960. Part I: The age of the Caliphs. Part II: The Mongol period.

The purpose of the *Handbuch* is to give, in concise language, a survey by a scholar of authority of the content and position reached in the principal branches of Oriental studies. It is hoped that these will be of value also to those working in related branches of study. Each division (Abteilung) consists of a number of volumes (Band) which may be further divided into sections (Abschnitt), and these in turn into fascicles (Lieferung) or half-volumes (Halbband) in each of which chapters will be written by prominent specialists. Thus the first Abteilung, Near and Middle East, has as its first volume (Band) the subject of Egyptology: this is described in two sections (Abschnitt) which are concerned respectively with Egyptian writing and language, and Egyptian literature. Five scholars contributed to the first section and seven to the second: we may note among the chapters discussions of the history of Egyptology, Egyptian libraries and book production, and books and book titles.

The *Grundriss der indo-arischen Philologie und Altertumskunde* (Encyclopaedia of Indo-Aryan research) is in fact a series of individual monographs in German or English by German, Indian and British writers, treating of all aspects of Indo-Aryan philology and antiquities.

Grundriss der indo-arischen Philologie und Altertumskunde (Encyclopaedia of Indo-Aryan research). Begründet von G. Bühler, fortgesetzt von F. Kielhorn, herausgegeben von H. Lüders und J. Wackernagel. Berlin und Leipzig.

I. Band. Allgemeines und Sprache.
    1. Heft. (a) *Georg Bühler. 1837–98.* Von Julius Jolly. 1899.
        (b) *Geschichte der Sanskrit-Philologie und indischen Alter-tumskunde.* Von Ernst Windisch. 2 pts. 1917–20.
    3. Heft. (b) *Die indischen Wörterbücher (Kosa).* Von Theodor Zachariae. 1897.
    4. Heft. *Vedic grammar.* By A. A. Macdonell. 1910.
    6. Heft. *Vedische und Sanskrit-Syntax.* Von. J. S. Speyer. 1896.
    7. Heft. *Pali Literatur und Sprache.* Von Wilhelm Geiger. 1916.
    8. Heft. *Grammatik der Prakrit-Sprachen.* Von R. Pischel. 1900.
  10. Heft. *Literatur und Sprache der Singhalesen.* Von Wilhelm Geiger. 1900.
  11. Heft. *Indische Paläographie von ca. 350 a. Chr. – ca. 1300 p. Chr.* Von Georg Bühler. 1896.

II. Band. Literatur und Geschichte.
    1. Heft. Vedische Literatur (Sruti).
        (b) *The Atharvaveda and the Gopatha-Brahmana.* By Maurice Bloomfield. 1899.
    2. Heft. Epische und klassische literatur.
        (d) *Das indische Drama.* Von Sten Konow. 1920.
    3. Heft. Quellen der indischen Geschichte.
        (b) *Indian coins.* By E. J. Rapson. 1898.
    5. Heft. *Ethnography (castes and tribes).* By Sir Athelstane Baines. With a list of the more important works on ethnography by W. Siegling. 1912.
    8. Heft. *Recht und Sitte, einschliesslich der einheimischen Littera-tur.* Von Julius Jolly. 1896.

III. Band. Religion, weltliche Wissenschaften und Kunst.
    1. Heft. (a) *Vedic mythology.* By A. A. Macdonell. 1897.
        (b) *Epic mythology.* By E. Washburn Hopkins. 1915.
    2. Heft. *Ritual-Litteratur, Vedische Opfer und Zauber.* Von Alfred Hillebrandt. 1897.
    4. Heft. *Sāmkhya und Yoga.* Von Richard Garbe. 1896.
    6. Heft. *Vaisnavism; Saivism and minor religious systems.* By Sir R. G. Bhandarkar. 1913.
    7. Heft. *Die Lehre der Jainas nach der alten Quellen dargestellt.* Von Walther Schubring. 1935.

8. Heft. *Manual of Indian Buddhism*. By H. Kern. 1896.
9. Heft. *Astronomie, Astrologie und Mathematik*. Von G. Thibaut. 1899.
10. Heft. *Medicin*. Von Julius Jolly. 1901.

OTHER REFERENCE BOOKS

Two other reference books covering large areas of Asia are worthy of mention:

The Asia who's who. 3rd edition. Pan–Asia Newspaper Alliance, Hong Kong. 1960.

Handbook of Oriental history, by members of the Department of Oriental History, School of Oriental and African Studies, University of London. Edited by C. H. Philips. London: Royal Historical Society. 1951.

The *Asia who's who* gives short biographies of some 2,500 persons prominent in affairs and resident in nineteen countries of Asia from Afghanistan eastwards to Japan. An appendix includes persons from the Communist Asian countries of China, North Korea, North Vietnam and Outer Mongolia. The entries for each country are preceded by the name of the sovereign or president, followed by those of holders of office in the cabinet of the day.

The *Handbook of Oriental history* gives for each of its five sections the Near and Middle East, India and Pakistan, South-East Asia and the Archipelago, China and Japan, information on questions of romanization, names and titles, and place-names, as well as a select glossary, an explanation of calendars and systems of dating in use, and a list of the principal dynasties and rulers.

[7]

Periodicals

HISTORY OF THE ORIENTALIST PERIODICAL

The first Orientalist periodicals were issued in Asia. The Batavian Society of Arts and Sciences (Bataviaasch genootschap van kunsten en wetenschappen), founded by the Dutch in 1778, began to publish volumes of short essays (Verhandelingen) from the following year, and the series continued until the year 1950, when the Dutch East Indies gained their independence and became known as Indonesia. Vols. I–VI and VIII (published originally in 1779–92 and 1816) were issued in a second edition in the years 1820–27, the first two volumes in a third edition in 1825–26, having also been issued in a Dutch edition in 1781 and 1787. The first volume contains a total of thirteen articles on geographical, historical and scientific subjects, as well as a preface (Voorbericht) on the present state of the Society, the names of the Society's officers, its constitution, an address given by the President (Mr J. C. M. Rademacher) at the first annual general meeting held on the 8 March, 1779 and a list of members. In India, *Asiatick miscellany*, edited in Calcutta under the sponsorship of Sir William Jones by F. Gladwin, lasted only for three volumes (1785–89). It carried also a title in Arabic, Awāmir al-ta'ālif fī nawādir altasānīf, and consisted of 'original productions, translations, fugitive pieces, imitations and extracts from curious publications'. This was followed by the organ of the Asiatic Society of Bengal, *Asiatick researches* (1788–1839), a predecessor of the Society's *Journal and proceedings*, which has continued in an unbroken line, with some variations of title, to the present day. (See the introduction to vol. 1, pt. 1 of *Index to the publications of the Asiatic Society, 1788–1953*, pp. vii–viii.) These Asian periodicals, although they spread their net fairly wide, were, naturally enough, primarily concerned with the areas in which they were published.

The first Orientalist periodicals of a truly general character were the journals and transactions of the national Oriental societies of Europe and America which were founded in the first half of the nineteenth century: the *Journal asiatique* (Société asiatique), 1822– , the *Transactions* (1827–33) and *Journal* of the Royal Asiatic Society, 1834– , the *Zeitschrift der Deutschen Morgenländischen Gesellschaft*, 1845– , and the *Journal* of the American Oriental Society, 1849– . All of these are still current.

At a later date, Oriental departments in European universities began to issue journals principally as vehicles for the publication of research carried out under their auspices, but never restricted to this material. First in the field was the *Vienna Oriental Journal*, which later translated its title to *Wiener Zeitschrift für die Kunde des Morgenlandes*, 1887– . This was followed by the *Mitteilungen des Seminars für orientalische Sprachen* (later, Ausland-Hochschule), of the University of Berlin, 1898–1937, the *Rivista degli studi orientali*, 1907– , of the Oriental School (now Institute of Oriental Studies) in the University of Rome, the *Bulletin of the School of Oriental* (later, *and African*) *Studies* of the University of London, 1917– , the *Annali* of the University Oriental Institute of Naples, 1928– , and the *Annales de l'Institut de Philologie et d'Histoire Orientales et Slaves* of the Free University of Brussels, 1932– .

Institutions outside universities also publish journals: *Archiv orientalni* of the Oriental Institute of the Czechoslovak Academy of Sciences in Prague has been published since 1929, while two others are of quite recent origin, *East and West*, a journal in the English language published by the Italian Institute for the Middle and Far East (ISMEO) since 1950, and the *Mitteilungen* of the Institut für Orient-forschung, an institute under the aegis of the Deutsche Akademie der Wissenschaften in Berlin, since 1953. All current Russian Oriental journals depend upon institutes of the Academy of Sciences, following the pattern usual in all Eastern European countries.

Two well-known journals of an independent character, not attached to any society, institute or university department, are *Le Monde oriental* published in Sweden during the period 1906–41, originally at private expense but later with the aid of a government subvention, and *Le Muséon*, a review of Oriental studies published in Belgium since 1882.

REVIEWING JOURNALS

Oriental studies also has its reviewing journal of the 'Literaturzeitung' genre: the *Orientalistische Literaturzeitung* published under the auspices of the Berlin Academy, has been issued since 1898, first as a monthly, later as a bi-monthly bibliographical magazine. In addition to the large number of signed reviews carried in each issue, regular features are a short research article, and a selection of contents lists of Oriental and other relevant learned periodical publications. The Netherlands Institute for Near Eastern studies in Leiden has published its reviewing journal *Bibliotheca Orientalis* since 1944.

LISTS OF ORIENTALIST PERIODICALS

No complete or near-complete list of Orientalist periodicals has yet been published. Gabrieli's *Manuale di bibliografia musulmana* (Roma, 1916) gives on pp. 27–43 a long list of journals supposedly of value for the Islamic scholar, which include many Oriental journals of a general character, but this is by no means complete and has many surprising inclusions and omissions. The best published sources are the catalogues of Orientalist libraries, such as those of the Royal Asiatic Society (*Catalogue*, 1940, App. II, pp. 524–41), the American Oriental Society (*Catalogue*, 1930, pp. 15–37) and the School of Oriental and African Studies. A supplement to Gregory's *Union list of serials* containing periodicals and series in Oriental languages, is being compiled in the Library of Congress.

For purposes of comparison we mention here two lists of periodicals for African studies compiled in the U.S.A.:

Serials for African studies. Compiled by Helen F. Conover. Library of Congress, Washington, D.C., 1961.

A Checklist of serials for African studies . . . Prepared by Peter Duignan and Kenneth M. Glazier. 1963.

Several countries in Asia have published guides to currently issued periodical publications. For India we have:

Nifor guide to Indian periodicals 1955–56. National Information Service, Poona, 1956.

This truly remarkable publication gives all possible information that might be required about 2,127 periodicals and daily newspapers, published in English, Hindi, and twenty-five regional languages. These are classified under eighty-five heads which provide easy access to lists of periodicals concerned with many different subjects, including in their number Government publications (35); Associations, institutions and organizations, publications of (7); Indology and Orientology (42); and News magazines (56). We are then offered language and subject classifications of periodicals and daily newspapers, periodicity and geographical classifications, and a survey of Indian periodicals giving statistical data in twelve tables.

As though this were not adequate for most requirements, India also provides through its *Annual report of the Registrar of newspapers for India*, published by the Ministry of Information and Broadcasting, a work in two volumes of some thousand pages giving information on currently published periodicals. ('Newspapers' includes 'General Interest Newspapers' and periodicals, both classes are surveyed in this work on the basis of the UNESCO classification into these two categories.) The eighth annual report shows that as at 31 December, 1963, there were 503 daily newspapers in existence, published in twelve languages, and 7,287 periodicals, of which some fifteen hundred were school or college magazines, publicity journals, house organs, periodicals carrying serialized fiction, journals on astrology and other miscellaneous materials.

Serials in Malaya and Singapore were listed in an article by Lim Wong Pui Huen:

'Current Malay serials.' *Majallah Perpustakaan Singapura*, 2, 2, October, 1962, pp. 75–94.

This lists 221 Malay and English titles (including monograph series, other than those produced by commercial publishers, with serial numbering). Excluded are popular and school magazines, company reports, newspapers, annual reports and other routine publications by government departments, and serials in Chinese and Tamil.

Guide to Malay periodicals 1876–1941, with details of known holdings in Malaya, by William R. Roff. (Papers on South-East Asian subjects, 4.) Eastern Universities Press, Singapore, for Department of History in the University of Malaya at Kuala Lumpur, 1961.

Roff's Guide lists in chronological order all Malay journals and newspapers published in Malaya since 1876, and indicates where files are available. 147 periodicals in all are included, and these were published between 1876 and 1941 in the Peninsular Malay States and Straits Settlements. Also included are six titles published in the English language by Malays and devoted to Malay and Islamic interests. *Tarikh surat khabar* by Muhammad bin Dato Muda was used as the basis for this work. To the 128 listed in this work, Roff has added twenty-four titles and has indicated as far as they are known, holdings in Malaya (University of

Malaya, Singapore; National Library of Singapore; Government
Records, Kuala Lumpur; Dewan Bahasa dan Pustaka, Kuala Lumpur;
and four private collections). He also gives, in an appendix, details of
fourteen journals published in Indonesia, Cairo and Mecca, which
circulated in the Peninsula.

The Centre for South-East Asian Studies in the Social Sciences in the
Department of History of the University of Singapore has recently
(1964?) published a duplicated list of current official serials of the Malaysian governments 'held at the University of Singapore'.

Malayasian [sic] *serials; a check list of current official serials of the
Malaysian governments*, by Niranjan K. Hazra, Edwin Lee Siew Cheng.

For Chinese and Japanese periodicals there are several lists usable by
those with no knowledge of these languages:

Chinese periodicals in British libraries. Handlist no. 1. Compiled by
E. D. Grinstead. British Museum [1962].

Hong Kong. Union Research Institute. *Catalogue of Mainland Chinese
magazines and newspapers held by the Union Research Institute.* March,
1962.

Catalogue des périodiques chinois dans les bibliothèques d'Europe, par
Y. Hervouet. Préparé avec la collaboration de J. Lust et R. Pelissier.
(École pratique des Hautes Études, VIème section. Le monde d'Outre-
Mer passé et présent, Quatrième série, Bibliographies, II.) Paris, 1958.

Grinstead's handlist (which is undergoing revision) serves as a union
catalogue of the holdings of the larger collections in Great Britain, and
contains some one thousand titles represented by volumes and parts in
libraries in London, Oxford, Cambridge, Durham and Manchester. In
addition, there are given in appendices the titles of scientific periodicals
held by the British Museum (Natural History), and the National Lending Library of Science and Technology, the latter being a revised catalogue, complete to June, 1962. The eighteen Nanyang newspapers in
the British Museum are listed in the preface.

The Union Research Institute's catalogue contains the names of
magazines and newspapers procured from, not to say smuggled out of,
Communist China, up to the end of 1962.

Hervouet's list contains 600 titles of periodicals in the Chinese
language in a single transliterated alphabetical arrangement. The holdings (mostly fragmentary) of thirty-five libraries in Western Europe are
given.

For Japan there is a plethora of such lists, which could without doubt be considerably added to by a specialist:

Directory of Japanese learned periodicals (1957 [2nd] edition). *Index.* Compiled by Frank Rodgers. Urbana, Illinois. (Rodgers)

Bibliographical list of Japanese learned journals – humanities and social sciences. No. 2. 1959. Ministry of Education, Bureau of Higher Education and Science, Science Information Section. 1959. (Preface dated: January, 1960.) (Min. Ed. – Hum. Soc. Sci.)

Bibliographical list of Japanese learned journals – natural and applied sciences. Ministry of Education, Bureau of Higher Education and Science, Science Information Section. 1962. (Duplicated typescript.) (Min. Ed. – Sci.)

Directory of Japanese scientific periodicals 1962. Natural sciences, medical sciences and industry. Compiled jointly by National Diet Library and Ministry of Education. National Diet Library, Tokyo, 1962. (N.D.L.)

Japanese scientific and technical serial publications in the collections of the Library of Congress. Science and Technology Division, Library of Congress, Washington, 1962. (L.C.)

Rodgers is the predecessor of Min. Ed. – Hum. Soc. Sci. and Min. Ed. – Sci. It contains some 3,000 entries, arranged by U.D.C., but without 'minute subdivision'. The former of the two Ministry of Education publications lists 1,170 titles in the humanities and social sciences, in which categories are included a series of thirty-seven studies on areas (Japanology, Koreanology, Orientology, Sinology). All possible information is given, including 'indication of biblio-dynamical elements in the journal during the publishing year'. By this happy turn of phrase is meant 'indexes of periodical articles, literature reviews, book reviews, special or subject bibliographies, library accessions, cumulative indexes, classification code used for features listed above, structure of journal from point of view of column'.

Of the three lists of scientific journals, Min. Ed. – Sci. lists 1,175 learned journals in the pure and applied sciences published by universities, learned societies and research institutions. To this is added an alphabetical list of 800 journals in 177 subdivisions from 'acoustic material' to 'zootechnics'. N.D.L.'s list of 2,241 titles covers the U.D.C. subjects in classes 5 and 6 (except for those numbered 614, 614·8, 614·84, 64, 65, 67, 68 and 69). Of the great welter of Japanese scientific and technical journals, L.C.'s list shows that the National Library of the U.S.A.

possessed in 1962 no fewer than 1,620 of these titles, of which 1,316 are in the Japanese language.

An earlier list, giving 549 titles of periodicals in the Japanese language or published in the Japanese Empire, is:

Bibliographie des principales publications éditées dans l'Empire japonais. (Bulletin de la Maison Franco–Japonaise, Série française, tome III, nos. 3–4, Tokyo, 1931.)

Restricted to specialized periodicals of a scholarly character, this bibliography covers all subjects, including the pure and applied sciences, as well as the publications of learned societies, bibliographical lists and publishers' yearbooks.

We give here a list of the most important scholarly periodicals which regularly publish research articles on all branches of Asian or Oriental studies. For each title is given the name of the issuing body, if this is not apparent from the title, and the date of origin (and of completion if the journal has ceased publication).

Acta Orientalia. Societates Orientales Batava Danica Norvegica (*now* Danica Norvegica Svecica.) 1923–

Acta Orientalia Academiae Scientiarum Hungaricae. 1950–

Annali (R. Istituto Orientale di Napoli) (*now* Istituto Universitario Orientale du Napoli.) 1928–

Annuaire de l'Institut de Philologie et d'Histoire Orientales et Slaves. (Université libre de Bruxelles.) 1932–

Archiv Orientální. Orientální Ustav, Prague. 1929–

Asiatische Studien/Études asiatiques. Zeitschrift der Schweizerischen Gesellschaft für Asienkunde/Revue de la Société Suisse d'Études Asiatiques. 1947–

Bulletin of the School of Oriental (and African) Studies. 1917–

East and West. Istituto Italiano per il Medio ed Estremo Oriente. 1950–

Epigrafika Vostoka. Akademiya Nauk SSSR, Institut Arkheologii. 1947–

Folia Orientalia. Académie Polonaise des Sciences, Section de Cracovie, Commission Orientaliste. 1959–

Giornale della Società Asiatica Italiana. 1887–1935.

Glasgow University Oriental Society, Transactions. 1901–

Journal of the American Oriental Society. 1849–

Journal Asiatique. (Société Asiatique.) 1822–

Journal of the economic and social history of the Orient. 1957–

Journal of the Manchester University Egyptian and Oriental Society. 1911–54.

Journal of the Royal Asiatic Society of Great Britain and Ireland. 1834– (Preceded by: *Transactions* 1827–34.)

Kratkie Soobshcheniya Instituta Narodov Azii (formerly *Instituta vostokovedeniya*). Akademiya Nauk SSSR. 1951–

Mitteilungen der Ausland-Hochschule an der Universität Berlin (formerly *Mitteilungen des Seminars für Orientalische Sprachen, Berlin*.) 1898–1940.

Mitteilungen des Instituts für Orientforschung. Institut für Orientforschung. Deutsche Akademie der Wissenschaften zu Berlin. 1953–

Le Monde Oriental. 1906–41.

Le Muséon: Revue d'études orientales. 1882–

Narody Azii i Afriki: istoriya ekonomika, kul'tura. (Akad. Nauk SSSR, Inst. narodov Azii, Inst. Afriki.) 1964– (formerly *Problemy Vostokovedeniya*, 1959–61; and before that, *Sovetskoe vostokovedenie*, 1940–58).

Oriens. Milletlerarasi Şark Tetkikleri Cemiyeti Mecmuası (International Society for Oriental Research). 1948–

Orientalistische Literaturzeitung. Deutsche Akademie der Wissenschaften zu Berlin. 1898–

Przegląd Orientalistyczny. Polskie Towarzystwo Orientalistyczne. 1948–

Rivista degli studi orientali. Università di Roma, Scuola Orientale (*now* Istituto di Studi Orientali). 1907–

Rocznik Orientalistyczny. (*Polish archives of Oriental research.*) Polska Akademia Nauk, Komitet Orientalistyczny. 1914–

Studia et Acta Orientalia. Société des Sciences Historiques et Philologiques de la R.P.R. (Bucarest), Section d'Études Orientales. 1957–

Studia Orientalia. Societas Orientalis Fennica. 1925–

Uchenye Zapiski Instituta Vostokovedeniya. Akademiya Nauk SSSR, Institut Vostokovedeniya. 1950–60.

Wiener Zeitschrift für die Kunde des Morgenlandes (formerly *Vienna Oriental Journal*). Orientalisches Institut der Universität Wien. 1887–

Zapiski Vostochnago Otdeleniya (Imperatorskago) Russkago Arkheologicheskago Obshchestva. 1886–1920. (Continued as: *Zapiski Kollegii Vostokovedov pri Aziatskom Muzee Akademii Nauk SSSR.* 1925–30. Continued as: *Zapiski Instituta Vostokovedeniya Akademii Nauk SSSR.* 1932–39.)

Zeitschrift der Deutschen Morgenländischen Gesellschaft. 1847–

Three other periodicals which cover roughly two-thirds of Asia, i.e. Eastern and Southern Asia, omitting only the Near and Middle East, should also be mentioned:

Harvard Journal of Asiatic studies. Harvard–Yenching Institute. 1936–

Journal of Asian studies. Association for Asian Studies (formerly *The Far Eastern Quarterly*). 1941–42.

T'oung Pao: archives concernant l'histoire, les langues, la géographie, l'ethnographie et les arts de l'Asie Orientale. Publiée avec le concours du Centre national francais de la recherche scientifique et de l'Organisation néerlandaise pour le développement de la recherche pure. 1890–

The service performed by these periodicals to Oriental studies consists in the publication of articles based on original research and the provision of information on new developments in these studies. These purposes are achieved by publishing, in addition to articles of a learned character, shorter notes or miscellanies on minor points, criticism of new publications by means of reviews by other scholars, and by giving publicity to these works by means of brief notices or lists of new titles received. Occasionally abstracts or summaries of new books and periodical articles are a regular feature.

Some journals in addition to all these things carry news of the Orientalist profession and similar features. This is especially true of the *Journal of Asian Studies* (formerly *The Far Eastern Quarterly*), which for many years has made a feature of publishing a 'Bibliography of Asian studies' in a special annual issue. In all of its volumes since 15 (1955–56) there has been a section entitled 'Notes of the profession' which gives information on Asian collections in various libraries in America and Europe, on the provisions for Asian studies made by universities in France, Germany, England and America, and on other matters of interest for the librarian and bibliographer. Also noteworthy is the article in volume 18 (1958–59) by Patrick Wilson entitled 'Survey of bibliographies on Southern Asia.'

Thus the learned periodical makes a significant contribution to the bibliography of our subject: perhaps the most important aspect of its function is to keep scholars up to date with developments in their field of study.

By concept the periodical article is, especially in the humanities, a kind of feeler put out before the publication of a definitive book in which the material with any accretions accumulated as a result of this preliminary publication will be included. In many fields, however, and especially in Oriental studies where costs of publication are high and the potential market rather low, the periodical article often is used for the definitive publication and sometimes approaches book size.

CATALOGUES OF PERIODICAL ARTICLES

Because Orientalist journal articles have a longer useful life than do those written in more cultivated fields such as the natural and applied sciences, some bibliographers have thought it valuable to compile catalogues of articles on a particular subject contained in a wide range of periodicals. Thus, M. Schwab in his:

Répertoire des articles relatifs à l'histoire et à la littérature juives parus dans les périodiques de 1783 à 1898. Publié sous les auspices de la Société d'Études Juives. Paris, 1900.

gives in its 600 closely-written pages a catalogue of articles in 94 periodicals and collective publications arranged by author, and a subject index. *Index Islamicus,* 1906–55 (compiled by J. D. Pearson with the assistance of Julia F. Ashton) contains over 26,000 entries for articles in some 10,000 volumes of about 500 periodicals, as well as those published in 120 Festschrift volumes and 70 publications of national and international conferences. The *Supplement 1956–60* adds some 7,000 titles to this total. In a similar way, Iraj Afshar in *Index Iranicus* (Teheran, 1961), has listed nearly 6,000 articles in the Persian language published in periodicals and collective publications between 1910 and 1958; and Lust's *Index Sinicus* (1964) records nearly 20,000 titles of articles on China published in Western languages between 1920 and 1955.

Several countries publish lists or abstracts of articles contained in their periodical press. These provide incidentally lists of at any rate the most important periodicals published in these countries:

Türkiye makaleler bibliiyografyası. Bibliographie des articles parus dans les périodiques turcs. (Milli Kutüphane Bibliyografya Enstitüsü Yayĭnlarĭ. Bibliothèque Nationale, Institut de Bibliographie Publications.) Ankara, 1954–. [Quarterly, arranged in DC order. Everything in both Turkish and French. Eighty-six periodicals included in 1963, I issue.]

Guide to Indian periodical literature. Prabhu Book service, Gurgaon. 1964–. [Monthly, covering all aspects of Indology, arranged

I

alphabetically by subject, to be cumulated annually. Sixty-four titles in list of periodicals surveyed in vol. I, no. 5, July, 1964.]

Indonesian abstracts: abstracts on current scientific literature. (Madjelis ilmu pengetahuan Indonesia. Council for Sciences of Indonesia.) Djakarta, 1958–. [Quarterly in the English language providing abstracts of current Indonesian scientific articles in the fields of the social sciences, mathematics and natural sciences, applied sciences, medicine, technology, geography, biography, history. Arranged in U.D.C. order, Indonesian titles translated into English. List of abbreviated titles in July, 1963 issue includes eighteen periodicals.]

Index of Indonesian learned periodicals 1960– (Indeks madjalah ilmiah). Madjeli's ilmu pengetahuan Indonesia (Council for Sciences of Indonesia.) Djakarta, 1961– [The fourth issue, for 1963, lists 509 periodical articles, classified by U.D.C. The titles, which are given both in Indonesian and English translation, are taken from thirty-five periodicals. A list of current Indonesian learned periodicals is prefixed to the Index: this contains 120 titles.]

Index to Philippine periodicals. Edited by Maxima M. Ferrer and Venancia T. Guillermo. Inter-departmental Reference Service, Graduate school of Public Administration, University of the Philippines, Manila. 1956– [Semi-annual, with entries under authors and subjects and some titles in a single alphabetical arrangement. List of periodicals indexed includes 117 titles, each issue shows actual coverage of volumes and issues. About 14,000 titles in vol. 8, 1st semi-annual issue, 1963.]

City of Johannesburg Public Library. *Index to South African periodicals*. Edited by J. D. Wackrill. [Annual, begun in 1940, the items published in first decade having been cumulated into a four-volume work published in 1953. Arranged in a single alphabetical sequence of authors and subjects, using Library of Congress subject headings. Scholarly journals, particularly the scientific and technical, have been indexed fully: the more general and popular selectively. Special attention paid to articles which may in future contribute to the history of any aspect of South African life. Critical reviews of books by South African authors are entered at 'Books, Reviews'. List of periodicals indexed contains 265 titles.]

Japanese periodicals index. Natural sciences. National Diet Library. [Provides titles in English of articles published in some 500 scientific and technological, and some 300 medical journals.]

The Japan science review; law and politics lists books and articles from some seventy-five journals in these fields. It has been published since

1950, but the first number contained a 'Retrospect and prospect of the legal and political sciences in Japan.' The bibliographies started in the second number, and covered the period 1946–50. The companion series (humanistic studies, formerly literature, philosophy and history) contains abstracts and reviews of a number of dissertations in the various fields which have been recommended by nineteen member societies of the Union of Japanese Associations of Humanistic Studies.

INDEXES TO PERIODICALS

The editors of Orientalist periodicals have long felt it essential to publish indexes to the contents of their journals. These sometimes take the form of alphabetical, or classified inventories, of the titles of articles, book reviews and the books reviewed, as the indexes to JA, JRAS, JASB, and Przegląd orientalistyczny recorded below. On the other hand, the forty-year index to JAOS and the centennial index published by ZDMG inventorize their contents in much greater detail. In addition to the indexes of authors of articles, notes and reviews, of authors of books reviewed, and of topics and subjects dealt with in the various articles, JAOS gives a complete index of words in the various languages that have been the subject of comment or discussion and passages of works, sacred and profane, from the literary heritages of the various Oriental cultures. ZDMG's *Generalindex*, Band 1–100, furnishes lists of obituary notices, of the indexes published as articles or part of articles in volumes 61–700, and of the annual scientific surveys ('wissenschaftliche Jahresberichte') which were a feature of volumes 61–74 of the journal and which recorded the literature published during the years 1906 to 1919.

LIST OF INDEXES TO GENERAL ORIENTALIST PERIODICALS
(superseded indexes not included)

Journal asiatique

Table alphabétique, tom. 1–11. Paris, 1829.

Table des matières, sér. 2–3 (1828–42) in sér. 3, tom. 14 (1842), pp. 453–584.

„ „ „ sér. 4–5 (1843–62) in sér. 5, tom. 20 (1862), pp. 393–498.

„ „ „ sér. 6 (1863–72) in sér. 6, tom. 20 (1872), pp. 261–533.

Table des matières, sér. 7 (1873–82) in sér. 7, tom. 20 (1882),
   pp. 277–534.

„ „ „ sér. 8 (1883–92) in sér. 8, tom. 20 (1892),
   pp. 341–540.

„ „ „ sér. 9 (1893–1902) in sér. 9, tom. 20 (1902),
   pp. 357–529, 531.

Table générale des matières, sér. 10 (1903–12) Paris, 1912.

„ „ „ „ sér. 11 (1913–22) Paris, 1922.

„ „ „ „ sér. 12 (1923–32) Paris, 1932.

„ „ „ „ sér. 13 (1933–42) Paris, 1942.

„ „ „ „ sér. 14 (1943–52) Paris, 1954.

Journal of the Royal Asiatic Society

1. 1827–88, i.e. to *Transactions* I–III (1827, 1830, 1835); *Journal* I–XX (1834–63); *Journal*, N.S. 1865–88. (Reprinted from *Journal*, 1888.)

In this are rearranged in one alphabetical list all the separate indices which have been appended to each volume. In the list of authors, which has been added, those who wrote in the 'Asiatick Researches' are also included. An earlier index, to *Transactions* and *Journal* I–VIII, published in *Journal* VIII (1846) is therefore superseded.

2. 1889–1903. (Reprinted from *Journal*, 1904.)

Arranges authors, subjects and topics in one sequence.

3. Centenary volume. 1823–1923. Compiled and edited by F. E. Pargiter. London, 1923.

A catalogue of articles and miscellaneous notes (except notes of no permanent importance) published in the hundred years of the Society's existence in *Transactions* and *Journal*, according to regions and authors. Index I covers all countries except India, and has sections for 'Miscellaneous' and for 'Sea, geography, travel, and commerce'. Index II covers India, subdivided into twenty-eight subjects and provinces. Index III lists authors and their contributions, including those who have been the subject of obituary notices. An appendix gives the names of Presidents, Directors, Treasurers, Secretaries and Librarians of the Society, and lists the chief collections of Oriental manuscripts belonging to the Society.

4. Index to the contents of the *Journal* for the decade 1920 to 1929. London (1934).

Lists the Society's own publications in the series *Oriental translation fund*, *Asiatic Society monographs*, *Prize publication fund*, *James G. Forlong fund*, and gives titles of articles and miscellanea *in order of publication*, a list of plates *in order of publication*, and an index of authors, subjects and reviews.

5. Index of the contents of the *Journal* for the decade 1930–39. London (1940).

List of publications of the Society, followed by a subject index of articles (Archaeology, Assyriology, Buddhica, Ethnology, Etymology, Historiography, Indica, Inscriptions, Islamica, Linguistics, Medical, Music, Numismatics, Philology, Philosophy, Religion, Sinica, Tibetica) with a list of authors' names and their articles, arranged in sections, as follows: Africa, excl. Egypt; Arabia and Islam; Armenia, Georgia, Caucasia; Asia Minor, Central Asia; China; Egypt; India (subdivided); Iran (subdivided by period); Iraq (subdivided by period); Linguistics and lexicography, excl. India; Malay peninsula; Miscellanea; Palestine and Syria; Turkey. This in turn is followed by Lists of reviews, obituaries, lectures; Authors of reviews, obituaries and lecturers; References in text of *Journal* (a kind of name and topic index), and a section headed 'General information'.

6. List of articles in the *Journal* . . . 1940–50.

Reprinted from *Journal*, April, 1952, pp. 96–101). Classified by region and subject (archaeology and art, Buddhism, geography, Islam, miscellaneous, music, numismatics, obituaries).

[No index was published for the decade 1951–60; each volume published from 1961 onward contains a so-called index which in reality is a List of articles and reviews.]

Journal of the Asiatic Society (of Bengal).

Index to the publications of the Asiatic Society (of Bengal) 1788–1953. Compiled by Sibadas Chaudhuri. Calcutta, 1956.

James Prinsep in 1837 brought out a very carefully prepared analytical index of the first eighteen volumes of the *Asiatick Researches*. In 1836 Raja Rajendra Jala Mitra's index to the last two volumes of the *Asiatick Researches* and the first twenty-three volumes of the JASB was published.

The Centenary review from 1784–1883, published in the Centenary volume, 1885, indexed the publications issued during the first hundred years of the Society's existence. It is now proposed to bring the Index of the *Journal* (inclusive of the Index in the Centenary volume) up to date and to cover all publications of the Society since its inception. Vol. 1, Part 1 contained an introduction on the history of the Society and its publication series, and an author index to *Asiatick Researches*, *Journal* (three series up to 1953), *Memoirs* and Miscellaneous Publications, containing 5,139 entries. Part 2 contains the index to the series

Bibliotheca Indica and *Monographs*, an author index to Notices in the Proceedings, and an analytical classified index. Vol. 2 will be devoted to a subject index, with the following subdivisions: Religion and philosophy; Language and literature; History and social sciences; Art and archaeology; Anthropology; Science; Miscellaneous.

Przegląd orientalistyczney.

Indèks artykulow 1948–58.

Journal of the American Oriental Society

Index to vols. 1–20 (1843–99) in vol. 21, first half, 1902, pp. Index to vols. 21–60 (1901–40). Compiled by E. H. Shafer, H. E. Fernald, I. Dyen, H. W. Glidden. (American Oriental series, vol. 40.) New Haven, 1955. (Superseded the index to vols. 21–40, 1901–20, compiled by R. K. Yerkes and published in vol. 44, pp. 313–84.)

Zeitschrift der Deutschen Morgenländischen Gesellschaft

Generalindex, Band 1–100. Wiesbaden, 1955. Contains indexes to articles and book reviews (by author of books reviewed) in volumes 1–100, obituary notices in volumes 1–100, and a subject index to volumes 61–100. Ten-year indexes covering volumes 1–60 had been published previously. A list of special indexes appearing in volumes 61–100 is also included.]

T'oung Pao

Index général 1890–1944. Leiden, 1953.
Most scholars would agree that *T'oung Pao* (meaning 'notices') is the foremost scholarly journal for Far Eastern, South-East Asian and South Asian studies. Founded by the great French scholar and bibliographer Henri Cordier, for many years it was edited by him and by Paul Pelliot. The index covers the first forty-seven volumes, published between the years 1890 and 1944, and was edited under the supervision of J. J. L. Duyvendak and P. Demiéville. The first part of the index contains in one alphabetical sequence: i. all the names of authors who contributed articles with the titles of their contributions; ii. all titles of books or articles reviewed, or which formed the subject of notices or critical notes; iii. a great number of proper names and technical terms mentioned in the articles, reviews, or critical notices.
To this is added an 'index complémentaire par matières', in which the material is arranged under a variety of subjects (including congresses and conferences, research and teaching, correspondence,

bibliography and obituary notices), each entry referring to the author or title of an article, review or notice containing information on the subject. All of this material relates to the Far East in general or to China, and this is followed by entries arranged under the names of other countries and regions, including most of the countries of Asia outside the Middle East.]

NEWSPAPERS

As the tendency for Oriental studies to move away from purely philological pursuits into the more workaday world of the social sciences increases, the newspaper is likely to become ever more demanded by users of our libraries, both for current reading and for retrospective searching by historians and others. To maintain a current newspaper collection is an expensive undertaking, to preserve it for posterity even more so, whether binding or microfilming be the method used. American libraries have been for some time coming to grips with this special problem, and plans have been made for co-operative acquisition and storage of these materials – plans in which libraries in all other countries might well become involved. On this read the paper given by Fussler to the Conference on American library resources on Southern Asia, and published in *Library J.*, 81 (1956), pp. 126–33 as 'New patterns for library co-operation'.

The estimated numbers of daily newspapers published in the various countries in Asia, are as follows:

(These figures have been taken from a wide variety of sources and represent the most up-to-date information available at the time of writing.)

MIDDLE EAST

Aden 17, Afghanistan 15, Cyprus 21, Iran 15, Iraq 18, Israel 54, Jordan 8, Kuwait 11, Lebanon 51, Saudi Arabia 14, Syria 18, Turkey 62. Total: 294.

SOUTH ASIA

Ceylon 15, India 591, Nepal 13, Pakistan 100. Total: 719.

SOUTH-EAST ASIA

Burma 40, Cambodia 11, Indonesia 94, Laos 1, Malaysia 64, Philippines 42, Thailand 39, South Vietnam 22. Total: 313.

FAR EAST

China 800, Formosa 31, Hong Kong 16(?), Japan 107, North Korea 11, South Korea 13, Macao 1, Mongolia 3, Ryukyus 13. Total: 1,055.

Newspapers on microfilm. Fifth edition. Compiled under the direction of George A. Schwegmann. Library of Congress, Washington, 1963.

Newspapers on microfilm in its fifth edition lists among the 16,000 entries that had come to the notice of the Microfilm Clearing House a total of 455 titles of Asian newspapers, 155 African and 44 Oceanic, of which microfilm copies, negative and positive are known to exist, whether in a large selection of libraries in the U.S.A., the Midwest Inter-Library Center, which has control of a co-operative scheme for the provision of foreign newspapers, or in possession of the microfilm companies themselves. Among the Asian countries represented by the largest numbers of titles are China (both sides, 86), India (61), Indonesia (41), Japan (53), the Asiatic parts of the U.S.S.R. (66), and Vietnam: as might be expected, compared with the Far East and Southern Asia, the Near and Middle East is poorly represented, with 29 titles for ten countries (Israel being top with 8 titles). For Africa, the Republic of South Africa leads, with 31 titles, followed by Nigeria (20), the U.A.R. (18), Ghana (17), Sierra Leone (12): countries not represented included Central African Republic, Dahomey, Chad, Mali, Madagascar, Mauritania, Nyasaland, and the Spanish territories. The Library of Congress has also published:

African newspapers currently received in selected American libraries. Washington, D.C., 1956. (New edition expected in 1964.)

For newspapers emanating from certain countries in Asia and Africa available in Great Britain see:

Union list of Commonwealth newspapers in London, Oxford and Cambridge. Compiled by A. R. Hewitt, University of London; Athlone Press for Institute of Commonwealth Studies, 1960.

NEWS SUMMARIES

Asia has its own 'Keesing's' in the *Asian recorder*, published weekly since 1957 in New Delhi, with quarterly indexes cumulated annually. News items affecting all countries in Asia are extracted from newspapers, periodicals, the radio, and embassy or government department sources, and are arranged alphabetically by country, with a special section 'Asia outside Asia' for events affecting Asia which happen outside that continent, and another special section on sport.

Summaries of the Chinese Press are provided in:

Survey of China mainland press. American Consulate-General, Hong Kong.

News from Hsin-hua news agency. China. No. 1, 7 October, 1957–76 Chancery Lane, London, W.C.2.

The Indian Press digests project is a department of the Center for South Asian Studies, Institute of International Studies, University of California at Berkeley. It publishes a 'Monograph series' based partly on a regular survey of Indian newspapers. Six volumes had been published by 1963.

Bulletin de la presse arabe, founded in 1948, is published every two days, by Le Bureau des documentations syriennes et arabes, in Damascus. The news items are translated into French and arranged by subject under nine rubrics.

News items relating especially to the Muslim Middle East are given in the Italian monthly journal *Oriente moderno* (Istituto per l'Oriente, Rome) in each of its two sections, political–historical and cultural. *Cahiers de l'Orient contemporain*, published by the Documentation française for the Centre d'études de l'Orient contemporain of the Institut d'études islamiques of the University of Paris, provides a regular four monthly chronology of events in the Muslim Middle East and North Africa, with references to newspaper reports.

NEWSPAPER CUTTINGS

Institutions all over the world collect clippings from newspapers in their spheres of interest or range of study. An example of this in Great Britain is the Press Library at the Royal Institute of International Affairs (Chatham House) which since 1924 has closely analysed and indexed cuttings from daily newspapers in western European languages. All aspects of international affairs, including political and economic developments in Asia and Africa, are represented.[1]

Since 1906 *The Times* newspaper of London has been keeping cuttings from its own pages which are pasted on to large sheets and bound up in guard-books for the use of its Intelligence Department. These

[1] See Geoffrey Whatmore's *News information*, Crosby Lockwood, 1964.

guard-books cover Africa; Arabia, Iraq, Syria, Lebanon; China; Congo Free State; Egypt; Ethiopia; Japan; Korea; Malaya, Siam and Indonesia; Morocco; Palestine; Persia; Turkey, as well as the Second World War, International, and League of Nations, and a wide range of subjects from Aircraft accidents through Medicine and Murders to Weather. The volumes begin at various dates from the early twentieth century to the late 1950's.

Recently, by arrangement with *The Times*, University Microfilms Ltd. has microfilmed all of these volumes and offers them for sale as paper-bound xerographic copies at £20 each, or £23 per volume for 'library-bound volumes'. The original volumes containing material on Japan from 1906–36 and China from 1907–31 are in the Library of the School of Oriental and African Studies.

GAZETTES

A special type of newspaper is the official gazette published by national or local governments and serving to promulgate orders, decrees and judicial decisions, to publish the texts of constitutions, legislative bills and treaties and many similar purposes. They are very voluminous in character being issued with great frequency, sometimes in fact once a day. The New York Public Library some years ago embarked upon a project of microfilming these documents and making the films available for sale to other interested persons. The microfilmed gazettes date mostly from the late 1950's, but some earlier years are represented. Two published lists record gazettes filmed up to December, 1962. Efforts were made to film as many gazettes as possible of African and Asian countries which gained independence during 1962. The lists indicate the volumes available, the number of feet of microfilm taken up and the price. Orders for complete sets or individual volumes may be addressed to the Photographic Service Division of the Library. Countries and states concerned number 34 in Asia, 63 in Africa and 12 in Oceania.

The New York Public Library National and Local Gazettes Microfilming Program. *Cumulative list of national and local gazettes filmed December, 1961.*

— *Supplementary list of national and local gazettes filmed as of December, 1962.*

[8]

General Bibliographies

In this chapter we shall concern ourselves with bibliographies which cover the whole realm of Oriental studies, with the whole continent of Asia, or with substantial regions of Asia, such as the colonial bibliographies.

There is no counterpart for Asian studies to the *Bibliography of African bibliographies* published by the South African Public Libraries. Besterman, among the 85,000 entries for abstracts, indexes, catalogues and bibliographies in his monumental and invaluable *World bibliography of bibliographies* (third and final edition, 1955) includes 2,212 titles relating to Asia, 101 to the Pacific, and 416 to Africa. These relate to individual countries and regions of those continents, to all aspects of Oriental and Asian studies and to individual Orientalists or Africanists. Many of the entries, however, represent summaries and digests of legislation or law reports, types of publication which would not normally be regarded as constituting bibliographies.

A list of 'bibliographical aids' designed for the study of social sciences, but also useful in other disciplines, is given in the publication:

Oversikt over samhällsvetenskapliga bibliografiska hjälpmedel. A survey of the bibliographical aids in the social sciences. Av Lars Frykholm. Stockholm, 1960.

This supplies a total of some 250 titles relating to Asia, the British Commonwealth, the Near East, the Orient, the Soviet Union and the Pacific.

WORLD BIBLIOGRAPHIES BY SUBJECT

Much material on Asia and Africa is obviously to be extracted from the principal bibliographies devoted to subjects or disciplines, which naturally include titles relating to the regions with which we are concerned. Thus, for instance, bibliographies of geography and social anthropology must inevitably contain a substantial amount relating to single regions or countries, for the vast majority of social anthropologists and geographers concern themselves at any one time with a single natural region or political unit. In the same way most historians specialize in the history of a region, which may be a whole continent, or a part of it, or a single country, and a large proportion of linguists occupy themselves with the study of a single language, a generic group of languages, or a complex of languages spoken in a particular region. On the other hand, philosophers, for instance, tend to concern themselves with theories and universals to a much longer extent than do those who propound the other disciplines.

A number of important subject bibliographies published at regular intervals has been examined with a view to ascertaining the amount of material on Asia and Africa which they contain, and the results will be given in the succeeding paragraphs. As a general rule it may be affirmed that the 'disciplinary' bibliographies contain material not in the 'regional' bibliographies, for, as has been said before, the world of scholarship is still largely divided into two, sometimes opposing, camps, that of the subject specialist and that of the regional or 'area studies' exponent. In order to approach completeness in the bibliographical coverage of an area or region, and especially in Asian and African studies, it is necessary to consult the two types of bibliography.

THE PRINCIPAL SUBJECT BIBLIOGRAPHIES IN THE HUMANITIES AND SOCIAL SCIENCES, AND THE PROPORTION OF ITEMS RELATING TO ASIA AND AFRICA

HISTORY OF RELIGIONS

International bibliography of the history of religions 1960–61. Compiled under the responsibility of the Secretary-General of the International Association for the History of Religions, Professor-Doctor C. J. Bleeker, by Salih Alich. Published in connection with *Numen* with the support of UNESCO and under the auspices of the International Council for Philosophy and Humanistic Studies by the International Association for the History of Religions. Leiden: Brill, 1964.

The aim of the bibliography is 'to include references to scholarly publications in any language on the history and analysis of religions'. Asian and African material is arranged under the rubrics 'Prehistoric and primitive religions, Religions of the Ancient Near East and Middle

East, Judaism and Ancient Israel, Eastern Christianity, Islam, Hinduism, and East Asian religions'. This material occupies 57½ pages out of the total of 91½ pages in the book, or 62·8 per cent of the whole.

PHILOSOPHY

Société philosophique de Louvain. *Répertoire bibliographique de la philosophie.* Publié sous les auspices de l'Institut international de philosophie avec le patronage de l'UNESCO. Tome XIII (1961). Louvain.

This is limited, in general, to literature (whether in the form of books or periodical articles) published in the principal languages of Europe with the exception of Russian. Of the various subject sections only that on the history of philosophy specifically mentions Asia and Africa: a total of 262 entries occur under these headings out of a total of 6,064 in the book, or 4·3 per cent.

HISTORY OF SCIENCE

'Eighty-eighth critical bibliography of the history of science and its cultural influences (to 1 January, 1963).' *Isis*, 54, no. 178, December, 1963, pp. 515–667.

In 'the chronological classification' of this bibliography, sections are included on the Ancient Near East, Islam and related cultures, India and the Far East. These sections occupy approximately 5 per cent of the total space.

ART AND ARCHAEOLOGY

Comité international d'histoire de l'art et Bibliothèque d'art et d'archéologie de l'Université de Paris. *Répertoire d'art et d'archéologie.* Publié sous la direction de Pierre Lelièvre. Rédigé par Mme. Lucien-Herr et Mlle. Claude Lauriol. Tome LXIV, Année, 1960. Paris, La Haye, 1963. [Financed by UNESCO, CNRS, EPHE (VIe section).]

The *Répertoire* contains many scattered references to Asian art in the general section (Histoire générale de l'art) and in the chronological sections Antiquity, and Middle Ages and Renaissance. The bulk of the entries on this subject, however, come in the final section, on Islam, India and the Far East. In all, 1,509 titles were detected out of a total of 11,652 – nearly 13 per cent.

GEOGRAPHY

Association de géographes francais. *Bibliographie géographique internationale, 1961.* Publiée sous les auspices de l'Union géographique internationale avec le concours de l'Organisation des Nations Unies pour l'Éducation, la Science et la Culture (UNESCO). Paris (1963).

In the regional part of this bibliography, Asia, Africa and Oceania take up 194½ pages out of 874, or 22·2 per cent.

HISTORY

International bibliography of historical sciences. Twenty-ninth volume, 1960 . . . Edited with the contribution of the national committees by Michel Francois and Nicolas Tolu for the International Committee of Historical Sciences, Lausanne. Published with the assistance of UNESCO and under the patronage of the International Council for Philosophy and Humanistic Studies. Paris, 1962.

Entries for Asia occur in sections D (Peoples of the Ancient East), I (History of the Middle Ages: Islam), K (Modern times: Individual countries), and for Africa and Oceania as well as in P (History of relations between modern states: 2, Colonial history). Sections R, S, U are entirely devoted to these regions. 730 entries out of 7,276 appear in the volume for 1960; this represents 10 per cent of the whole.

SOCIAL SCIENCES

The International Committee for Social Science Documentation publishes a series of four annual bibliographies:

International bibliography of sociology.
International bibliography of political science.
International bibliography of economics.
International bibliography of social and cultural anthropology.

The volume for 1961 (published in 1963) was examined in every case.

I.B. Sociology has Africa, Asia, Middle East and Pacific subdivisions subsumed only in section C (Social structure) at C.11 (Population changes: studies by countries), C.32 (Civilizations and national characteristics) and C.712 (Ethnic groups: Descriptive studies by countries). As with all the bibliographies, however, many references to the regions are to be found in all divisions. 273 books and 416 articles were discovered out of a total of 4,925 – 8·4 per cent.

In *I.B. Political science*, the figures are: Asia, 226 books, 494 articles, Africa 116 and 192, Pacific 0 and 7, totalling 1,035 entries in all. Out of a total of 4,304 numbers in the bibliography this represents 24·1 per cent. Subdivisions for 'National studies' occur in a great many sections, while section F is devoted entirely to 'Area studies'.

I.B. Economics has sections for Africa, Asia and the Middle East in the two divisions F.1 (Present economic conditions) and 0.12454 (International economics: Problems of Eurafrica). These sections yield 972 references out of a total of 8,139 entries in the book, corresponding to 11.9 per cent.

I.B. Social and cultural anthropology contains 3,646 items arranged systematically by subject. The 'Classification scheme', which serves as a contents list, incorporates sections for Asia, the Middle East, Africa and the Pacific in the following divisions:

Material and methods of anthropology
Archaeological material
Historical material
Linguistic material
Morphological foundations
General and comparative studies
General ethnographic studies of peoples and communities
Religion, magic and witchcraft
Problems of knowledge, arts and science, folk traditions
Artistic and literary expression
Fables, tales, legends, literary materials
Problems of acculturation and social change, contact situations

Together with the entries for the regions which appear in other divisions of the bibliography, the total figures are:

				Books	*Articles*	*Total*
Asia and Middle East			...	275	1,118	1,393
Africa ...	...	...	...	146	937	1,083
Pacific ...	...	...	...	40	314	354
		Total	...	461	2,369	2,830

The total figure for the three regions represents 77·6 per cent of the whole, by far the highest percentage of all the bibliographies adduced as evidence in this chapter.

LAW

Index to foreign law periodicals. Volume 4, 1963. Published by the Institute of Advanced Legal Studies, University of London, in co-operation with the American Association of Law Libraries, 1963.

This joint Anglo-American venture, though described as an index to 'foreign' periodicals, numbers 4 British and 9 United States journals among a total of 276 law periodicals indexed. The articles are arranged under subject headings, with country divisions wherever appropriate. 758 entries on Asia and 174 on Africa are given, or roughly 8·1 per cent of the total.

LINGUISTICS

Permanent International Committee of Linguists. *Linguistic bibliography for the year 1959 and supplement for previous years*. Published by the Permanent International Committee of Linguists with a grant from the United Nations Educational, Scientific and Cultural Organization. (Title also in French.) Utrecht–Antwerp: Spectrum, 1961.

In the chapter on general linguistics, works relating to Asia, Australia and Africa, appear under the rubric 'Onomastics'. Writings on Asian and African languages appear in the sections devoted to the following groups: Indo-European, Asian and Mediterranean, Hamito-Semitic, Caucasian, Altaic, Dravidian, Burushaski, South-East Asia, Austronesian, Papuan, Australian, Negro-Africa, Creole. The entries in all of these groups occupy roughly 71 pages, or 21·5 per cent of the whole.

It may be of some interest to indicate by means of a table, in descending order of magnitude, the amount of Asian and African material to be found in the current bibliographies in the principal spheres of study in the humanities and social sciences.

	Per cent
Social and cultural anthropology	77·6
History of religions	62·8
Political science	24·1
Geography	22·2
Linguistics	21·5
Art and archaeology	13·0
Economics	11·9
History	10·0
Sociology	8·4
Law	8·1
History of science	5·0
Philosophy	4·3

GENERAL ORIENTALIST BIBLIOGRAPHIES

Two bibliographers attempted from their different points of view to list all publications in the field of Oriental studies which had appeared since the invention of printing in the West in the fifteenth century. To a large extent the works of these two authors supplement one another, Ternaux-Compans consisting of books about the countries of Asia and Africa in European languages, Zenker of books in all the languages of the East.

Bibliothèque asiatique et Africaine ou catalogue des ouvrages relatifs à l'Asie et à l'Afrique qui ont paru depuis la découverte de l'imprimerie jusqu'en 1700, par H. Ternaux-Compans. Paris, 1841.

Bibliotheca Orientalis. Pars 1. Libros continens arabicos persicos turcicos inde ab arte typographica inventa ad nostra usque tempora impressos. Edidit J. T. Zenker. Lipsiae, 1840.

A description of the Zenker bibliography is given by Chauvin in the preface to his *Bibliographie des ouvrages Arabes on relatifs aux Arabes . . .* Part I (1892), pp. xxiv–xxx. In spite of its title the first attempt of 1840 did not proceed beyond a listing of Arabic books, arranged in alphabetical order. There were to have been added further parts containing the Persian and Turkish books, a second volume containing books on the remaining parts of Asia, and a third containing grammars, chrestomathies and dictionaries of all Oriental languages. His only sources were previously published catalogues and bibliographies: the only libraries to which he had access were inadequately provided with Oriental books.

The work received scathing reviews from Wüstenfeld and von Hammer. Not discouraged by these, however, Zenker reorganized his material, began again from the beginning, and published in 1846, this time in French, the first volume of a new edition, the second appearing fifteen years later in 1861:

Bibliotheca Orientalis. Manuel de bibliographie orientale. I. Contenant (1) les livres arabes, persans et turcs imprimés depuis l'invention de l'Imprimerie jusqu'à nos jours, tant en Europe qu'en Orient, disposés par ordre des matières; (2) table des auteurs, des titres orientaux et des éditeurs; (3) un aperçu de la littérature orientale, par J. Th. Zenker.

Bibliotheca Orientalis. Manuel de bibliographie orientale. II. Contenant (1) Supplement du premier volume; (2) Littérature de l'orient chrétien; (3) Littérature de l'Inde; (4) Littérature des Parsis; (5) Littérature de l'Indo-Chine et de la Malaisie; (6) Littérature de la

K

Chine; (7) Littérature du Japon; (8) Littérature mantchoue, mongole et tibétaine; (9) Table des auteurs, des titres orientaux et des éditeurs. Par J. H. Zenker. Leipzig, 1861.

Ternaux-Compans, who appears to have been a commercial publisher, originally intended to produce a catalogue of works relating to the history of Turkey in Europe, but having been forestalled in this by Hammer-Purgstall in his history of the Ottomans he decided to list, in chronological order, all printed books on Asia and Africa published up to the year 1700. In the main body of the work 2,803 titles were listed, with a further 381 in a *Supplément*, making 3,184 in all. For each title in a language other than French, a translation into that language is provided.

His intention to publish a third contribution containing works on the history, geography and philosophy of the East, as well as other works relating to objects other than philology or literature, and a fourth containing extracts and translations of Oriental works scattered among various writings, was never realized.

The second recension of Zenker's work differs in arrangement from the 1840 specimen. In the 1846 and 1886 volumes, the titles are listed in accordance with the classification used by Tashköprüzade for his *Miftāh al-Sa'āda* which is based on a fourfold division of all knowledge into writing, word, thought and law. The enumeration of the sciences is given on pp. xviii–xliii. Within the several sections of the classified chapters the titles of books are given in chronological order in so far as this does not separate the different works of a single author. The first volume contains 1,859 titles published up to about the year 1844, the second 6,972 titles up to about the year 1857.

The sources used in this second venture remain the same as in the previous one, being catalogues and bibliographies published previously. (He mentions Garcin de Tassy,[1] Gildemeister,[2] the catalogue of the Sprenger Library, Long[3] and the catalogue of publications of the Mekhitarists of San Lazaro among his sources.) He seems not to have thought it necessary to examine books in libraries or in booksellers' shops. This makes his work in many ways unsatisfactory and inadequate. It was manifestly impossible to compress into the pages of four volumes a complete list of books in all the languages of the East published since the invention of printing. Thus says Chauvin, but it seems only fair to

---

[1] *Histoire de la littérature hindoui et hindoustani.*
[2] *Bibliothecae Sanskritae specimen.*
[3] *General catalogue of Oriental works (Agra).*

say that Zenker himself acknowledged the deficiencies of his work and hesitated long before publishing it lest some person more competent to do so should publish a similar bibliography. All in all his work lists 6,972 volumes. In the second volume the chronological arrangement is at best approximate.

PERIODICALLY ISSUED BIBLIOGRAPHIES

The first beginnings in a long sequence of periodically published bibliographies compiled by German Orientalist scholars may be detected in the series of annual progress reports (*Wissenschaftliche Jahresberichte*) published by the German Oriental Society. On its formation in 1845 the Deutsche Morgenländische Gesellschaft included among its statutes a requirement that the managing committee (*Vorstand*) should produce, to be read at each annual conference, a report on the activity of the Society, and on the state of Oriental studies in general (*über den Zustand der orientalischen Studien überhaupt*), and that this report should be printed and distributed free of charge to all members. An account of the somewhat chequered bibliographical history of these reports is given in Beiträge, D. of the 'Protokollarischer Bericht über die in Dessau . . . 1884 abgehaltene Generalversammlung der D.M.G.' (Minutes of the general assembly held in Dessau 1884) appended to *ZDMG* 38 (1884), pp. xxi–xxxv. These published reports are available either as separately published supplements to the *ZDMG* or as integral articles of the same journal, for the years 1846–67 (except 1848) and 1876–81. They took the form of discursive surveys of advances made in all branches of Oriental (and African) studies, compiled originally by a single prominent scholar but later by a group of such persons, with bibliographical details of works referred to given in the form of footnotes (the report of 1849 being an exception). As time went by, it became increasingly difficult to produce these reports, especially with the total of bibliographical detail aimed at, and many appeared after long delay, some remained partially complete in manuscript and some never appeared at all. Many committees were set up to deal with a very difficult situation until at the Dessau annual conference in 1884 the decision was taken to abandon the reports in the form they had hitherto taken, but to give whenever possible surveys of progress in the individual branches of Oriental studies, and to support the Kuhn and Klatt *Literaturblatt*, which began to appear in 1884. Much later, for the period 1903–19 (except for 1910) the *Wissenschaftliche Jahresberichte* reappeared as an annual contribution to the *ZDMG*, but without the bibliographical apparatus.

LIST OF THE WISSENSCHAFTLICHE JAHRESBERICHTE

Year covered and author	ZDMG vol.	Sep. publ. (date)	No. of bibl. entries
1846 (Fleischer)	In: *Jhb. f. 1846*, pp. 67–146		
1847 (Fleischer)	2, pp. 447–491		364
1849 (Fleischer)	4, pp. 72–82		none
1850 (Rödiger)	5, pp. 417–466		347
1851 & 1852 (Rödiger)	8, pp. 637–719		585
1853 (Arnold)	10, pp. 603–648		341
1854 (Rödiger)	9, pp. 321–356		228
1854 (2nd half, 1855 Rödiger)	10, pp. 691–799		557
1856 (Gosche)	11, pp. 253–311 585–667		590
1857–58 (Gosche)	14, pp. 135–241 17, pp. 95–213		1,689
1859–61 (Gosche)		1868	1,926
1862–67 (Heft 1) (Gosche)	Suppl. to 33	1871	933
1876 Oct.–1877 Dec. (2 Hefte) (Kuhn, Socin)	Suppl. to 33	1879	2,793
1878 (Kuhn)	Suppl. to 33	1883	1,503
1879 (Kuhn, Müller)	Suppl. to 33	1881	1,397
1880 (Kuhn, Müller)	Suppl. to 34	1883	1,752
1881 (Kern, Praetorius, Baethgen, Klatt, Kautzsch, Ethé, Hommel)		1885	1,166
1907	62, pp. 155–202		
1908	63, pp. 212–251		
1909	65, pp. 157–174		
1911	66, pp. 341–361		
1912	67, pp. 386–404		
1913	68, pp. 421–456		
1914	69, pp. 209–222		
1915	70, pp. 274–297		
1916	71, pp. 271–295		
1917	72, pp. 292–310		
1918	73, pp. 200–210		
1919	74, pp. 304–317		

Beginning in 1876, when for nine years no *Wissenschaftliche Jahres-berichte* had appeared (the last to be published having covered the period 1862–67), for the next eight years until 1883 a bibliographical service was provided by

Bibliotheca orientalis oder eine vollständige Liste der in Jahre 1876 (–1883) in Deutschland, Frankreich, England und den Colonien erschienenen Bücher, Broschüren, Zeitschriften u.s.w. uber die Sprachen, Religionen, Antiquitäten, Literaturen, Geschichte und Geographie des Ostens. Zusam-mengestellt von Karl Friederici. London [etc.], n.d.

Published with the imprint 'Leipzig, London, Paris and New York', the title-page is sometimes in English, sometimes in both German and English, as may also be the invariably brief prefaces and the rubrics to the various sections. The English title-page, when this appears, reads:

Bibliotheca orientalis or a complete list of books, papers, serials and essays published in 1876 in England and the Colonies, Germany and France on the history, geography, languages, religions, antiquities and literature of the East. Compiled by Charles Friederici.

Each single annual part, which was arranged in a general section and individual country divisions proceeding westwards from China and Japan to the Near East and Africa, contained an average of about 1,200 titles (without comments) on the subjects and languages appropriate to the countries mentioned on the title-page, and was provided with an index of places and races of people and (from the second volume on-ward) one of authors. Its aim was stated (in the issue of 1877) to be 'to place in the hands of all who take an interest in Oriental studies a complete list of books, papers etc. on the various branches of Oriental research'. Attempts were made to include all essays, articles and com-ponent parts of collective volumes, and despite the geographical limita-tions indicated by the title, American periodical literature was claimed (again in the 1877 volume) to be 'fully quoted'. A useful feature was the practice of listing the contents of periodicals *seriatim* in the general sec-tion as well as individually at the appropriate places in the regional arrangement. In the issue for 1879 it was found necessary to reduce the list by some 250 items by the omission of 'purely geographical books' on the grounds that this was already made up in a complete list every year by Professor Koner, and that the bibliography was intended to be 'in the first place . . . a register of linguistic publications only'.

In 1883 the publication was discontinued because of the appearance of Kuhn's *Literatur-Blatt* to cover the literature from October of that year onward.

> *Literatur-Blatt für orientalische Philologie;* unter Mitwirkung von Dr Johannes Klatt in Berlin hrsg. von Prof. Dr Ernst Kuhn in München. 1(–4) Band. Leipzig, n.d.

This journal, a substantial part of each issue of which was given up to listing Orientalist and Africanist publications, covered the literature on these subjects which appeared from October, 1883 to 1886. In addition, occasional lists were given of new publications from Colombo, Rangoon, and places in India, as well as Oriental editions of Arabic and Persian texts. Arranged on roughly the same lines as the *Bibliotheca orientalis* of Friederici, the annual volumes included 1,946, 4,898, 4,608 and 3,676 items respectively, and some issues at least an unnumbered series of reviews. The last volume contains an 'alphabetisches Register' to the four volumes published and declares the intention of the two compilers in a note dated October, 1888 to bring the publication to an end because of the appearance in that year of the first issue of *Orientalische Bibliographie* edited by August Müller.

> *Orientalische Bibliographie* . . . hrsg. von A. Müller. Berlin, Paris, London, New York, 1888–1928. 25 vols. and one part. This sometimes appeared with a title-page in English as follows: *Oriental bibliography* (founded and edited by August Müller).

With this publication the series of German Orientalist bibliographies reached its zenith. For the literature of the field until the year 1911 only the most pedantic will need to look further. Founded by August Müller in 1887, it was edited by him with the help of collaborators until his death in 1893. Then for two years it was compiled by Lucian Scherman and edited by E. Kuhn, and in 1896 was taken over completely by Scherman until its demise in 1928. Coming out four times, twice, or latterly three times a year, until 1906 it appeared invariably during the year after the period covered by the bibliography. The three volumes for 1906–8 were published two years in arrear, and because of war-time difficulties, the two volumes for 1909–10 only in 1912–15. The volume for 1911, the publication of which was begun in 1917, was not completed until 1922. An attempt was made in 1926 to bring out a volume for that year, but only Sections I and II were published and those in 1928, the volume never being completed.

In each issue the titles of monographs, parts of works, essays in periodicals and indeed all contributions to the knowledge of Asia and Africa were arranged in six main chapters – General, North and Central Asia and Europe (including Mongols and Manchus, Finno-Ugrians, Turks, Central Asia and Tibet), East Asia and Oceania (including Madagascar), Indo-Germanic peoples, Semites and Africa, each chapter being subdivided into a varying number of appropriate subsections. The number of entries contained in the first annual volume was 4,635, and from then on in each year from five to seven thousand titles were recorded, the peak being reached in the volume for 1911, with 7,307 titles. In addition each volume contained, appended to various subject divisions, large numbers of reviews of books which were not included in the general numeration. Thus for the period 1887–1911 it may be said that the documentation for Asian and African studies was well-nigh complete and to be found in a single publication.

Various attempts have been made to continue the *Orientalische Bibliographie* or to re-start or replace it. Scherman had hoped when the volume for 1926 was completed, to go back and deal with the literature of the years 1912–25. This he never succeeded in doing. In 1948 the International Congress of Orientalists, meeting in Paris, received a proposal from M. Gaudefroy-Demombynes that the *Orientalische Bibliographie* should be revived, and be published in two sections, the first to include works in any language on linguistics, archaeology, history, science, philosophy and religion, sociology and folklore of Asia, Africa and Oceania, the second works in any of the classical languages of Asia and Africa constituting the contemporary literature of Eastern lands, and including poetry, novels, drama and criticism, as well as learned works on non-Oriental countries. He suggested that means should be sought of eliminating unimportant books and that all national committees participating in the International Conference should prepare lists of printed books and articles published in their countries during the period 1938–48 and should decide on the material to be eliminated and employ signs to indicate the value of items included.

The Congress resolved in plenary session to instruct its permanent international committee to work out a plan for the compilation of the Oriental bibliography and to endeavour to secure funds to pay for its publication. In 1952, however, the International Union of Orientalists indicated that 'a general bibliography in its field could hardly be envisaged. It would for the time being limit its activities to Egyptian, Ethiopian and Buddhist bibliographies'. (*UNESCO, Bulletin for Libraries VII*, nos. 5–6, 1953, par. 305.)

In 1946, at a conference held in Cambridge to commemorate the bicentenary of the birth of Sir William Jones, it was unanimously decided to promote the establishment of an Oriental bibliographical journal in English. The School of Oriental and African Studies undertook to publish an annual bibliography of Oriental and African Studies to be called *The Oriental Year*, of which the first volume was to be published toward the end of 1949, to cover the literature of the year 1948. Many prominent English scholars served on the editorial board of the project, which unfortunately proved abortive. The material collected for the year 1948 was printed off on good paper from the galleys, and a small number of sets distributed to subscribers.

At the XXVIth International Congress of Orientalists held at New Delhi in January, 1964, a resolution was passed in plenary session requesting all member countries of the Congress to publish annually national lists of publications on Asia, it being realized that the publication of a complete international bibliography is nowadays quite impracticable. By producing lists for each country it should be possible to achieve complete or nearly complete lists, and to produce them much more promptly than could be done by an organization working outside the country of origin. These national lists could be consolidated into one master international bibliography if this should be thought desirable. Some lists have already been produced for African studies in the U.S.A. (1961 and 1962) and Germany (1962); a list for Britain (1963) is undergoing compilation. Lists of books about Asia published in Britain regularly form part of the *Bulletin of the Association of British Orientalists*.

In the early volumes of the *Rivists degli studi orientali* a good deal of space was given up to the 'Bullettino', or 'Bollettino' as it was called after the first year of its publication. This was an annual report of progress made in the various branches of Oriental, rather than Asian studies, and was in the form of a discursive account with the titles of works referred to given in footnotes, similar to the reports in the *Wissenschaftliche Jahresberichte*. The Bulletin was divided into five sections: i. Africa (including Ancient Egypt and Coptic); ii. Semitic languages and literatures; iii. Asia Minor, Elam, etc., Georgian language and literature; iv. Armenian and Indo-Iranian languages and literatures (including Ancient India); v. Central Asia and the Far East (including Turkish of all varieties). An index of authors was published in each volume of the Rivista.

The Bulletin appeared in volumes I–IV and VI–VIII of the Rivista, as shown in the following table:

Part 1. (Africa) Vol. I (1907), pp. 141–64; II (1908–9), pp. 99–129; III (1910), pp. 123–76; IV (1911–12), pp. 135–91; VI (1914–15), pp. 215–316; VII (1916–18), pp. 01–088; VIII (1919–20), pp. 01–059.

Part 2. (Semitic) Vol. I, pp. 228–414; II, pp. 257–505; III, pp. 301–513; IV, pp. 349–552; VI, pp. 551–922; VII, pp. 089–0235; VIII, pp. 060–075 (Semitic-general only).

Part 3, 4. (Asia Minor, Elam, etc., Georgian; Armenian, Indo-Iranian, Indian) Vol. I, pp. 499–572; II, pp. 605–715; III, pp. 649–844; IV, pp. 775–1003; VI, pp. 1089–1281; VII, pp. 0235–0339 (part 4 only; absent in VIII).

Part 5. (Turkish, Central Asia, South-East Asia, Far East) Vol. I, pp. 654–701; II, pp. 835–79; III, pp. 933–89; IV, pp. 1083–96 (absent in VI–VIII).

Bibliografiya Vostoka (*Bibliography of the Orient*) was a bibliographical periodical entirely in Russian issued by the Institute of Oriental Studies in Leningrad in ten parts (6 volumes) from 1932 to 1937. Regular features were (in the words of the English translations given for the Russian titles), Literary reviews (bibliographical surveys), Thematical bibliography (bibliographies of special topics), Manuscript collections and topics, Reviews of books, Annotations on books, Bibliography of the reviews and newspapers (contents lists), and General bibliography. (Three articles listing books and articles in Russian relating to the Orient outside Russia published during the years 1931 to 1933.)

As this is the only bibliographical journal of its kind ever to have been issued in the field of Oriental studies, it has been thought worth while to list the English titles of all the bibliographies, catalogues, bibliographical articles and surveys listed in all issues of the journal.

PART I (1932)

Literary Reviews

N. A. Belgorodsky. Reports of the Persian Ministry of Finance.

Thematical Bibliography

P. E. Skachkov. Lenin on the Orient.

N. N. Poppe. New works on the latinization of the Mongolian written language.

N. A. Belgorodsky. Contemporaneous Persian almanachs.

Manuscript Collections and Archives

I. J. Kratchkovsky. Arabian manuscripts in Tübingen.

M. Isakson. National funds of the Central Archives of the UsbekSSR in Tashkent.

PARTS 2–4 (1933)

Literary Reviews
> S. F. Oldenbourg. On some new Indian works concerning Indian history and economics.
> I. J. Kratchkovsky. New materials from Yemen.
> A. I. Vostrikov. Some remarks on the bibliography of Tibetan literature.
> N. A. Belgorodsky. Persian custom-house report 1930–31.
> A. D. Novichev. Some remarks on the feudalism in Turkish Kurdistan.

Thematical Bibliography
> A. K. Arends and N. A. Belgorodsky. Bibliographical materials on Persian oil.

Manuscript Collections and Archives
> P. E. Skatchkov. Hyacinth Bitshurin (1777–1853). Archives materials for his biography.

PARTS 5–6 (1934)

Literary Reviews
> V. M. Alexsejev. On the new synonymic dictionaries of the Chinese written language.
> E. E. Berthels. The press of Afghanistan.
> N. A. Belgorodsky. Persian custom-house report 1931–32.

Thematical Bibliography
> N. N. Poppe. The bibliography of Mongolistic literature on linguistics for the period 1917–32.

Manuscript Collections and Archives
> S. A. Kozin. Asiatic archives in the Institute for Oriental Studies of Academy of Sciences of U.S.S.R.

PART 7 (1934)

Literary Reviews
> A. Petrov. The philosophy of China in the Russian sinology.
> K. Flug. Contributions to the history of China in the period of Ing-shang.

Thematical Bibliography
> L. Douman. The Russian and foreign literature concerning the Dungan insurrection of the years 1861–78.
> K. Flug. Contributions to the bibliography of the Tai-Ping movement.

Manuscript Collections and Archives

K. Flug. Summary of the non-Buddhist part of the Chinese manuscripts fund of the Institute of Oriental Studies.

A. Kovalevskij. Description of the oriental manuscripts of the Central Library of the State University in Kharkov.

Appendix

Bibliographical works on the Orient.

PARTS 8–9 (1935)

Literary Reviews

I. Kratchkovsky. First issue of Arabian verses in Russia.

L. I. Duman. Some Chinese sources for studying Hsin-Kiang of the XVIII–XIX centuries.

Thematical Bibliography

V. A. Kazakevitch. Bibliography of P. Koslov's works.

E. A. Obermiller. Methods of studying Tibetan medical literature.

L. F. Wexler. Aboul-Kasim Ferdowsi.

Manuscript Collections and Archives

A. J. Borisov. Mu'tazila Manuscripts of the State Public Library in Leningrad.

K. Flug. Short description of ancient Buddhist manuscripts in collections of the Institute for Oriental Studies of the Academy of Sciences.

Appendix

A. G. Bisnek and K. I. Shafranovsky. Bibliography of Bibliographies of Middle Asia.

PART 10 (1936)

Literary Reviews

I. J. Kratchkovsky. N. Marr and the Arabian literature.

D. V. Semenov. French scientists on the present state and future of the Arabian language.

Thematical Bibliography

George W. Bounakov. An Yang finds and American sinology.

S. B. Karnejev. Persian Poetry. Studies in the bibliography of the Russian translations.

Manuscript Collections and Archives

J. N. Marr. List and description of some objects newly entered in the Asiatic Museum – Persian Collections.

I. I. Ginzburg. Short review of Hebraic funds of the Manuscript Section of the Institute for Oriental Studies, Academy of Sciences U.S.S.R.

K. Flug. Two notes on new manuscripts in the Manuscript Section of the Institute for Oriental Studies. I. Liao tchai tu sho. II. Yun lo ta tien.

A. A. Petrov. Manuscript concerning China and Mongolia in the Central Archives of Tatar ASSR and in the Kazan University Library.

Appendix
A. Tveritinova. Catalogue of Turkish books on history preserved in Leningrad libraries.

The *Annual bibliography of Oriental studies*, (Japanese title, *Shōwa sanjūyonendo Tōyō-shi kenkyū Bunken Ruimoku*), has been published by the Research Institute for Humanistic Studies in Kyoto University since 1934. It is a bibliography of books, articles and book reviews on Oriental culture published in Japan and overseas and is divided into two sections, one for Japanese, Chinese and Korean materials, the other for European, each section being in two parts, books and articles. The issue for 1961 (published in March, 1964), included 792 books and 2,572 articles in the Japanese, Chinese and Korean section, and 1,023 books and 1,203 articles in the European section. Material relating to Japan itself is excluded.

NATIONAL ORIENTALIST BIBLIOGRAPHIES

The ever-increasing flood of publications on Oriental and Asian studies, in the emerging countries, in those with a tradition of interest in these studies and in those newly come to them, makes it unlikely, perhaps, that any individual or organization will ever again be able to undertake the compilation and publication of a current bibliography covering the whole field, and it may be that as Orientalists turn their attention to more and more specialized fields, so will the bibliographies serving them become more and more specialized. Yet something may well be lost in this excessive fragmentation.

GERMANY

National Orientalist bibliographies are much easier to compile, and it is perhaps by a combination of these that we may approach nearest to the ideal of a general Orientalist bibliography in the future. Such publications go back a long time. In 1870, C. H. Herrmann published, as the first part of a complete catalogue of the philological literature published in Germany during the previous twenty years, his:

Bibliotheca orientalis et linguistica, Verzeichniss der vom Jahre 1850 bis incl. 1868 in Deutschland erschienenen Bücher, Schriften und Abhandlungen orientalischer und sprachvergleichender Literatur hrsg. von Carl Heinrich Herrmann. Halle a/S., 1870.

It has a general section in which linguistic and Orientalist periodicals published during the period are listed with their contents, and eight other chapters devoted to peoples of Semitic, African, Finnish-Tatar, Mongolian, Malayo–Polynesian, American and Indo-Germanic origin. It is the first part of a tripartite catalogue of philological writing; the two remaining parts, concerned with classics and classical philology, were published in 1871–73.

Westdeutsche Bibliothek (Sammlung der ehem. Preussischen Staatsbibliothek). *Orient-Literatur in Deutschland und Österreich, 1945–50.* Marburg (Lahn) (1950).

The publications of Germany and Austria on Asian subjects for the years 1945–50 are listed in the above work, published by the Oriental Department of the Westdeutsche Bibliothek in Marburg (Lahn). The 610 book titles included are arranged in three main sections by subject: Language and literature, religion, history, geography and ethnography, law, economics, art, medicine, natural sciences and technology and belles-lettres. To these are added a further section on bibliography and periodicals and a supplement.

POLAND

Three works, in Polish, French and German respectively, record the Orientalist and Africanist post-war publications in Poland and of Polish scholars.

Polska Akademia Nauk, Komitet Orientalistyczny. *Bibliografia polskich prac orientalistycznych (1945–55).* Warszawa, 1957. (Polish Academy of Sciences, Orientalist Committee. Bibliography of Polish works on Orientalist studies.)

'Dix ans d'études orientales en Pologne Populaire.' *Rocznik orientalistyczny* 20 (1956), pp. 7–14.

'Die polnischen orientalistischen Arbeiten in den Jahren 1953–58. W. Zajączkowski.' *Folia Orientalia* 1 (1959), pp. 163–73.

The first-named title is a plain bibliographical list of 707 titles of works by Polish Orientalists and by non-Orientalists when these collaborated with Orientalists. The other two are bibliographical essays incorporating many titles in the body of the articles and in footnotes. The French article is a report presented to the XXIII International Congress of Orientalists at Cambridge in 1954 and was drafted by J. Reychman, W. Jabloński, S. Strelcyn and A. Zajączkowski.

Oriental publications issued by the Éditions Scientifiques de Pologne (Państwowe Wydawnictwo Naukowe) up to 1964 have been listed in a *Catalogue des publications orientalistes*, published by the firm, undated, but presumably in 1964. It includes lists of the contents of the periodical *Rocznik orientalistyczny* from volume 15 (1949) to 28, 1 (1963), of monographs published in the series 'Prace orientalistyczne' (Oriental publications of the Committee for Oriental Studies of the Polish Academy of Sciences – Komitet Orientalistyczny Polskiej Akademii Nauk – volumes 1–7), and other (unnumbered publications), with extracts from reviews in western European languages.

ITALY

But it is Italy that provides the most extensive and continuous record of the publications of the Orientalists of any country from the earliest times in the series of works listed below.

Origine e progresso dello studio della lingua orientali in Italia. F. Predari. Milano, 1842.

Materiaux pour servir à l'histoire des études orientales en Italie. Angelo de Gubernatis. Florence, Rome, Turin, 1876.

'Gli Studi orientali in Italia durante il cinquantenario 1861–1911 (bibliografia)'. 2 pts. *RSO* 5, 1913–27.

Bibliografia degli studi orientalistici in Italia dal 1912 al 1934. G. Gabrieli. Roma, 1935.

Commissione Nazionale Italiana per l'UNESCO. *Contributo italiano alla conoscenza dell' Oriente: repertorio bibliografico dal 1935 al 1958.* Firenze, 1962.

In Predari's work a large number of early contributions to Oriental studies are arranged under the various Oriental languages. This work was extended and brought up to date by the Indianist De Gubernatis, in his survey published on the occasion of the Third International Congress of Orientalists at St Petersburg.

The third contribution was the work of several professors of the Oriental School in the University of Rome. Unlike its predecessors it is devoted solely to bibliography, a projected 'synthetic' history of Oriental studies in Italy having been abandoned. Its publication was protracted over a period of fourteen years because of the First World War. It is arranged in nine sections, under the headings, Africa, Semitic languages, Linguistics (Glottologia), Armenian, Persian, Indian languages, Turkish, East Asia, Byzantine studies, with an appendix to all sections; in each section the works are arranged under their authors in alphabetical order, for many of whom biographical details are given. An index of names is provided only to the appendix.

Gabrieli's work contains an elaborate introduction in which is found a brief description of the history of Oriental studies in Italy, the present state of teaching in the various cities, names of institutions and their publications, a list of Orientalist periodicals current and deceased, and a list of Orientalists arranged under the language families in which they were interested, as Arabists, Semitists, etc. The main body of the work, which is in two parts, contains a general bibliography and a subject bibliography under the headings Languages and literatures, Oriental linguistics and History of religions, under each heading the material being arranged alphabetically by author. It contains in all about 2,400 items.

The most recent bibliography is published by the Italian National Commission for UNESCO within the framework of that body's 'East–West major project'. It is intended to be a continuation of the work of Gabrieli, though unlike that one, which contains all contributions in Italian, this one is restricted to the writings of Italian Orientalists, including those published in other countries, and brings the record down to the year 1958. It is the work of ten scholars, co-ordinated and edited by Olga Pinto and Lionello Lanciotti and includes, in addition to works of Orientalist studies in the strict sense of the term (i.e. those based on documents written in an Oriental language or those for which knowledge of an Oriental language is a prerequisite), works about Asia and Africa compiled by scholars in the various disciplines, as well as popular works and those dealing with the history of missions. The bibliography proper is preceded by two short notices: (1) on the Italian contribution to the exploration of Africa and Asia and archaeological and cultural expeditions sent into those continents, especially to Egypt and East Africa from the beginning of the twentieth century, and (2) a summary list of institutions concerned with Oriental studies, comprising university departments where Oriental and African languages are taught, institutes specializing in the study of the East, and museums containing important collections of objects from the East.

The bibliography contains some 3,000 entries, of which perhaps 600 are books, and 2,400 periodical articles.

HUNGARY

'Dix années d'orientalisme hongrois (1940–50). Denis Sinor.' *Journal asiatique* 239 (1951), pp. 211–35.

Hungarian publications on Asia and Africa, 1950–62; a selected bibliography. Budapest, Hungarian Academy of Sciences, 1963. (Title etc. also in Hungarian.) Compiled by Eve Apor and Hilda Ecsedy. Edited by Louis Bese.

Sinor's survey is concerned mainly with writings by Hungarian nationals and those of foreign scholars published in Hungary on Central Asian, Turkish and Far Eastern studies, but works in other fields are briefly mentioned.

The bibliography compiled by the Oriental Department of the Library of the Hungarian Academy of Sciences, lists the titles of 717 books and articles on Asia (including Oceania) and fifty-seven on Africa (including Egypt), selected out of a total of nearly a thousand writings contributed by Hungarian Orientalists. It covers 'scholarly works as well as popular scientific publications, textual analyses of scholars, artistic translations of works by classical and contemporary writers or poets, written in Hungarian or a foreign language'. The titles are arranged by region and country, with a section on European–Asian relations which includes works about Hungarian Orientalists. A list of periodicals and serial publications is also given. The titles of works written in the Hungarian language are provided with English translations and brief annotations.

SCANDINAVIA

Scandinavian books and periodical articles on all branches of Oriental studies as well as writings by Scandinavian scholars published in other countries, published during the period 1910–25 are listed in:

'Nordisk orientalisk bibliografi für åren 1911–20. En översikt av Ernst von Döbeln.' *Svenska Orientsällskapets* Arsbok 3 (1925), pp. 51–88.
— 1921–25, *Id.*, 1926/27, pp. 93–113.

U.S.S.R.

Russian publications on Oriental subjects published since the Revolution of 1917 are referred to in articles by Borovkov (in Russian, 30 years) and Guboglu (in French, 40 years).

'Vostokovedenie v SSSR za 30 let. A. K. Borovkov.' *Izvestiya Akad. Nauk SSSR. Otdelenie literatury i yazyki*, tom 6, vyp. 5 (1947), pp. 395–407.

'Quarante ans d'études orientales en U.R.S.S. (1917–57), par Mihail Guboglu.' *Studia et Acta Orientalia* 1 (1958), pp. 281–316.

A bibliography (in Russian) of the publications of the Asiatic Museum and the Institute of Oriental Studies of the Academy of Sciences of the U.S.S.R. (1917–58) appeared in volume 3 (1950) of the *Ocherki po istorii russkogo vostokovedeniya:*

'O. E. Livotova. Bibliografiya izdaniy Aziatskogo muzea i Instituta vostokovedeniya.'

A description of the achievements of Russian Orientalists between the twenty-fifth and twenty-sixth International Conferences (1961–63), with references to the books published during those years is given in the publication:

Soviet Orientalogy between the XXV and XXVI Congresses of Orientalists. Moscow, 1963.

CZECHOSLOVAKIA

Ten years of Oriental studies in Czechoslovakia are summarized in an article by Průšek:

'Deset let naší orientalistiky. Jaroslav Průšek.' *Archiv orientanli* 23 (1955), pp. 271–311.

JAPAN

Japanese publications on Oriental studies have been enumerated in a whole series of publications compiled in European languages for the benefit of foreign scholars.

A list of these bibliographies is given in the publication:

A Survey of Japanese bibliographies concerning Asian studies. Compiled and published by the Centre for East Asian Cultural Studies, Tokyo. 1963.

This work, the 'fruit of the assiduous efforts' of Mr H. Okamoto and colleagues from the National Diet Library, contains some one thousand

L

titles of bibliographies published in Japan between 1900 and 1962 which are concerned with the humanities and social sciences. The Japanese titles are given in characters and Romanization, and an English translation is appended. An index of titles includes thirty-nine titles in English, French and German interspersed among those printed in Japanese characters. Among the works which may be used by those with no knowledge of the Japanese (not all of which are included in the *Survey*) are the following:

> Bibliographie sommaire des ouvrages d'orientalisme en langue japonaise (parus entre 1938 et 1950). (*Bulletin de la Maison Franco–Japonaise*, nouvelle serie, tome I, 1951.) Tokyo, 1952.

> [Titles of 1,787 books on Japanese history, literature, linguistics, ethnography and ethnology, as well as art and archaeology, Buddhism and Indology, and Sinology, are given in Japanese characters, Romanized transliteration and French translation.]

The same institution followed up this bibliography with another covering the years 1955 and 1956.

> *Bibliographie de l'orientalisme japonais*, rédigée par la Société Franco–Japonaise des Études Orientales sous la direction de ISHIDA Mikinosuke. (Publications de la Maison Franco–Japonaise.) 1955 (premier semestre). Tokyo, Paris, 1958. 1955 (suite) – 1956. Ib., 1962.

The two volumes contain 292 and 406 abstracts respectively of books and articles published in Japan on India, Central Asia, Manchuria and Mongolia, Korea, China, South-East Asia, Buddhism, Art and archaeology, i.e. those parts of Asia from India eastwards to China. Studies on Japan are omitted. Appendices contain titles of French Orientalist publications on the same area. A list of ninety-five periodicals from which articles were abstracted is given.

> *Bibliography of the humanistic studies and social relations.* Tokyo, 1952–

has been compiled annually (vol. 2 biennially) since 1955. The issue for 1961 comprises over 5,500 titles of books and articles from learned periodicals on the subjects of literature (including linguistics), history (and archaeology), philosophy and social relations (i.e. education, sociology, cultural anthropology and human geography). All regions of the world are covered, including Europe.

The Institute of Eastern Culture (Tōhō Gakkai) has published nine annual volumes since 1954 of its

> *Books and articles on Oriental subjects published in Japan during 1954* (–).

'The compilers have not attempted to make an absolutely complete list, but they believe that all of the most important studies are included.' Books and articles are arranged in two sequences, the articles being arranged by country and region, with sections on Asian relations with Japan (*later*, Relations between Japan and Asian countries), Buddhism and miscellaneous. As is usual in all these lists, names of authors are given both in Japanese and Roman characters. Many titles are annotated. Works on Japan are not included. From volume 7 onward, contents lists of books are given.

[9]

Bibliographies of parts of Asia

As has been already noted, Asia in the American sense begins at Pakistan and Afghanistan and carries through to Japan, the Near and Middle East being omitted. The predecessor of the *Bibliography of Asian studies* was the *Bulletin of Far Eastern bibliography*, which was first issued in 1936 under the editorship of Earl Pritchard. It was published by the Committee on Far Eastern Studies of the American Council of Learned Societies in five parts containing 2,872 titles and an index of authors, editors, translators, etc. and other persons named. Each issue was arranged in a single alphabetical sequence under authors. From the first books and articles on the Far East and South-East Asia were included and from the second volume for 1937 onward these were classified in regional divisions beginning with a section for Far East (general), continuing from there with the adjacent territories of the Far East and Central Asia, Japan and Taiwan, Tibet, South-East Asia and the Pacific Islands.

From 1941 the *Far Eastern bibliography* (as it was then called) was published in *The Far Eastern Quarterly* (later *The Journal of Asian Studies*) in each quarterly issue. The bibliography for 1947 and all subsequent years was also (later, solely) published as a separate part. The cover of the first part of the 1947 volume (which was in two parts) gives a summary of the annual volumes issued to that date as follows:

1936   (Vol. 1)   5 numbers.   2,872 items.   Index
1937   (Vol. 2)   5 numbers.   3,518 items.   Index
1938   (Vol. 3)   5 numbers.   3,422 items.   Index
1939   (Vol. 4)   5 numbers.   3,033 items.   Index
1940   (Vol. 5)   5 numbers, in 2 parts.   2,238 items.   Index
1941   Nov. 1941, Feb., May 1942, *FEQ.* 1,423 items. No index. Unbound, $1.00.
1942   Aug., Nov. 1942, Feb., May 1943, *FEQ.* 1,509 items. No index.

1943 Aug., Nov. 1943, Feb. 1944, *FEQ*. 1,028 items. No index.
1944 May, Aug., Nov. 1944, Feb. 1945, *FEQ*. 769 items. No index.
1945 May, Nov. 1945, May 1946, *FEQ*. 980 items. No index.
1946 May 1947, *FEQ*. 1,364 items. Index. Paper covers, $1.50.
1947 June 1948. Separate volume, 1,787 items. Index. Paper covers, $2.00.

Prior to 1941 the bibliography had fairly complete coverage of books and articles on the Far East in Western languages (except for Russian). Its coverage remained relatively good during 1941 and 1942, but for 1943, 1944 and 1945 it is very incomplete. The decline in the items noted in the bibliography was caused by (1) an actual decline in books and articles published, (2) failure of books and articles published abroad to reach the United States during the war years, and (3) inability of the compiler to cover the periodicals and books available, because of the pressure of other duties. The coverage of the 1946 and 1947 bibliographies is again relatively complete (except for Russian and Central European works), and items missed were to be noted in the later annual bibliographies. The aim was to make coverage of works in Western languages as complete as possible. No effort was made to cover Oriental language publications.

With volume XV of the *FEQ* the bibliography began to include items on India and the remaining parts of South Asia, as distinct from South-East Asia which had been included from the very beginning. In the following year (1956) the *FEQ* became the *Journal of Asian Studies*: the bibliography followed suit and from then on has been known as the *Bibliography of Asian Studies*.

Publications, which from their titles might be expected to be bibliographies of Asia in general, but which in reality have a much narrower range, are:

Asian bibliography is, in fact, the accessions list of the United Nations ECAFE Library. It has been published twice a year since 1952, and lists books added to the library by subject, with an index by country. Most of the books added are in the field of the social sciences, and related to the whole of Asia with the exception of the Near East.

The *Asien-Bibliographie* is published quarterly by a bookseller in Frankenau/Hessen. It lists books available in the German-speaking market on the regions of Asia, North Africa, Oceania and Old America. The same firm publishes *Bibliographia Asiatica*, a list of articles published in certain magazines and newspapers.

COLONIAL BIBLIOGRAPHIES

The bibliography of certain regions of Asia is tied up with that of the various European nations – and the U.S.A. – who have, or have had in the past, colonies, protectorates, mandated territories or the like in the Asian continent. Some of these nations have published bibliographies of colonial studies in general, and the principal ones of these will be described in the succeeding paragraphs. There are also libraries in these countries which have collected or still do collect, literature relating to these colonial territories and there are published catalogues of these libraries which constitute valuable sources for the bibliography of the regions.

COLONIES IN GENERAL

Bibliographie d'histoire coloniale (1900–30). Publiée par les soins de MM. Alfred Martineau, Roussier, Tramond. (Premier Congrès international d'histoire coloniale – Paris, 1931.) Paris, 1932.

In 1931 the Société de l'Histoire des Colonies organized a congress in Paris, for the express purpose of compiling a general bibliography of colonial history for the years 1900–30. It was attended by representatives of all colonial powers and of all those countries with responsibilities for dependent territories. In the resulting bibliography, published in the following year, the most important writings produced by each of the various countries or relating to the colonial power are listed in separate chapters, to which in some cases an introductory essay of some considerable length may be prefixed, sketching the history of the colonial literature of the country concerned, and provisions made for colonial studies in universities and other institutions.

A List of books and articles on colonial history and overseas expansion published in the United States 1900–30. Compiled by Lowell Joseph Ragatz. Ann Arbor, Mich., 1939.
— *in 1931 and 1932*. London (etc., 1933 and 1934).
— *in 1933, 1934 and 1935*. London (1935).

The American contribution to the *Bibliographie d'histoire coloniale* was the work of L. J. Ragatz. This was later reprinted as *Bibliographie d'histoire coloniale, 1900–30. États Unis.* (Paris, 1932) and as *Colonial studies in the United States during the twentieth century* (London, 1932). In 1939 it was republished in an edition containing a large number of titles not included in the original edition. Finally in 1963 the 1939 edition, together with the supplements for 1931–32 and 1933–35, was issued as an authorized reprint, produced by microfilm-xerography, by University Microfilms of Ann Arbor, Mich.

A bibliography of articles, descriptive, historical and scientific, on colonies and other dependent territories, appearing in American geographical and kindred journals. Compiled by Lowell Joseph Ragatz. Volume I, through 1934. (Volume II. Compiled by Janet Evans Ragatz, 1935 through 1950.) External Research Bureau, Washington (1951).

The bibliography 'through 1934' was originally compiled for an annual meeting of the Commission Internationale d'Histoire Coloniale which was to have been held in Prague in August, 1936. It was originally published in two volumes in 1935, and issued in a new edition together with an extension 'through 1950' in 1951.

How do these two works differ? The *List* contains 2,291 entries: these are arranged under General, and the various countries with colonial or dependent territories, including in addition to the main culprits, Germany, Russia, the United States, Denmark, Norway, Sweden and Japan. This work includes books, but probably over 90 per cent of the material relates to the American continent.

The *Bibliography*, which is restricted to articles in periodicals, goes back earlier than 1900, the date at which the *List* begins. Its two volumes contain 4,444 entries: the arrangement chosen for these is General, the Belgian, Danish, Dutch, French, former German, Italian, Japanese, Portuguese and Spanish Empires; Russia's extra-European possessions; the United States's outlying possessions and spheres of influence; the jointly-held regions (Anglo-Egyptian Sudan, Tangier, New Hebrides Condominium; and 'Debated territory' (Afghanistan, Iran, Mongolia and Sinkiang, Tibet)). In the *Bibliography* is evident a much better balance between American and non-American territories.

THE BRITISH COMMONWEALTH

Among the members of the British Commonwealth in the Near and Middle East are the Republic of Cyprus and the Federation of South Arabia; in South Asia, India, Pakistan, Ceylon and the Maldive Islands; in South-East Asia, Malaysia and Brunei; and in the Far East the Colony of Hong Kong. Burma was a member until it attained independence in 1948, and Great Britain held at one time mandates under the League of Nations over Iraq (or Mesopotamia, as it was then called), Egypt and Palestine.

Guide to resources for Commonwealth studies in London, Oxford and Cambridge, with bibliographical and other information, by A. R. Hewitt. University of London, Athlone Press for the Institute of Commonwealth Studies, 1957.

Mr Hewitt packed into his *Guide* much of the information collected by him over a number of years in the course of his duties as Secretary and Librarian of the Institute of Commonwealth Studies in the University of London. It is divided into three parts. The first gives a 'general survey of resources', beginning with a chapter on the general library picture in London, Oxford and Cambridge, going on to describe the principal manuscript and archive depositories and the main collections of certain types of printed material such as parliamentary papers and official publications, periodicals and newspapers, with a chapter on theses and research in progress. In addition the author has provided a 'concise survey of library resources by subjects' wherein the principal libraries specializing in history, political science, geography, law, sociology and tropical medicine are named, and a select list of bibliographies of reference books, the latter term comprising mainly biographical works. Part II lists the libraries in the three cities and gives details of their principal collections on the Commonwealth with very useful information on times of opening and services provided. A very short part III indicates universities in the U.K. providing facilities for Commonwealth studies and other organizations and institutions concerned with Commonwealth affairs.

The Guide is intended, in the author's words, as a help for advanced research workers, particularly those coming from overseas, to locate material for the study of the British Commonwealth. It may, however, be confidently asserted that other classes of persons will derive equal benefit from it: the research worker not yet 'advanced' for instance, will profit considerably from a careful study of the book in the very earliest stages of his research, the librarian of all types of library interested in the Commonwealth will find it indispensable in his daily work, and the most senior student of Commonwealth affairs will certainly obtain from it information on matters important to him and hitherto unknown.

For the history of the British Commonwealth recourse should be had to the monumental *Cambridge history of the British Empire*, published in seven volumes (vol. 3 was never published) between 1929 and 1936 in which each chapter is written by an acknowledged expert in the subject treated, and is provided with a full bibliography listing the sources in manuscript and all forms or printed book on which it is based. The most extensive collection of books and periodicals is held by the Library of the Royal Commonwealth Society, which will be described in a later chapter. The Library's *Subject catalogue* may well be considered to take the place of a complete bibliography of the Commonwealth up to the year 1930. In addition, the Society published a series of bibliographies between 1915 and 1943, as listed below:

1. *Foreign colonization.* W. C. Hill. 1915.

2. *Recent publications in the Library illustrating constitutional relations between parts of the British Empire.* E. Lewin. 1926.

3. *Recent publications in the Library illustrating constitutional relations between European and coloured races.* E. Lewin. 1927.

4. *Communications in the Overseas Empire, with special reference to Africa.* E. Lewin. 1927.

5. *Warren Hastings.* V. Ward. 1932.

6. *Constitutional relations of the British Empire (publications 1926–32).* E. Lewin. 1933.

7. *Italian colonization in Africa.* D. H. Varley. 1936.

8. *African native music.* D. H. Varley. 1936.

9. *Recent publications on Africa, South of the Sahara.* E. Lewin. 1943.

10. *Best books on the British Empire, a guide for students.* E. Lewin. 1943.

11. *Pacific regions,* by E. Lewin. 1944.

12. (2nd ed. of no. 10, 1945.)

13. *Best books on Australia and New Zealand.* E. Lewin. 1946.

Hewitt also compiled the:

Union list of Commonwealth newspapers in London, Oxford and Cambridge. University of London, The Athlone Press for the Institute of Commonwealth Studies, 1960.

This lists collections of 2,426 newspapers to be found in some sixty libraries, archive depositories, and agencies in London, Oxford and Cambridge. (It is unlikely that many collections of value exist outside these three cities.) All territories within the British Commonwealth, with the exception of the United Kingdom, are included. Of former members, Burma is included up to 1947, but Eire before its secession is not. Newspapers published in Egypt and Palestine will not be found in the list, but those of the Sudan up to 1955 are included.

The largest collection is in the British Museum Newspaper Library at Colindale, in fact the *Union list* is basically the catalogue of that institution, with fairly substantial additions from the Public Record Office (limited to the period 1824–57), the India Office Library, the Bodleian, Rhodes House and Cambridge University Library, and minor contributions from others. Exact details, in so far as these could be deduced from catalogues and lists provided by the libraries themselves, are given for dates covered and changes of title are recorded. The arrangement is alphabetically by territory and place of publication, with an index of titles.

OTHER COLONIAL POWERS

The French former colonial empire in Asia was in Indo-China, with some possessions in India. A bibliography was published by Favitzki.[1]

The former Dutch East Indies (now Indonesia) is well documented in the catalogue of the Colonial Library, and in the *Repertorium* of Hooykaas and Hartmann. These will be considered in detail in the volume on South-East Asia in this series:

Catalogus der Koloniale Bibliotheek van het Kon. Instituut voor de Taal-, Land- en Volkenkunde van Ned. Indië en het Indisch Genootschap. 's-Gravenhage, 1908. [With supplements, 1915, 1927, 1937.]

Repertorium op de Koloniale literatuur, of systematische inhoudsopgaaf van hetgeen voorkomt over de Koloniën (beoosten de Kaap) in mengelwerken en tijdschriften, van 1595 ter 1865 uitgegeven in Nederland en zyne overzeesche bezittingen, door J. C. Hooykaas. Amsterdam, 1877. [With supplements by A. Hartmann and others to 1932.]

A catalogue of the books in the Library of the Sociedade de Geografia de Lisboa on the Portuguese overseas territories by Júlio Gonçalves is appearing in the pages of the Society's *Boletim.* The sections covering the literature on the former possessions in India, Macao, Timor, Angola are included in the following volumes:

[1] Favitski de Probabysz (Comte de): *Répertoire bibliographique de la littérature militaire et coloniale française depuis cent ans.* Paris, Liège, 1935.
A select bibliography was published by the Ministère des Colonies in 1945 under the title: *Cinq cent livres sur la Communanté française.*
Neither Favitski's work, said to contain titles of 8,021 works, nor the *Cinq cent livres* has been seen by me. The information is taken from Maldès, vol. 2, p. 204.

'Júlio Gonçalves. Bibliografia do Ultramar portugues, existente na Sociedade de Geografia de Lisboa.'

I. Estado da Índia. *Boletim* Ser. 78, nos. 1–3, 4–6, 1960. 43 pp.

II. Macao. Sér. 79, nos. 7–9, 1961. 27 pp.

III. Timor. Sér. 80, nos. 1–3, 1961. 19 pp.

IV. Angola. Sér. 80, nos. 7–12, 1962; Sér. 81, nos. 1–6, 7–9, 10–12, 1963; Sér. 82, nos. 1–3, 1964. 122 pp.

[10]

Select Bibliographies

Many lists have been compiled of books and other documentary materials regarded as most suitable for introducing certain classes of persons, usually pupils at school, students at universities or members of the general public, to the study of Asia and Africa. Examples of these, restricted entirely to those intended for the English-speaking world, and published in the last seventeen years, are listed below, with short comments. They all cover the whole area of Asia with the exception of that compiled by Kublin (no. 5 below), which omits the Middle East: nos. 6 and 7 contain also titles relating to Africa.

1. *Books on Asia.* Compiled by I. H. Baqai. (Asian Relations Conference, March–April, 1947.) Indian Council of World Affairs (1947).

2. *A Select list of books on the civilizations of the Orient:* Prepared by the Association of British Orientalists and edited by W. A. C. H. Dobson. Oxford, 1955.

3. *Introduction to Asia; a selective guide to background reading.* Prepared by L. King Quan. The Library of Congress, Reference Department, Washington, 1955.

4. A *Selected bibliography of books, films, filmslides, records and exhibitions about Asia.* United States National Commission for the United Nations Educational, Scientific and Cultural Organization. (Washington, 1957.)

5. *An Introductory reading guide to Asia.* Compiled by Hyman Kublin. The Asian Society, New York, 1958. (– Revised edition, 1959.)

6. A *Select bibliography: Asia, Africa, Eastern Europe, Latin America.* American Universities Field Staff, Inc. New York (1960). (– Supplement, 1961, Ib., 1961. – Supplement, 1963, Ib., 1963).

7. *Asia and Africa; a select bibliography for schools.* Second edition. (Compiled by E. H. S. Simmonds.) School of Oriental and African Studies, University of London (1963).

Baqai's *Books on Asia* was prepared in consultation with the Research Associates of the Asian Relations Conference secretariat, in the hope that it might be of some use to the many students of public affairs 'beginning to be interested in Asia and her problems'. Bibliographies were supplied on request by the Director-General of Education, Kabul; the Librarian, Royal Empire Society; the National Book League; the Ministry of Foreign Affairs, Baghdad; the American University of Beirut; and the Secretary of the Arab League, London. The titles, about a thousand in number, are arranged by country within the larger area divisions of Asia in general, Western Asia (Middle East), Central Asian Republics (Afghanistan, India, Nepal, Tibet, Ceylon), Eastern Asia (Far East), and South-East Asia. In addition, there are sections containing titles relating to the Pacific Ocean (including the Islands), and the Pacific War (i.e. as part of the Second World War). Materials in all the principal languages are listed, including some few examples in Turkish and Russian. About a half of the titles are provided with brief annotations. Most of the titles are for relatively new books, and greatest weight is placed on political, economic and sociological subjects.

A group of scholars meeting at a conference held by the Association of British Orientalists decided that it would be useful to 'gather together in a single publication the basic bibliographies' of their various studies. They had in mind not only the needs of students embarking on these courses, but also the interests of a wider public curious to know more about Asia. By choosing out of a great mass of specialized writings books reliable as to scholarship and readable as to content, they hoped to persuade those who could be troubled to deliberate that orientalism was something more than 'an eccentric amusement, an esoteric confabulation of dons and dervishes'. They were anxious to prove that Oriental studies deserved to occupy a more central place in our educational scheme of things than the periphery to which they have been hitherto relegated. *The Civilizations of the Orient* was the result.

The titles, numbering 870 in all, are arranged in a series of four main divisions dealing with the civilizations of Ancient Egypt and the Ancient Near East and Middle East, Islam, Indian and Further India (perhaps the last occurrence of this outmoded title), and the Far East. To each of the divisions are prefixed brief introductions on the scope and range of the subject under review, and many titles are given terse annotations. Other features incorporated in the booklet are particulars of the principal societies in Great Britain concerned with Oriental civilizations (with addresses and names of secretaries), Oriental studies

in the universities of Great Britain, and a list of Oriental booksellers. A
new edition was under consideration by the Association in 1964.

Quan's *Introduction to Asia* is intended 'to help the public understand
the problems and aspirations of Asia, their causes, their historical
growth, their cultural background and their relations to the West'.
Standard and authoritative works on all the countries of Asia are included, preference being given to 'informative and easily understand-
able sources rather than to technical treatises'. To this end lengthy
notices are appended to most of the titles. It is limited for the greater
part to titles in English, with only a few in other Western languages.
781 titles of books published up to 1953 are included, with a further
thirty embodied in a supplement representing books acquired by the
Library of Congress up to the year of publication. Each main country
in the geographical divisions has the common subdivisions of 'General
background, Historical background, Contemporary political and economic scene, Arts and letters (including languages). It is not restricted
to United States publications. Library of Congress call-marks are given.
A selected bibliography . . . was prepared in connection with the Sixth
National Conference of the United States National Commission for
UNESCO, for which the theme chosen was 'Asia and the United
States: what the American citizen can do to promote mutual understanding and co-operation'. The list, compiled on the basis of the
judgement of many contributing organizations and institutions was intended to be useful to a wide general public. 194 films, thirty-five recordings of Asian music and a number of travelling art exhibitions are
listed in addition to the 199 titles of books relating to countries from
Afghanistan to Japan.

The Asia Society sponsored an introductory reading guide compiled
by Professor Hyman Kublin. This was intended 'to aid the layman and
the teacher to acquire basic information about the peoples and civilizations of Asia'. It was thought that it might also be of use to librarians
wanting to build up small but basic collections of books on Asia possessed of 'relatively permanent value'. The 115 titles in the original
edition had been augmented to 145 in the revised edition of 1959. The
countries covered extend from Afghanistan to Japan, the Near and
Middle East being omitted.

The American Universities Field Staff's *Select bibliography* was compiled by a large group of scholars who listed some 6,000 titles representing what they regarded as the most useful books and journals available
for college study and general reading about the civilizations of Asia,

Africa, Eastern Europe and Latin America. The titles are arranged in regional and cultural sections within the major geographical areas, these sections in turn being subdivided by subject. Library of Congress catalogue card numbers are given and prices of each book listed in the *Cumulative Book Index*. University Microfilms undertook to supply a microfilm copy of any title out of print. The work is intended to be used as a bibliographical guide for checking and developing library collections supporting institutions providing undergraduate instruction in Asia. For Asia 2,748 titles are provided, with brief explanatory notes as required. The *Supplement 1961* provides further titles numbered 2,749–870, and *Supplement 1963* numbers 2,871–3,042. Two further selections are made by indicating roughly 10 per cent of the titles with the letter A to indicate top priority and roughly twenty with the letter B to indicate second choices. A rather devastating review by K. G. Tregonning was printed in the *Majallah Perpustakaan Singapura* (*Singapore Library Journal*), vol. 1, no. 2, October, 1961, pp. 90–91. Tregonning declares that 'the compilation had been neatly spiked on one of the horns of a dilemma'. Furthermore, that 'any lecturer with the briefest knowledge of the area can supply his librarian with a more useful list. If it is a fact that these four regions were blank areas of college ignorance before, all that this book is likely to do is to replace that ignorance by confusion'.

The object of the S.O.A.S. bibliography is stated to be 'to aid schools in their selection of appropriate and reliable books on Asian and African subjects'. In all, 158 books are included. These deal with history, geography, economics, political and social problems, and the literature and arts of the five regions Middle East, South Asia, South-East Asia and the Pacific, Far East and Africa, with about thirty titles for each region. To these are added further sections on Problems of development and on Race relations. Where possible, autobiographies written by leading personalities in Asia and Africa, and accounts of family life have been included. Forty-one starred entries are recommended for initial purchase: the cost of these at the prices quoted would be £39 19s. 6d.

It will have been noticed that the lists vary in size from those which list a hundred to two hundred items, through those with some eight hundred or a thousand, to that of the American Universities Field Staff which comprises some 2,750 titles on Asia and some 700 on Africa. (The smallest also provides a selection of forty titles and the largest an initial selection of some 250 or 500 books.)

They are produced in India, the United States and the United

Kingdom, are directed variously at school children, university students and members of the general public, and designed primarily to stimulate interest in the various regions of Asia and Africa. With one exception (Baqai) they restrict themselves to the listing of books in English and the best-known European languages. One work (UNESCO) provides also a catalogue of films, music recordings and travelling art exhibitions at the disposal of United States citizens. In some cases prices are given. The main differences are set out in the following table:

1. Baqai, 1947	For students of public affairs.	c. 1,000 titles
2. Dobson, 1955	Orientalist students and wider public.	c. 870 ,,
3. Quan, 1955	For general public.	811 ,,
4. UNESCO, 1957	For 6th Nat. Conf. 'Asia & the U.S.'	199 books, 194 films, 35 recordings, travelling art exhibitions.
5. Kublin, 1958	For layman and teacher (Middle East omitted)	115 books
6. Amer. Univ. Field Staff	For college study and general reading.	3,042 (Asia), First priority A, 10 per cent, second Priority B, 20 per cent).
7. S.O.A.S. (1963)	For schools.	158 (41 starred.)

PART THREE

STOREHOUSES OF THE LITERATURE

[11]

Libraries

Something of this writer's attitude toward books and, indeed, of his philosophy of librarianship may be gained (by those who are curious about it) from the article cited below, which was originally a paper read before a plenary session of the International Congress of Orientalists. In it is set out the view that as writings on Asia and Africa proliferate to an ever-increasing extent, co-operation between libraries which are endeavouring to obtain, preserve and issue this literature becomes of ever-increasing importance. This co-operation may be brought into play in the matter of selection of books for purchase, should certainly obtain in the fields of inter-library loans, which may be facilitated by the compilation of union catalogues. There should perhaps be two cycles of library co-operation: the one embracing those libraries which do not lend to other libraries, and whose book collections are for reference only; the other those which are predisposed in favour of the circulation of books by loan among the main libraries in the country.

Libraries should be regarded as centres for supplying information on all questions addressed to them to which the answer is to be found in books in their collections. They should contribute to the propagation of knowledge about Asia and Africa among the general public by being willing to compile lists of books recommended for this purpose. They should also assist the scholar and research worker by the compilation of comprehensive retrospective and current bibliographies to enable them to survey as rapidly and thoroughly as possible the contributions of past generations of scholars to their field, and to keep abreast of current production.

'The rôle of the library in Oriental studies.' By J. D. Pearson. *Proceedings of the Twenty-Third International Congress of Orientalists*, Cambridge, 1954, pp. 34–42.

THE ORIENTALIST LIBRARIES OF THE
UNITED KINGDOM

The libraries in Great Britain which own the largest collections of books in Oriental languages or about Asia are of varied origin and character. These are:

1. The British Museum, Department of Oriental Printed Books and Manuscripts.
2. The Bodleian Library (Oxford); Oriental Department.
3. The University Library, Cambridge; Orientalia Department.
4. The India Office Library, London.
5. The Library of the School of Oriental and African Studies, University of London.
6. The Library of the Royal Asiatic Society, London.
7. The Library of the Royal Commonwealth Society, London.
8. India House Library.
9. The University Library, Durham; Oriental section.
10. The John Rylands Library, Manchester.
11. The Library of Selly Oak Colleges, Birmingham.

The first three of these are 'copyright libraries': the British Museum, the national library, receives a free copy of every book published in the country, which publishers are required by law to deposit: the universities of Oxford and Cambridge are entitled to claim free copies, a privilege shared with the National libraries of Scotland and Wales, and (as a curious anachronism) the library of Trinity College, Dublin. Other libraries of universities, or of colleges of universities are Durham and S.O.A.S. The India Office Library is attached to a government department, now the Commonwealth Relations Office. India House is the London office of the High Commissioner for India. There are two libraries of societies: the Royal Asiatic and the Royal Commonwealth. Selly Oak Colleges is an establishment primarily concerned with the training of missionaries. The John Rylands Library is an independent foundation which is open to the public.

THE BRITISH MUSEUM

The British Museum Library; a short history and survey, by Arundell Esdaile. London (1946). (2nd impression, 1948.)

'The catalogues of the British Museum. 3, Oriental books and manuscripts, by F. C. (*now* Sir Frank) Francis.' *J. Documentation*, 1951, pp. 170–83. (Reprinted as a separate pamphlet, 1959.)

'The Department of Oriental Printed Books and Manuscripts of the British Museum. Contributed by K. B. Gardner, E. D. Grinstead, and G. M. Meredith-Owens.' *J. Asian studies*, 18, 2 February, 1959, pp. 310–18.

The foundation and growth of the British Museum and its Library were described by Esdaile, who gives an account of the 'foundation collections' of Sir Robert Cotton, the Harleys, Earls of Oxford and Sir Hans Sloane, all of which contained some Oriental printed books and manuscripts, and of their acquisition for the British people. The method adopted in order to secure funds for the establishment of a home for these collections was a lottery conducted under the august sponsorship of the Archbishop of Canterbury and his fellow trustees. The history of the collections of Oriental printed books, with a good general account of the rise and growth of the collections in the various languages will be found on pages 294–321. More information on the history of the collections may be found in the introductions to the various catalogues of manuscripts, where traditionally is prefixed an account of the history of the collections described. The development of the collections between 1753, when the Museum possessed only a fair number of Hebrew MSS., and thirty-four Turkish MSS. in the Harleian collection, and 1959, when the Museum's collections of manuscripts on Southern and Eastern Asia alone were shown to number 15,271 means that the Museum's stock of MSS. is greater than any other in this country and is scarcely to be matched elsewhere.

This steady development of the Oriental collections is in no small measure the result of efforts made by the many eminent Oriental scholars whose services have been at the disposal of the Museum. Until 1867, the Oriental MSS., and until 1892, the Oriental printed books, were part and parcel of the general MS. and printed book collections and were administered by the Departments of MSS. and Printed Books respectively. The first Oriental scholars in the Museum seem to have been the Rev. C. G. Woide and the Rev. Thomas Maurice. Woide is better known as the editor of the facsimile edition of the New Testament section of *Codex Alexandrinus*, published in 1786, but his scholarship embraced also Coptic, and some of the fragments formerly owned by him are now to be found in the Bodleian Library. His papers were presented to the Museum in 1955 and bear the shelf-marks Add. 48700–16 (see *BMQ* 20, 1955, p. 32). Maurice was the author of two large works entitled *Indian Antiquities* and *History of Hindustan*, and of *Sanscreet fragments*, and was the first in a line of distinguished Indologists who have served the Museum, a line which includes the honoured names of F. A. Rosen (who was employed in the 1830's, principally, it seems, on the Catalogue of Oriental MSS.), Charles Bruce (the first to have charge of the Sanskrit printed books), Dr Ernst Haas (who brought out the first printed catalogue of Sanskrit books), Cecil Bendall, E. J. Rapson, John Allan (like Rapson, of the Department of Coins and Medals), and L. D. Barnett (*d.* 1960), the range of whose linguistic achievements is illustrated by the vast array of catalogues of printed books and manuscripts for which he was responsible.

The list of other Orientalists employed before the Department was set up includes the name of the Rev. Josiah Forshall, who, with F. A. Rosen, compiled the first catalogue of the Oriental MSS.; he later became Secretary to the Museum, and was a great power in the Museum until his mind became deranged in 1850. But the best-known name is that of William Cureton. To him, more than any other, is due the credit for the growth of the Near Eastern collections in the second third of the nineteenth century: for from 1838 onward there came into the Museum some 581 Syriac, Karshuni and Mandaean MSS., mostly from the Convent of St. Mary Deipara in the Nitrian Desert, which included fragments of the celebrated version of the Syriac New Testament by which Cureton's name has been immortalized.

In 1867 the Department of Oriental MSS. was set up under Charles Rieu, who originally came to the Museum as a supernumerary in 1847, having studied under Silvestre de Sacy. Rieu's assistant for nine years was William Wright and in that time the two scholars brought out between them the major portion of the Near Eastern catalogues, characterized by that wealth of scholarly description to which few libraries can aspire in these days of enforced austerity. Rieu himself brought out the Arabic, Persian and Turkish catalogues, while Wright made himself responsible for the Syriac and Ethiopic ones before his retirement from the Museum to become Sir Thomas Adams Professor of Arabic in the University of Cambridge, a chair in which he was later to be succeeded by his former Keeper, Rieu.

Rieu was followed as Keeper by R. K. (afterward Sir Robert) Douglas, in whose day (1892) the Oriental printed books were united with the manuscripts to form the Department of Oriental Printed Books and MSS. Douglas produced catalogues of the Chinese and

Japanese books. His assistants were A. G. Ellis, who catalogued the Arabic books and produced a 'descriptive list of the Arabic MSS.'; G. Margoliouth, who brought out the large four volume catalogue of the Hebrew MSS., having previously compiled a hand-list of them, and a 'descriptive hand-list' of the Syriac MSS. acquired since Wright's catalogue was issued; L. D. Barnett and L. Giles, both of whom succeeded to the Keepership and who continued to serve the Library in retirement. Giles was succeeded in the Keepership on his retirement in 1940 by A. S. Fulton, and he by J. Leveen, who retired in 1957. The present Keeper is Mr K. B. Gardner, who is assisted in his work by a specialist staff of scholars competent in the languages concerned and proficient in the techniques of librarianship.

The total number of books in the Oriental Department is estimated to be about 150,000. An 'Oriental Students' Room' is provided for readers of manuscripts. This contains a collection of the principal reference works, catalogues and aids to study. As no general access is given to the shelves, the system used for classifying the books is of little interest to the ordinary visitor, but the catalogues are all the more important for that reason. It has long been the Museum's policy to issue catalogues which are monuments of precise description with meticulous attention to detail. Throughout the English-speaking world, at least, a statement in a British Museum catalogue is generally taken as authoritative and requiring no checking. Mr F. C. (now Sir Frank) Francis, formerly of the Printed Books, and now Director of the Museum, has enumerated *The Catalogues of the Oriental Printed Books and Manuscripts* in a series of lists of the Museum catalogues published in the *Journal of Documentation* in 1951. The catalogues were also listed by Esdaile, by Pearson in his *Oriental manuscript collections* (1954), and in the *JAS* article referred to above. This article concludes by giving a 'statistical summary of manuscripts' which furnishes figures for (1) the Stein collection (9,361, the largest number being Chinese), (2) the Nevill collection (2,227, of which 1,625 are Sinhalese), and (3) other manuscript collections.

The only catalogue of manuscripts published since 1954 is Dr Lionel Giles's *Descriptive Catalogue of the Chinese manuscripts from Tunhuang in the British Museum*. 1957. Hand-lists of manuscripts in Persian, Syriac and Ethiopic are in course of preparation and are to be published shortly. They will include brief details of manuscripts acquired since the publication of the last printed catalogue in each case, and will be arranged under subject with author and title indexes but without the original oriental characters. It is not therefore necessary to give here the list of British Museum catalogues of manuscripts, but an up-to-date list of languages for which printed book catalogues are available is given for general convenience.

Hebrew	J. Zedner. 1867, reprinted 1963.
	S. van Straalen. 1894.
Syriac	C. Moss. 1962.
Georgian and other Caucasian	D. Lang. 1962.
Arabic	A. G. Ellis. 2 vols., 1894–1901.
	Vol. 3: Indexes, by A. S. Fulton. 1935.
	Supplement by Fulton and Ellis. 1926.
	Supplement by Fulton and Lings. 1960.
Persian	E. Edwards. 1922.
Sanskrit and Pali	E. Haas. 1876.
Sanskrit, Pali and Prakrit	C. Bendall. 1893.
	Supplement by L. D. Barnett. 1908.
	Supplement by L. D. Barnett. 1928.
Saurashtra	L. D. Barnett. 1960.
Bengali	J. F. Blumhardt. 1886.
	Supplement. 1910.
	Supplement by J. F. Blumhardt and J. V. S. Wilkinson. 1939.
Hindi, Panjabi, Sindhi and Pushtu.	J. F. Blumhardt. 1893.
Hindi.	Supplement. 1913.
Hindi, Bihari, and Nepali	L. D. Barnett. 1957.
Urdu (Hindustani)	J. F. Blumhardt. 1889.
	Supplement. 1909.
Marathi and Gujarati	J. F. Blumhardt. 1892.
	Supplement. 1915.
Assamese and Oriya	1900.
Panjabi	L. D. Barnett. 1961.
Canarese (Kannada, Badaga and Kurg.)	L. D. Barnett. 1910.
Tamil	L. D. Barnett and G. U. Pope. 1909.
	Supplement by L. D. Barnett. 1931.
Telugu	L. D. Barnett. 1912.
Sinhalese	M. de Z. Wickremasinghe. 1901.
Burmese	L. D. Barnett. 1913.

Chinese   R. K. Douglas. 1877.
                        Supplement. 1903.
                        MS. Supplement by L. Giles.
Japanese   R. K. Douglas. 1898.
                        Supplement. 1904.

All the catalogues of the Museum, printed or otherwise, have continuations which are available in the department. A catalogue of MSS. arranged in purely numerical or press-mark order, irrespective of language, is kept in the Students' Room; this is up to date, or, at the most, a year behind time; in addition, there is a 'classified inventory' which gives a list of the MSS. arranged under languages, which serves as an index to the numerical register of manuscripts. Important MS. accessions are described in the *British Museum Quarterly*.

The printed book catalogues are invariably constructed in three parts, the main entries appearing under authors, with a general index of titles, and a subject index.

Until recently the only catalogues immediately available to readers were the printed ones, which naturally become more and more out of date as time goes by, and the inherent difficulties in the requirement of the services of experts knowing what (for the West) are unusual languages and in the especial problems inevitably present in the cataloguing of Oriental books tend toward long delays occurring between the publication of an original catalogue and its supplement. Catalogues in process of formation, in the form of collections of slips ultimately forming copy for the printers, existed in the Department but were normally not accessible to readers, who had perforce to ask for a title of a book to be looked up in the catalogue by a member of the Departmental staff.

In the last few years a card catalogue has been begun for the Museum's intake of new books and this is accessible to all in the Students' Room. Entries for this (as for other purposes) are reproduced from the original typewritten slips by xerography in the number of copies provided. Ultimately it is hoped that extra copies may be made on behalf of other libraries in this country and possibly elsewhere.

As has already been stated, the Museum, by virtue of being a 'copyright library', is entitled to a free copy of every book or periodical published in the United Kingdom, and this right is strictly enforced. In addition, the Museum buys large numbers of books published in other countries every year: enforced economies during and just after the war, together with the unprecedented rise in book production all over the world have had the result that the Museum can no longer justifiably claim to acquire everything of importance for scholarship and containing new information based on the results of research, or all important new editions of older works. This affects both the Western collections and the Eastern: in both numbers of periodicals essential for research purposes are missing. Lack of expert staff has also resulted in serious deficiencies in some departments, such as Japanese, for which no competent scholar was available since Douglas's time until the appointment of K. B. Gardner in 1954. It is sincerely to be hoped that more enlightened official policy will enable these deficiencies to be made good.

Permission to work in the Museum Library is invariably granted on application to all serious students, though it is technically necessary to give evidence that the material sought is not accessible in other libraries. The Act of Parliament which regulates the affairs of the Museum permits it to lend books for exhibition, but not for consultation, and the Museum is incapable, therefore, of playing the same part in inter-library national and international co-operation as is played by the national libraries of other countries such as the Library of Congress.

THE BODLEIAN LIBRARY, OXFORD

Annals of the Bodleian Library, Oxford, by W. D. Macray. 2nd ed., enlarged, and continued from 1868 to 1880. Oxford, 1890.
History of the Bodleian Library, 1845–1945, by Sir Edmund Craster. Oxford, 1952.
'The Oriental manuscript collections of the Bodleian Library, by A. F. L. Beeston.' The *Bodleian Library Record* 5, 2, October, 1954,

The early history of the Library of the University of Oxford and its re-foundation by Sir Thomas Bodley in the seventeenth century are related in Macray's *Annals* and in Esdaile's *Great libraries of the world*. Macray gives a wealth of information on the early collections of Orientalia, as may be discovered by looking up the names of Oriental languages in the index to his book. Sir Edmund Craster's *History of the Bodleian Library 1845-1945* describes the recent history of the Library and the growth of its collections, including the Oriental printed books and manuscripts.

Although it was only on Craster's assumption of office in 1931 that the Department of Oriental Books was set up, parallel to the Departments of Western manuscripts and Printed Books, each being in the charge of a sub-librarian, throughout the greater part of the nineteenth century one of the two sub-librarians had been a scholar versed in Arabic or the other Semitic languages. Nicoll, compiler of part of the second volume of the Arabic MSS. catalogue, was appointed in 1814 and stayed until his election to the Regius chair of Hebrew in 1822. He was succeeded by Stephen Reay who combined the duties of sub-librarian with those of the Laudian professorship of Arabic for thirty-two years. Later Oriental scholars who occupied this post with distinction were Robert Payne Smith, later to become Regius Professor of Divinity and Dean of Canterbury, who compiled the Syriac MSS. catalogue, Max Mueller (for a year or two only), J. W. Nutt and Adolf Neubauer, author of the Hebrew catalogue, whose reputation for scholarship was such that he was appointed to the second sub-librarian-ship at a time when the senior sub-librarian was also a Hebrew scholar. An eminent Hebrew scholar in the person of Sir Arthur Cowley was Bodley's librarian from 1919 to 1931. (An earlier distinguished orient-alist to occupy this post was Thomas Hyde, Librarian from 1665 to 1701.)

Beeston in his article gives an account of the history of the principal manuscripts in the collections administered by the Department of Oriental Books, and of the catalogues provided for their study, be-ginning with Bernard's Catalogue of 1697. He also describes the way in which the manuscripts are classified, and gives some indications as to how new accessions made since catalogues were published are dealt with: the *Summary catalogue of western MSS.*, despite its title, lists Ori-ental items, and is valuable as indicating the provenance and history of individual manuscripts. A card index of Arabic manuscript accessions since 1836 is available in the library. Chinese manuscripts are entered with printed books in that language, but may be distinguished through the custom of using buff cards for the manuscript material. Statistics are given which show the numbers for the various languages of manu-scripts entered in published catalogues, of those included in unpublished indexes available in the library, and of those as yet uncatalogued. Since 1914 all important manuscript accessions have been described in the *Bodleian Quarterly Record* and its successor, the *Bodleian Library Review*. Information is also to be found in the annual *Report of the Curators*.

For the convenience of the Orientalist in the Bodleian a special read-ing room, the Rawlinson Room, is provided. Here all MSS. and most of the printed books are delivered for the use of readers, the exceptions being those on India, Pakistan and Burma, which are in the Indian Institute nearby, founded in 1880 to supply a centre for Indian studies

in the University and since 1927 under the direct control of the
Bodleian curators. In the Rawlinson Room may be found also the prin-
cipal reference books and periodicals important for Oriental studies,
with catalogues of MSS. and printed books. The only catalogue of its
Oriental printed books published by Bodley so far is that of the
Hebrew books, which Cowley brought out in 1929. Its illustrious predecessor, by Steinschneider, scarcely needs to be mentioned here. The
Rawlinson Room also contains the card catalogues for the printed
books in Arabic, Armenian, Chinese, Ethiopic, Georgian, Hebrew,
Japanese, Persian, Syriac, Turkish and other languages which are kept
up to date, as are those for Indian languages in the Indian Institute,
where they and the entries for Western books are all arranged in one
alphabet.

Genuine scholars are always made welcome at the Bodleian. Though
the lending of books was expressly forbidden by its founder, in later
years some relaxation of this rule has been instituted. It still remains
necessary, however, for any proposed loan to be sanctioned by the
Curators, who are only disposed to grant the privilege to institutions
approved by them.

The present Keeper of Oriental Books is Mr N. C. Sainsbury. His
predecessor was Dr A. F. L. Beeston who, following the ancient tradition, was translated to the Laudian Professorship of Arabic in 1955.

OTHER OXFORD LIBRARIES

Many of the Oxford colleges possess a number of manuscripts in
Oriental languages, which in a great many cases have been deposited in
the Bodleian. Most of these are described (somewhat inadequately) in
H. O. Coxe, *Catalogus codicum MSS. in collegiis Oxon.* and in Kitchin's
catalogue of the library of Christ Church. Recently the Oriental Institute was built in Pusey Lane: to this were transferred collections of
books on the Near East and the Far East to provide a lending library for
students and teachers. (The Indian books are preserved in the Indian
Institute, which is an integral part of the Bodleian. So, too, is the library
of Rhodes House, with its important collections of manuscripts, documents and printed books relating to all parts of the British Commonwealth other than India, and to colonial subjects in general.)

The new foundation of St. Antony's College has a Middle Eastern
Section, with a library which contained in 1964 about 4,500 books and
bound volumes of periodicals, as well as a large collection of pamphlets,
offprints, press-cuttings and newspapers.

In 1963 the University appointed a Middle Eastern Bibliographer, whose function will be to collect publications issued in the Middle East for a half-dozen libraries in Oxford, not including the Bodleian.

THE UNIVERSITY LIBRARY, CAMBRIDGE

C. Sayle: *Annals of Cambridge University Library, 1278–1900.* Cambridge, 1916. (Reproduced from '*The Library*' of 1915.)

The University collection of books at Oxford dates back to 1337, but 1424 is the date usually assigned to the commencement of Cambridge University Library. Nevertheless Cambridge's Oriental collections go back to a very respectable antiquity; a 'Catalogue of the Hebrew books in the Public Library of Cambridge' was compiled by Abraham Wheelock, Librarian from 1629 to 1653 [now MS. Dd. 3. 7].

Cambridge also had its Macray in the person of Charles Sayle, former Secretary to the library and an eminent and tireless bibliographer, in whose *Annals* we find recorded the earliest reference to an Oriental matter under the year 1588 (a year better known for another highly important event in English history) when William Chaderton, Bishop of Chester, and formerly President of Queen's College, gave the Bomberg Bible. This entry is soon followed by that recording the death of Erpenius in 1624 and the exertions of the Duke of Buckingham to ensure that his MSS. were acquired for the University Library, where they duly arrived in 1632. But a brief and more connected account of the principal Oriental collections in the Library is to be had in the preface to Browne's *Persian Catalogue.*

The Cambridge University Library is the only one of the 'copyright' libraries with important Oriental collections to have a system of 'open access' to a large proportion of the shelves. Unlike the two larger libraries already described, in Cambridge it is the custom for a reader, having found the book he wants in the catalogue, to fetch it himself from the shelves, and to read it either at a table conveniently situated among the bookshelves, or in the imposing Reading Room seating over 200 readers. Furthermore, if he is a member of the University, he is permitted, on giving due recognizances, to take the book home with him.

With the possibility of visiting the bookstacks open to him, the reader has a more than academic interest in the system used for classifying the books, and it is thought worth while on this account to give a brief description of it as far as it affects books on Oriental languages and literature. The general book-classification scheme is a decimal one, utilizing the numbers 1 to 999, of which 800–849 are reserved for Oriental (and other non-European) languages and literatures. Works on other subjects such as law, history, anthropology, archaeology, religions and philosophy with special reference to Oriental countries must be looked for in the sections allocated to these subjects, as is customary in large general libraries. Periodicals are classified by the same series of numbers, with the prefix P for current and important journals, L for the less erudite, Q for those which have ceased publication, and T for those which for their rarity, value, multiplicity of plates or other special features are thought to demand restriction of access. Thus the visitor will find the printed books on Oriental linguistics and literature mainly in classes 800–849 and the most important current periodicals in the field in P800–849.

A smaller number of printed catalogues has been issued by Cambridge than by the other two great libraries who, like it, are entitled to claim any British publication under the authority of the Copyright Act. This lack of catalogues applies both to MSS., and to printed books, for which all that is available is the printed catalogue of the Wade Collection of Chinese books, with its supplement, and the hand-list of the Turkish books bequeathed to the Library by E. J. W. Gibb. At Cambridge, however, unlike some other libraries, cataloguing of printed books is up to date and entries for practically all the Oriental books are placed in the General Catalogue (of authors only) very soon after they are received, the only exception being the Chinese (and formerly the Japanese) books which have separate card catalogues. Recently a beginning was made with the printing of slips for the Japanese books and the insertion of them in the General Catalogue. A consolidation of the slips so printed up to 1960 has been published by E. B. Ceadel:

Classified catalogue of modern Japanese books in Cambridge University library. Eric B. Ceadel. Cambridge (1961).

Entries for books in the other Oriental languages are made in the eneral catalogue of the library which is formed by cutting up sheets of new titles printed as required, and pasting them into guard-books. Books in Near Eastern languages have their titles printed in the character used, with no transliterations, but for Indian and languages spoken farther East, transliterations of titles alone are given. There are no title or subject catalogues available at the moment.

As a beneficiary under the terms of the Copyright Act Cambridge can be relied upon to have any British publication, though its funds for the purchase of the works of foreign authors are severely limited. Fortunately this deficiency is offset to some extent by the use of the income from the Browne Memorial Fund, from which source it is enabled to buy important contributions to Islamic studies in both Western and Oriental languages.

Books are lent freely to members of the University, but the library plays no part in national or international library co-operation schemes. Books and MSS. are, however, on occasion lent to other institutions for limited periods. All applications for these loans must be recommended by the Library Syndicate, and approved by Grace of the Senate.

The Orientalia section is at the time of writing under the charge of Mr D. G. Crane, who has the assistance of Miss J. Thompson. Miss M. Scott is in charge of the Chinese books. The Library Syndicate appoints every year a Curator of Oriental books, who normally provides some expert assistance in the cataloguing of manuscripts or, occasionally, printed books.

OTHER ORIENTALIST LIBRARIES IN CAMBRIDGE

The Faculty of Oriental Studies possesses a small library of Oriental books which are used mainly by undergraduate and post-graduate students.[1] Many of the colleges own important collections of Orientalia, and descriptions of these can be found in the revised and enlarged edition of A. N. L. Munby's *Cambridge college libraries; aids for research students* (Cambridge, 1962). From this work it will be seen that significant Orientalia collections exist in the libraries of Christ's (the William Robertson Smith Oriental library bequeathed in 1894, the Coptic bequests of Sir Stephen Gaselee and the Rev. Forbes Robinson); Clare (books in Hebrew and Near Eastern languages from the library of Humphrey Prideaux, 1648–1724); Corpus Christi (some 250 Oriental manuscripts collected in India in 1864, now deposited in the University Library, a collection of Coptic manuscript fragments given by Sir Edwyn Hoskyns, 1884–1937, and a miscellaneous collection of books about Oriental literature and archaeology, many relating to India, and books and pamphlets on the Jews, collected by the Rev. Dr H. P. Stokes, 1849–1931; Emmanuel, which received a hundred Hebrew

---

[1] See 'The Departmental libraries of the University of Cambridge, by D. W. Butcher'. *J. Documentation* 7 (1951), p. 237, no. 38.

books in 1685 under the will of Edmund Castell, and Girton, which possesses the Mary Frere Hebrew library, containing books and manuscripts which were described by H. M. J. Loewe in a catalogue published in 1915. King's has a collection of Arabic and other Near Eastern manuscripts given by E. Pote in 1788: the catalogue was published in *JRAS*, 1867; Trinity has significant collections of manuscripts in Sanskrit, Arabic and Hebrew, with catalogues by Aufrecht, Palmer and Wright, and Loewe; Westminster College contains the collection of Oriental manuscripts assembled by Mrs Margaret Gibson (1843–1926), and Mrs Agnes Smith (1843–1920), which includes Genizah fragments bound in fifteen volumes and a few complete manuscripts. Most of the Islamic manuscripts were included in Browne's *Supplementary hand-list of the Muhammadan manuscripts . . . in the libraries of the University and Colleges* of Cambridge; some additions are noted in Pearson, *Oriental manuscripts collections*.

THE INDIA OFFICE LIBRARY

S. C. Sutton: *A Guide to the India Office Library*. London, 1952.

S. C. Sutton: 'The India Office Library.' *J. Asian stud.* 18, 3, 1959, pp. 425–28.

A. J. Arberry: *The Library of the India Office. A historical sketch.* London, 1938.

The history of the India Office Library was written by Professor A. J. Arberry during his tenure of the office of assistant librarian: many distinguished scholars, in addition to him have spent part or all of their careers in its service. A revised edition of the *Guide to the Library*, by S. C. Sutton, the present librarian, is in the press: in it may be found full particulars of the collections and their catalogues.

The Library was founded by the Honourable East India Company in 1801 to serve as a repository for the varied collections committed to its charge by its servants in the East. In 1858 on the transfer of the Company's powers and effects to the Crown, responsibility for the Library was taken over by the newly created Department of State, the India Office, and in 1867 the Library was moved to its present quarters in King Charles Street, off Whitehall. In 1947, on the abolition of the India Office as a result of the Indian Independence Act of that year, the Library was embodied in the Commonwealth Relations Office and came directly under the control of the Secretary of State for that department. It has, however, retained its old name.

The Library's resources were put in 1964 at about 21,000 Oriental

MSS. and many thousands of fragments, some 8,000 MSS. in European languages, and about 260,000 printed books, some 170,000 of which are in Oriental languages. In addition, the Library possesses a large collection of paintings and drawings, including some thousands of Indian and Persian miniatures;[1] a collection of photographic negatives and prints mainly of archaeological interest; and various 'miscellaneous properties' such as coins, textiles samples and epigraphic material. The average annual increase of printed books to the Library is in the region of 1,500 to 2,000. Its acquisition policy is to collect everything of importance in Western and Oriental languages relating to the Indian subcontinent, together with all modern Arabic and Persian works on the history, religions and classical literatures of the Arabs and the Persians, and such works dealing with other parts of the East as have a bearing on the countries and peoples of India and Pakistan. Over a long period, from 1867 to 1948, the Library enjoyed the right, bestowed upon it by the (Indian) Press and Registration of Books Act (Act XXXV of 1867), of claiming a free copy of every printed or lithographed work published in British India and Burma.

The Library has for long adhered to a policy of publication of printed catalogues for its collections, a policy which has the great advantage of enabling a knowledge of the contents of the collections to be widely disseminated, and which has proved of special value in respect of its huge collections in modern Indian languages which are not widely represented in other libraries. On the other side of the scale, however, there is the disadvantage inherent in the system of the catalogue's never being fully up to date, which involves those who are able to visit the Library in a search through two or more series of catalogues in order to be sure that all sources are tapped, and there is also the possibility that cards for some of the more recent accessions will not be available for the reader. This can be illustrated in particular by the catalogues of the 'European Collection'. A printed catalogue was issued in 1888 with a supplemental list and an index, a supplement in 1895, a second supplement in 1909 and a series of eighteen lists of accessions for the period 1911 to 1936.

As explained in Sutton's *Guide*, the printed catalogues (for Western language books only) were cut up and pasted into guard-books to form the main catalogue of the Library (known as the 'Green Catalogue') to which additions were made from the printed lists of accessions from

---

[1] These figures have been computed from those given in the new edition of S. C. Sutton's *Guide*, the draft of which I have been privileged to examine.

N

1911 to 1936, in which year a card catalogue was begun. This 'Green Catalogue', together with the card catalogue, and a hand-list of the European manuscripts, has been photographed by G. K. Hall & Co. of Boston, Mass., and will shortly be offered for sale.

The principal catalogues issued so far for the Oriental printed book collections are those for the Persian books by A. J. Arberry in 1937, and for the Sanskrit and Prakrit books by Reinhold Rost, librarian 1869–93, in 1897. The latter catalogue, arranged in Sanskrit alphabetical order by titles, is undergoing revision, and three volumes of the four projected have so far (May, 1954) been issued. When completed, the catalogue will cover all accessions up to 1932, with some for the years 1933–35 which it will have been found possible to include. Catalogues for the printed books in modern Indo-Aryan languages were compiled by Professor Blumhardt. Many other catalogues, both of MSS. and printed books, Western and Oriental, are already in the press or in process of compilation: Mr Sutton's *Guide*, supplemented by the Annual Report, will give the latest position in each case. The Library also has a large possession of photostats and microfilms of manuscripts in Arabic, Persian and Indian languages belonging to other libraries; a list of these was published in the *Bulletin of the Association of British Orinetalists* 2, 1–2, 1964, pp. 6–19.

The records of the former East India Company, and of the India Office, its successor, have not been transferred to the Public Record Office, as are those of every other government department, but are controlled by the Library.

The India Office Library has always been known for the very liberal way in which it has lent its treasures to scholars all over the world. Fortunately, no signs of modification of this policy are apparent. The Library continues to lend generously both to all who seek its membership and to those who are precluded from joining by distance. Printed books may be borrowed through the post: MSS., however, are lent only to approved institutions such as university libraries. For some years now the Library has been engaged in preparing microfilm copies of its most precious MSS. which are lent whenever appropriate in place of the original manuscripts.

THE SCHOOL OF ORIENTAL AND AFRICAN STUDIES

The nucleus of the Library was formed at the time of the School's foundation in 1916 by the collection of Oriental books owned by the

London Institution. The University Library and the libraries of University and King's Colleges transferred to the School their Oriental books (other than those in Hebrew and Syriac) in exchange for the Western books from the London Institution Library. Foremost among these collections were the printed books and manuscripts, containing many rare editions and unique items, which had been presented to King's College in 1835 by the Orientalist and numismatist, William Marsden.

A description of the principal collections acquired by the Library at various times, and some estimates of the size of its contents, is given in a pamphlet headed 'The Library' which is reprinted from the School's *Calendar*. A document giving similar information was published in *J. Asian studies* 17 (1957), pp. 183–88.

Although primarily intended for the staff and students of the School and those of other Colleges in the University of London, the Library admits to membership all bona-fide students of Oriental, Asian and African affairs, and at the present time more than 700 persons outside the University have availed themselves of this membership. The Library also lends freely to scholars in other universities, and plays an important part in the national scheme for inter-library lending as an 'outlier' of the National Central Library. It was considerations such as these which led the Hayter Sub-Committee to declare that the Library was to be regarded as a 'national [*sc.* lending] library' in the fields which it covered.

In respect of book selection, the Library's policy is to attempt to acquire all significant publications relating to Asia, Africa and Oceania, written in all languages, in the fields of the humanities and the social sciences. (There are a few relatively minor exceptions to this general statement. Some branches of Oriental studies, such as Egyptology and Biblical and Rabbinical Hebrew, are covered only sketchily, as teaching of these subjects is given elsewhere in the University. Similarly, by agreement with the Institute of Advanced Legal Studies and the London School of Economics, certain aspects of colonial, British Commonwealth, and international law are regarded as being the prerogative of those institutions.)

The School's collections in August, 1964, numbered some 263,500 pieces. Of these, some 70,000 were in Chinese. The Library possesses about 1,700 manuscripts in Oriental languages, though it has never gone out of its way (or had the necessary funds) to collect rare and valuable items. Such manuscripts as it possesses have come by way of gift. There are two important collections of documents in Western languages: the papers of Sir William MacKinnon, first president of the British East Africa Company, and the papers of Sir Frederick Maze, Inspector-General of the Chinese Imperial Maritime Customs from 1929 to 1943. The printed books collection is increasing at the rate of some ten thousand volumes a year, and this figure may confidently be expected to continue to rise in an exponential curve for some years to come, as the nations of Asia and Africa, and the interest shown in them outside those continents, continue to develop.

In 1957, the Eastern art collections of the Courtauld Institute were deposited on permanent loan in the Library and merged with the art books already there. The Courtauld collection comprises about 3,000 volumes, with the main emphasis on China. It includes a large collection of sale and exhibition catalogues. In the section devoted to painting and calligraphy there is a collection of photolithic reproductions of Chinese materials, the publications of the Palace Museum in Peking prior to 1939 being almost complete. Periodicals in Western and Far Eastern languages are presented. The most important periodical in Chinese is *Yü kung* (Chinese Historical Geography), which is complete and is the only set in Great Britain.

Additional teaching and study material is provided by the steadily growing collections of lantern slides, transparencies and photographs.

All the art collections are housed in an annexe adjoining the Percival David Foundation (No. 53 Gordon Square). Mention should also be made of the Library of the Foundation, which contains about 5,000 works in Chinese, Japanese and European languages, dealing mainly with Far Eastern art and culture.

Access is freely granted to about three-fifths of the Library's shelves: this proportion would be much higher were it not for difficulties caused by shortage of accommodation. The aim is to make the whole of the Library accessible, with the obvious exception of MSS. and valuable works for which extra security is essential. Works in Western languages are kept as a rule distinct from those in Oriental languages and translations therefrom, though the two categories are kept as closely together as is possible in order to mitigate any inconvenience caused by this arrangement. The principal sections of the classification are: I – Far East. II – South-East Asia. III – Sanskrit. IV – India, Pakistan, Ceylon. V – Arabic. VII – Persian. VIII – Turkish, Near East in general. IX – Phonetics and Linguistics. X – Islam, Law. XI – Generalia. XII – Modern Indian languages. XIII – African languages. C – Chinese. D – Japanese. FA–FZ – Art. U–W – Africa. W.G. – Religion, philosophy, anthropology, folklore.

The card catalogue maintained in the Library is completely up to date. The main catalogue contains entries for all the books in the Library, MS. and printed, in all the languages catered for (a language index to the School's collections contains some 2,500 cards), with the exception of Chinese and Japanese, for which separate catalogues exist. Cataloguing is based on the code used by the British Museum: the catalogues are arranged by author, title and subject in three separate alphabetical arrangements. Of the subject catalogue it should be mentioned that the arrangement is in general by language and country: for each language and country a stereotyped list of subjects is used as far as is appropriate. (There are many objections to this method: it entails, for instance, making an arbitrary and quite impracticable distinction between 'religion' and 'philosophy' which cannot be substantiated for most of the Eastern religious systems.) Monthly lists of accessions to the library, containing reproductions of the catalogue entries for both new books and older ones recently acquired, are distributed to all libraries which have evinced an interest in them: they are designed mainly to serve the needs of the academic staff of the School but have been found useful by other institutions.

The Library's catalogues, including those for the Chinese and Japanese books, were photographed by G. K. Hall & Co. and issued for sale in twenty-six volumes in 1964 (though dated 1963). The volumes containing the entries in the subject catalogue under General, Africa, Near and Middle East, South Asia, South-East Asia and the Pacific Islands, and the Far East, are obtainable separately from Messrs. Hall, as are the author, title, Chinese, Japanese, and manuscripts and microfilms catalogues, and 'offprints' of the section for periodicals and serials.

Other catalogues in the Library include one drawn up for a collection of 'India papers', mostly publications issued under the aegis of the East India Company, an author and subject catalogue of periodical articles on the Far East and South-East Asia from 1920, and of South Asia from 1956 (these constructed as a comulation of the entries included in the Library's *Monthly list of periodical articles on the Far East and South-East (Southern) Asia*, which has been circulated to all interested persons and institutions since May, 1954), and an author catalogue of articles on Islamic subjects in periodicals and other collective publications from 1906 onward. A hand-written catalogue of the Library's large collection of offprints and older pamphlets is being constructed.

Several bibliographies and union catalogues have been compiled by members of the Library staff, sometimes in association with their academic colleagues. In addition to the *Monthly list of periodical articles* mentioned above, of which annual cumulations were published in the years 1954–56, the following list indicates the range of these works:

Oriental manuscript collections in Great Britain and Ireland, by J. D. Pearson. 1954.

Islamic art and archaeology. An annual record of publications, by J. D. Pearson and D. S. Rice. 1954 and 1955.

The Far East and South-East Asia: a cumulative list of periodical articles. May 1954–April 1955 (—May 1955–April 1956, May 1956–April 1957). [1955–57.]

A Bibliography of Oceanic linguistics, by H. R. Klieneberger.

Index Islamicus 1906–55; a catalogue of articles in periodicals and other collective publications, by J. D. Pearson with the assistance of Julian F. Ashton. 1958 [reprinted 1961].

Index Islamicus, supplement 1956–60, by J. D. Pearson. 1962.

Bibliographies of Mon–Khmer and Tai linguistics, by H. L. Shorto, Judith M. Jacob and E. H. S. Simmonds.

Index Sinicus, by John Lust, with the assistance of Werner F. Eichhorn. 1964.

Theses on African studies. 1964.

A guide to documents and manuscripts in Western languages in the libraries of Great Britain and Ireland relating to South and South-East Asia. Compiled by M. D. Wainwright and Noel Matthews, under the general supervision of J. D. Pearson. 1965. [Similar guides to Near and Middle Eastern, Far Eastern and African materials have reached an advanced stage of preparation.]

Although the School forms part of the University of London, its library is to all intents and purposes entirely independent of the University Library, though the two libraries work in close co-operation with one another. The Departmental libraries in the School, which consist of small collections of reference books and teaching materials, are nominally under the control of the School's library committee, but in practice are administered independently by the several Heads of Departments, sometimes through a lecturer detailed to act as departmental librarian. The main library at present orders all books for the departmental libraries, but apart from this there is complete decentralization. It is hoped, however, in the near future, to appoint a special departmental libraries officer to co-ordinate the keeping of records and the cataloguing of the books, thus ensuring that the main library catalogue keeps track of all of the books in the School.

Most of the books in Burmese bought by the School are added to the stock of the Burmese dictionary library for the use of the compilers of the Burmese dictionary being published by the Oxford University Press for the School. On the completion of the dictionary they will be incorporated in the collections of the main library.

THE ROYAL ASIATIC SOCIETY

The history of the Society, a list of important collections of books and manuscripts in its Library, and the names of former librarians, are given in the *Centenary volume* which the Society published in 1932. *A Catalogue of printed books published before 1932 in the Library of the Royal Asiatic Society* was published in 1940. This catalogue does not, however, list all the books in the Library. Bibles, pamphlets and reprints are omitted, as are books in Chinese, Siamese, Turkish (in part), the Schrumpf Armenian Collection (of which a list was published in *JRAS*, 1893), and the Burton Collection presented in 1939. The Chinese books (of which a catalogue was compiled by S. Kidd in 1838, and a card catalogue by Mr Shelley Wang in 1937) were transferred to the Library of Leeds University in 1964 as a consequence of the foundation of the Leeds Centre for Chinese Studies. The manuscripts and blockprints were catalogued by H. F. Holt in a work published in 1890.

The *Catalogue* also contains a brief but most useful explanation of the treatment of Oriental names and two valuable Appendices, one containing a list of gazetteers and the other of periodicals and their indexes. The titles of individual volumes comprised in monograph series are often given.

Most of the books added to the Society's Library are received either as copies sent by publishers for review in the Society's *Journal* or by exchange for the *Journal* itself and other publications of the Society. The Society has little money to spend on the upkeep of its library. Additions are listed in the annual report which now forms part of the second issue of the *Journal* in every year.

THE ROYAL COMMONWEALTH SOCIETY

The Library of the Royal Commonwealth Society (formerly the Royal Empire Society, and before that the Royal Colonial Institute) contains

what is probably the most extensive collection of printed materials
(with some manuscripts) in the country on the territories which now
form part of the British Commonwealth, of those which were formerly members, and of the colonial possessions of foreign powers. A
brief description of the Library and its contents was published by the
present librarian, Mr D. H. Simpson, in *Library materials on Africa*, 1,
iii, 1963, pp. 6–9. Following on four catalogues published in the years
1881, 1886, 1895 and 1901 the *Subject catalogue* was published in four
volumes from 1930 to 1937 and an extra volume, *Biography catalogue*,
in 1961.

*Subject catalogue of the Library of the Royal Empire Society, formerly
Royal Colonial Institute*. By Evans Lewin. 4 vols. (London), 1930–37.

1. The British Empire generally, and Africa. 1930.

2. The Commonwealth of Australia, the Dominion of New Zealand, the South Pacific, General voyages and travels and Arctic
and Antarctic regions. 1931.

3. The Dominion of Canada and its provinces, the Dominion of
Newfoundland, the West Indies and Colonial America. 1932.

4. The Mediterranean colonies, the Middle East, Indian Empire,
Burma, Ceylon, British Malaya, East Indian Islands and the Far
East, 1937.

In 1930 the Library contained upward of 200,000 books and pamphlets, but severe losses were suffered as a result of bombing during the
Second World War. The subject catalogue does not entirely supersede
that of 1901 and is not exhaustive, but very few publications 'of any
present use or importance' are omitted. Not all official literature on
Africa may be found in the catalogue, but most of that published since
1910, and a selection of earlier official publications were included. It
had been hoped eventually to publish a special catalogue of the official
literature of the Empire, and a volume listing the literature on the
First World War in the Library, but these have not as yet materialized.

The catalogue is arranged regionally by continent and individual
countries as far as this is practicable, each region being further subdivided in accordance with a fixed schedule of subject headings and
headings for geographical and political areas. Within the separate sections the material (books, pamphlets, titles of articles, papers read before societies, the analysed contents of numerous volumes of papers and
essays) is arranged in chronological order. Most useful are the analyses

of contents of learned journals which may be found under the heading 'Societies'.

Every month the Library issues *Library notes with list of accessions*. The Library notes part gives much useful information on collections in the Library.

INDIA HOUSE LIBRARY

India House Library is the library of the Office of the High Commissioner for India in Great Britain. It contains publications issued by the Government of India, Provincial Courts, the Stationery Office and unofficial books and periodicals.

In 1933 *A short catalogue* was published as a guide to publications in stock as at the end of 1932. It is arranged by subjects arranged in Dewey Decimal classification order, with author and subject indexes. No analytical entries for collective works are contained in this, but they are incorporated into the typewritten catalogue held in the Library. Sections for 'quick reference books' and bibliographies are included in the printed catalogue.

The office publishes regularly a *List of publications received in the Publications Branch*, which may be obtained from that source. This includes publications of the Central Government, and a list of unofficial publications received in the Library.

UNIVERSITY LIBRARY, DURHAM: ORIENTAL SECTION

No description of the Durham Orientalia collections has as yet appeared in print, the following notes being taken from a typewritten report written by the Librarian-in-charge late in 1960. The genesis of the collection may be attributed to the grant of funds in 1947 recommended by the Scarbrough Commission: by 1960 the collection had developed from the mere shelf of books which the University possessed in 1947 to approximately 52,500 volumes in the principal fields of Oriental studies cultivated in Durham, i.e. Egyptology, Assyriology, Hebrew and Old Testament studies, Islamic studies, Arabic, Persian, Turkish, Indian and Chinese studies. The Oriental Section was set up as a separate branch of the University Library in 1950, and since 1952 the collections have been housed in the premises occupied by the School of Oriental Studies at Elvet Hill.

In 1960 the Library received currently 152 periodicals, and subscribed to some twenty newspapers and popular magazines, which are kept permanently. It possessed thirty-nine volumes of manuscripts 'of Islamic character', forty-one of 'Indianist character', one each in Armenian, Ethiopic and English, and several albums of photographs taken by travellers in the East, and it served as a depository of microfilm copies of manuscripts made by the India Office Library of its own collections. Special collections of printed books include the entire Egyptological Library of Professor Battiscombe Gunn, the Cant collection of Chinese and Japanese works, the European part of the library of works on Chinese art and archaeology built up by the late Professor W. Percival Yetts, and the library of the distinguished Indian philosopher Swami Ananda Acharya, who died in 1945. But pride of place among the Durham collections must surely be granted to the 'Sudan archive', a collection of papers and printed material relating to the Sudan during the Condominium period, for which a typewritten handlist is available. Among the collections in the archive is an extensive collection of Mahdist manuscripts and rare lithographs, and the papers of Sir Reginald Wingate and Slatin Pasha.

THE JOHN RYLANDS LIBRARY, MANCHESTER

The John Rylands Library, Manchester: 1899–1935. A brief record of its history with descriptions of the building and its contents. By Henry Guppy. Manchester, March, 1935.

The John Rylands Library, Manchester; a brief descriptive account. Manchester (1954, reprinted 1955, 1958).

The 'brief descriptive account' of the John Rylands Library is very largely drawn from the history of the Library's first thirty-seven years written by its distinguished first librarian, Henry Guppy, whose work may be regarded as a model for a history and description of a library. The Library was founded and built in an imposing Gothic style as a memorial to her husband by Mrs John Rylands, and opened its doors to the public on the very convenient date of 1 January, 1900. The 'foundation collections' may be assumed to be the Althorp Library of the 2nd Earl Spencer, who had been under the tutelage of Sir William Jones, which had been bought by Mrs Rylands in 1892, and the Bibliotheca Lindesiana, which contained the collection of Eastern and Western manuscripts brought together by the 25th Earl of Crawford, which was bought in 1901. More information on the history of the collections, and discussions of matters relating to individual manuscripts may be found in the volumes of the *Bulletin* which the Library has published continuously since 1903, and which includes not only research articles on the Library's own books and manuscripts, but also monographs (which are available separately) by scholars in various fields of studies. Volume 25 of the *Bulletin*, which was published in 1941, in honour of Henry Guppy, contains an index to the first twenty-five volumes. It also contains an article by Sir Frederick Kenyon, formerly Director of the British Museum, entitled 'Testamentum bibliothecarii', which may be read with profit by all established librarians as well as by those contemplating a career in librarianship.

The Library's publications include catalogues of the Coptic manuscripts, Demotic papyri, Sumerian tablets, Arabic papyri, Arabic manuscripts and Samaritan manuscripts. No manuscript, printed book or map is permitted to leave the building for any purpose whatsoever.

THE SELLY OAK COLLEGES LIBRARY, BIRMINGHAM

The group of colleges comprising the Selly Oak Colleges in Birmingham, which provide training for those intending to become missionaries, enjoys the use of a central library which aims at providing facilities for advanced work in missionary and Oriental studies. It possesses more than 2,000 volumes in Arabic and Syriac and is building up the only counterpart in England to the Missionary Research Libraries in the United States. The Library possesses a small selection of grammars of African and Asian languages, and a few texts in these languages, and a strong collection of missionary writings on these continents, but pride of place must be given to the Mingana Collection of Arabic and Syriac manuscripts, for which catalogues have been published.

The collection, which was bought at the time of Mingana's death, by Dr Edward Cadbury, consists of some 660 Syriac, 270 Christian Arabic, 1800 Islamic Arabic, and a few Persian, Georgian and other Oriental manuscripts. Dr Cadbury also provided funds for the purchase of the Library of the Near Eastern scholar Eugen Mittwoch, which contains a goodly collection of Arabic and Syriac texts and works on Islam and its history.

The Library is described in a pamphlet issued by the Librarian dated October, 1947: another pamphlet dated May, 1940 describes the Mingana Collection of Oriental manuscripts. Books are lent to members of the Colleges, and to non-members at the discretion of the Librarian.

Other libraries of importance for Oriental studies exist at the universities where these studies are fostered. In Leeds the Department of

Semitic languages and literature possesses several hundred manuscripts in Arabic and Persian, for which catalogues have been drawn up by Dr John Macdonald, and in Hebrew and Samaritan. The University Library has recently acquired the valuable private library of Hebrew and Jewish books and manuscripts owned by Dr Cecil Roth, and the Chinese Library formerly belonging to the Royal Asiatic Society. Good working collections exist in the university libraries of Liverpool and Manchester and, in Scotland, at Edinburgh (where there is also a special Islamic Library in the Muir Institute), Glasgow and St Andrews. Library collections in the special fields allotted to the 'Hayter centres' at Sheffield (Japanese studies), Hull (South-East Asian studies) and the University of Sussex at Brighton (Indian and African studies) are being developed. A directory of libraries with important collections for African studies was published by the Standing Conference of Libraries with Materials on Africa in 1963.

THE CHESTER BEATTY LIBRARY

Formerly housed in London (at Baroda House, Kensington Palace Gardens) the Chester Beatty Library was transferred to Dublin, in the Republic of Ireland, when its owner moved his residence to that city in 1953. The Library, which is described in a pamphlet dated December, 1958, by the Honorary Librarian, Dr R. J. Hayes, claims to contain 'the greatest collection of Oriental manuscripts ever made by a private collector'. This collection includes Assyro-Babylonian clay tablets, Egyptian and Coptic papyri, Syriac, Coptic and Armenian manuscripts, Ethiopic and Turkish manuscripts and miniatures, the Arabic collection of over 2,500 manuscripts, Persian manuscripts, Indian manuscripts and miniatures (including about twenty Jain manuscripts, sixteen Nepali, and some in Tamil, Kanarese and Sinhalese), Burmese, Siamese, Tibetan and Mongolian collections, Batak manuscripts from Sumatra, Chinese and Japanese collections, large numbers of printed books on Oriental languages, art and other subjects connected with the manuscript collections, many books printed by Jesuit missions to the East, especially those printed at the missionary press in Peking in the seventeenth century, and Oriental *objets d'art*.

Sumptuous catalogues have been published for many of the collections. These include the Indian miniatures (1936), Arabic manuscripts (1955–), Turkish manuscripts and miniatures (1958), Armenian manuscripts (1958), Persian manuscripts and miniatures (1958–), and Batak manuscripts (1961). Several works in the list of publications are descriptions or editions of single manuscripts, and a series of monographs has included additional studies of individual Islamic manuscripts, and a discussion of some early bindings from Egypt.

THE HAYTER REPORT AND LIBRARY CO-OPERATION

The Hayter Sub-Committee, in full appreciation of the important part to be played by libraries in developing Asian, African, Slavonic and East European studies in Great Britain, devoted a whole chapter to the subject of libraries in its report. A very rough estimate was given of the total annual cost of important new books relating to Asia and Africa, and strong recommendations made that university libraries should co-operate much more than is at present their custom in matters of book selection and cataloguing. Since the Committee's estimate was published, a more detailed study has been made at S.O.A.S. of the cost of annual book accessions, using for this purpose all published national bibliographies, and all other available information. These studies show the estimated cost for books, both official and commercial publications, but excluding periodicals, to be rather in the region of £12,500, made up as follows:

			£
Books published in the Near and Middle East			800
,,	,,	,, South Asia	1,500
,,	,,	,, South-East Asia	500
,,	,,	,, The Far East	3,600
,,	,,	,, Africa	1,350
,,	,,	,, Europe	3,400
,,	,,	,, America, Australia, etc.	1,350
			12,500

If the important Orientalist periodicals were to be added, and a sum for selected newspapers and topical magazines, the annual total would certainly reach £15,000.

A certain amount of co-operation between libraries in respect of book selection goes on already. A scheme for sharing of responsibility for collection in certain subject fields has been mentioned in the paragraphs on the Library of S.O.A.S. Such schemes normally only work when the library relinquishing responsibility for a given area has no great interest in the area, or with libraries not attached to teaching and research establishments. As soon as a new post is created in one of the latter it is quite unrealistic to inform the occupant of it that books in his field are, by arrangement, collected by another library some distance away. More acceptable are arrangements where the actual work of book selection can be done by representatives of more than one library working together on the same lists and catalogues: such an arrangement exists between the British Museum and S.O.A.S. in the realm of Japanese, and could probably extend to other subjects, with more libraries taking part, but it should be noted that the B.M.–S.O.A.S. agreement is to some extent vitiated by the fact that the B.M. does not lend and S.O.A.S. does, so that, for instance, S.O.A.S. books can be dispatched on loan to Sheffield, whereas scholars from that University must needs come to London to consult the books which the B.M. has bought, or, possibly, accept the expense of photographic copies. It would seem that there needs to be book-selection agreement between libraries in two cycles, that of the non-lending group and those taking part in inter-library lending schemes.

On 1 January, 1965, a union catalogue of books acquired by most of the Orientalist libraries in Great Britain was inaugurated by S.O.A.S. For the present it is restricted to books published in Asia (except the U.S.S.R.) in any language, since 1949:[1] information is sent in by the participating libraries in the form of catalogue cards, slips or lists of accessions, and these are edited at S.O.A.S. to bring them into conformity with the cataloguing code agreed upon. S.O.A.S. undertakes, in addition, to collect all possible published or multiplicated copies of other library catalogues, and to provide information as to where loan or reference copies of books exist (a service in fact similar to that which the National Central Library performs for libraries generally but on a much smaller scale). In fact, it might well be thought that the N.C.L. would be the proper body to undertake the work of compiling such a union catalogue, but the multiplicity of languages with which Orientalist libraries have to contend makes it impracticable for any library not attached to an institution with a large staff of experts in all the languages, or with expert staff of its own, to contemplate it.

Ultimately it is hoped that the editor of the union catalogue will be able to issue at regular intervals accession lists of all entries inserted in the catalogue. These should have the effect of enabling libraries to see

[1] By March, 1965, some 2,000 cards had been entered in the catalogue.

on the one hand important books needed to be added to their collections, and on the other to demonstrate which books they do not need to buy because they are available in other libraries prepared to lend them. In administering the union catalogue, S.O.A.S. is able to draw upon the experience and advice of a joint committee consisting of members of the Libraries Group of the Association of British Orientalists (ABO) and the Standing Conference of National and University Libraries (SCONUL).

Periodicals are excluded from the union catalogue for the reason that it seems more practicable and convenient to publish union catalogues similar to that already issued by the British Museum, with the co-operation of other libraries, for Chinese periodicals.

The high cost of 'processing' books, especially those in Oriental languages – S.O.A.S. estimates the average cost of getting a book on to the shelves and into the catalogue, after it has been bought and paid for, to be 16s. 7$\frac{1}{2}$d. – obviously led the Sub-Committee to recommend possible centralized cataloguing of these books. A visit to the U.S.A., where a good deal of centralized cataloguing goes on, obviously impressed the Committee very greatly. But the high cost of getting such an arrangement off the ground would be very considerable. As the Hayter Report implies, the difficulties are well-nigh insurmountable. In this country, unlike in America, not all libraries have card catalogues. The two largest use cards of different sizes, neither of which is of the standard 5 × 3 in. dimensions. And most libraries would still need experts in Oriental languages even if the cataloguing were to be done in, and cards supplied from, a central source: for all the processes connected with the ordering and accessioning of the books in the first place, and with bringing it to a place accessible to the reader, and helping him to find it in the second, can only be performed by someone who is able to read the book, or at least the title-page. So that it seems on due consideration of the points for and against it, that centralized cataloguing is only feasible in a country as well endowed with financial resources as is the United States.

American Libraries

American institutions and organizations interested in Asia; a reference directory. Second edition. Compiled by the Asia Society, Inc. Editor, Ward Morehouse. Assistant editor, Edith Ehrman. New York, 1961.

Libraries for Japanese studies; a report of a survey by Naomi Fukuda. The International House of Japan Library, 1963.

'Far Eastern resources in American libraries. G. Raymond Nunn and Tsuen-hsuin Tsien.' Reprinted for private circulation from *Library Quarterly*, vol. XXIX, no. 1, January, 1959, pp. 27–42.

Library collections for area programs. [By Rolland E. Stephens. Unpublished report, 1964.]

Language and area study programs in American universities. Compiled by Larry Moses. Department of State, Bureau of Intelligence and Research, External Intelligence Division, 1962.

Hadi, M. M. el–: *Arabic library resources in the United States: an investigation of their evolution, status and technical problems.* [Not seen. Library school thesis. Title taken from *Library Qly.* 34, 4 (October, 1964), p. 392.]

The American libraries with extensive collections on Asia range from the national library, through an ever-increasing number of libraries of universities and colleges, to a small number of public libraries and the Library of the American Oriental Society. Most of these may be identified in the second edition of the Asia Society's 'reference directory' by checking all the page numbers listed in the table 'Summary of activities described in the directory' under the phrase 'libraries and library associations', where limited information on their collections is given.

Naomi Fukuda's report is of great interest as a survey made by a Japanese librarian of the Japanese collections owned by a large number of American university libraries (8 in the West, including the University of British Columbia in Canada; 5 in the Middle West; and 7 in the East, including the New York Public Library and the Library of Congress). For each library a wealth of information is provided; hours of opening, number of volumes in Japanese and incidentally in the other Far Eastern languages, subject analysis of the collections and policy of the library, number of current periodicals taken, the amount of the budget, staff, catalogues, classification systems, stacks and shelving (i.e. position of the Japanese or Far Eastern library in the university library complex), and the number of potential users including language students.

Nunn and Tsien discuss the Far Eastern resources of 'twenty major libraries which possessed 10,000 volumes or more of Far Eastern materials at the end of 1957'. The history and development of these collections is delineated with tables giving the holdings in numbers of volumes in all the Far Eastern languages at the end of 1957, and the growth of Far Eastern collections in American libraries from 1930 quinquennium by quinquennium to 1956 and 1957. In 1930 the total number of Far Eastern books in American libraries was estimated to be 387,000: in 1957 it stood at 2,453,000, an increase of over 600 per cent over the period of twenty-seven years. The 'subject strengths' and 'specialties' on China and Japan of the various libraries are then revealed, including manuscripts, early printing and other rarities. Finally an estimate is made of acquisitions of the extent of use made of the collections. A most useful bibliography refers to published catalogues and descriptions of the individual collections, reminding us in the process of the many articles on these collections which have appeared over the years in the *Far Eastern quarterly* (later, the *Journal of Asian studies*).

Stephens's report is about a journey of exploration made by him in the interests of Ohio State University to the following universities with 'well-developed programs in area studies' in the Middle West and East of the United States: Michigan, Chicago, Illinois, Indiana, Pennsylvania, Harvard, Yale, Columbia and Cornell. Between them these nine universities can muster thirty 'area studies programs' in East Asian, South-East Asian, South Asian, Middle East and East European studies. The report gives details of the holdings in number of volumes, the rate of annual increase and the funds available, and makes recommendations for the establishment of one of each of these centres in Ohio State University. I have been privileged to see and make use of a copy of this valuable report which was not published, though Stephens published a summary of his main observations, without the budget figures, in *College and research libraries* 24 (1963), pp. 383–91.

The Department of State's *Language and area study programs* includes

o

'Library facilities' among the rubrics under which information is given for the areas Africa, Asia (General), East Asia, South and South-East Asia and the Near East, but the information given on this topic is minimal.

THE LIBRARY OF CONGRESS

Among the divisions constituting the Reference Department of the Library of Congress is the Orientalia Division. This Division, in which thirty-three persons were employed in 1963, is divided further into sections covering the main regions of Asia. Its responsibilities include the acquisition of materials in Asian languages, and the recommendation of books in Western languages in Asian subjects for purchase or solicitation by other divisions of the Department. It also prepares bibliographies and other guides to research, and supplies information to members of Congress, institutions and the general public. (In 1962–63 it answered 22,758 'reference questions' addressed to it in person, 1,657 by correspondence, and a total of 20,039 by telephone from Congress, Government and other inquirers. Thirty bibliographies were prepared, containing 1,397 entries.) The cataloguing and classification of Asian language materials is undertaken by special units within the Descriptive and Subject Cataloguing Divisions of the Processing Department.

The total contents of the Oriental collections in 1963 numbered 950,466 volumes and pamphlets, and 1,423 bound newspaper volumes. The figure for volumes and pamphlets is broken down as follows: Far Eastern languages, 812,595, Near East 39,235, South Asia 18,047, South-East Asia 13,615, Hebraica 66,974. The additions to the collections in 1963 totalled 17,554 (Far Eastern 10,694, Near East 4,014, South Asia 279, South-East Asia 756, Hebraica 1,811). No additions were made to the collection of bound volumes of newspapers: all newspapers are now preserved in microfilm form and the existing stock of bound volumes is gradually being transferred to this form. As to the use made of these collections, the figures for circulation in 1963 were 59,877 volumes within the library, and 4,961 lent outside.

Some idea of the mammoth size of the Library's collections will be gained from the above figures: it should be recognized, however, that these only apply to books in Asian languages, and take no account of the even greater number of books about Asia written in Western languages which are preserved in the Library's general collections. No figures are available for these books, but in 1963–64 the number of items received from Asia alone through the operations of the Orientalia Exchange Scheme (a branch of the Gift and Exchange Division) numbered 82,517 pieces, an advance of 28,345 over the previous year. (In the same year 14,841 items were received from Africa, compared with 8,069 for the previous year.) In addition to these receipts, 8,315 books and pamphlets published in Asia were bought in 1963–64 and 579 published in Africa. The total cost of these materials amounted to $33,874.52 or roughly £12,100. The Library also received through the Public Law 480 Book Acquisition Scheme, about which more will be said later, 33,731 pieces.

Another department with interests in Asia and Africa is the Law Library, which has Divisions for Far Eastern Law and for Near Eastern and North African Law.

Most of the figures quoted above are taken from the *Annual Report of the Librarian of Congress* which furnishes every year a wealth of information on the operations of the Library. Others were kindly provided by Mr John Cronin, Director of the Processing Department, in a personal communication. Detailed annual reports on acquisitions by the Orientalia Division as well as by other acquisitive Divisions are given from time to time in the Library of Congress's *Quarterly journal of current acquisitions*.

Methods used by the Library of Congress to obtain books from various parts of the world will be described later. So much co-operation in this activity exists among American libraries that it is convenient to treat this subject as a whole later in this chapter.

PUBLIC LIBRARIES

Foremost among the public libraries with Oriental collections stands the New York Public Library, founded in 1895 out of three large private collections, which contains an Oriental Division and a Jewish and Hebrew Division within the framework of its Reference Department. The Oriental Division contained in 1960 about 65,000 items consisting of grammars, dictionaries and literary works in Oriental languages, as well as translations and works on Oriental studies in Western languages. The area covered is 'the Near, or the Middle, and the Far East', but there are said to be over 1,000 entries on India in the catalogue.

This catalogue was one of the first to be photographed and published by the firm of G. K. Hall & Co. of Boston, Mass., who also issued in the same way catalogues of two others of the Library's collections, the

Hebraica, and the Schomburg Collections of Negro history and literature. The Oriental catalogue, which was issued in sixteen volumes in 1960, is of the alphabetical dictionary type and contained at that time some 325,000 cards, including an estimated 15,000 cards for indexed periodical articles.

The Library also publishes a *Bulletin* (founded in 1897), which from time to time has included catalogues of books and articles on various sections of the Oriental Department, many of which have been issued separately as reprints.

Other public libraries with important collections of Orientalia are those in Boston, Philadelphia, Chicago, Cleveland and Denver. Each of these possesses a collection of Oriental manuscripts, those in Philadelphia and Cleveland being the most extensive. Cleveland's collection, known as the John Griswold White Collection of Folklore and Orientalia, Chess and Checkers, contained in 1961 some 105,000 volumes, about half of which relate to Asia. The Library claims to have the largest holding of Sanskrit literature in the United States, and substantial collections of books in other Indian languages. Two large and important libraries formerly in private ownership but now administered by trusts are the Pierpont Morgan Library in New York, well-known for its splendid collection of Coptic and other Oriental manuscripts, and the Newberry Library in Chicago, with collections on the Philippines, Portuguese colonies and the history of India. The Ames Library of South Asia, formerly at West St Paul, Minn., which in 1961 contained approximately 70,000 items in Western languages on South Asia, has now been conveyed in trust to the University of Minnesota.

UNIVERSITY AND COLLEGE LIBRARIES

The universities which possess in their libraries the most substantial collections for Asian and Oriental studies are: California (Berkeley), California (Los Angeles), Chicago, Claremont Graduate School, Columbia, Cornell, Harvard, Hawaii, Michigan, Pennsylvania, Princeton, Southern California, Stanford, Washington (at Seattle) and Yale, with those of British Columbia (Vancouver), McGill (Montreal) and Toronto in Canada.

Far Eastern studies have been the most cultivated hitherto in America and many of these universities have more or less closely integrated libraries of books in Chinese, Japanese and other Far Eastern languages, sometimes in separate buildings (Columbia, Harvard, Chicago, California, Berkeley, Stanford), elsewhere under the main library's roof, as at Princeton, Cornell, Michigan, Seattle, Los Angeles and elsewhere, and invariably, as are all departmental libraries in American universities, under the direct control of the central library and looking to it for such services as ordering, cataloguing and other 'processing' work.

Books in the other Oriental languages and those in European languages on Asia are invariably dispersed among the collections in the book stocks whether the Library of Congress classification, that of Melvil Dewey or a home-made one be preferred. Only at Chicago, in the Oriental Institute, and at the Institute of Islamic Studies of McGill University are there physically separate libraries covering the Near East. In no American university does there appear to be at present a free-standing library on South Asia.

The libraries at California (Berkeley) and Columbia are each known as the East Asiatic Library, Chicago's is known as the Oriental Institute, and contained in 1961 130,000 volumes on the Far East, and an extensive collection on the Near and Middle East, Cornell has the Wason Collection, Harvard the most extensive of all in the Harvard–Yenching Institute and Princeton the Gest Oriental Library. At Stanford the main Oriental collections are in the Hoover Institution on War, Revolution and Peace.

The University of California at Los Angeles, in its *Catalogue of the Library 1919–62* (Hall, 1963), has devoted volumes 127–29 to the Chinese, Japanese and Armenian collections. Claremont Graduate School has issued a series of four union lists of materials on the Pacific area held in thirteen libraries in Southern California. Columbia's East Asiatic Library has published its *Index to learned Chinese periodicals* (Hall, 1962).

Cornell has issued three catalogues in a bibliographical series of Indonesian materials in its collections which were published under the auspices of its South-East Asia Program. These are:

Bibliography of Indonesian publications; newspapers, non-government periodicals and bulletins 1945–58 at Cornell University, by Benedict R. Anderson. (Data paper, no. 33.) Ithaca, February, 1959.

A Bibliography of Indonesian government documents and selected Indonesian writings on government in the Cornell University Library, by Daniel S. Lev. (Data paper, no. 31.) Ithaca, 1958.

Preliminary checklist of Indonesian imprints during the Japanese period (March, 1942 – August, 1945), with annotations. John M. Echols. (Bibliography series.) Ithaca, 1963. [This includes lists of newspapers and periodicals published between 6 March, 1942 and 16 August, 1945 in the Cornell University Library.]

The Library of the Harvard–Yenching Institute at Harvard University has published classified catalogues of its Chinese and Korean books, and of its Japanese collected works and series. It was in this Library that the Harvard–Yenching system for the classifying of Chinese and Japanese works was produced by its librarian, Dr A. Kaiming Chiu.

The Hoover Institution ranks as 'an independent Institution within the frame of Stanford University'. The origin and growth of the collections, and the contents of the collections themselves (including those on East Asia, Middle East and Africa) are described in the pamphlet.

Hoover Institution on War, Revolution and Peace. Stanford University, Stanford, Cal. January, 1963.

Among the many publications issued by the Institution are two series, 'Collection surveys', and 'Bibliographical series'. In the former series was published as no. 3:

The Hoover Institution collection on Japan. Nobutaka Ike. Stanford University., 1958.

The titles relevant to Asia, and one to Africa, published in the Bibliographical series up to 1963 are:

Mote, F. W., *Japanese-sponsored governments in China, 1937–45. An Annotated bibliography compiled from materials in the Chinese Collection of the Hoover Library.* 1954.

Wu, E., *Leaders of Twentieth-Century China. An Annotated bibliography of selected Chinese biographical works in the Hoover Library.* 1956.

Nahm, A. C., *Japanese penetration of Korea, 1894–1910. A Checklist of Japanese archives in the Hoover Institution.* 1959.

Israel, J., *The Chinese student movement, 1927–37. A Bibliographical essay based on the resources of the Hoover Institution.* 1959.

Uchida, N., *The Overseas Chinese. A Bibliographical essay based on the resources of the Hoover Institution.* 1959.

Hsüeh, C., *The Chinese Communist Movement, 1921–37. An Annotated bibliography of selected materials in the Chinese Collection of the Hoover Institution on War, Revolution and Peace.* 1960.

Duignan, P., *Madagascar (the Malagasy Republic). A list of materials in the African Collections of Stanford University and the Hoover Institution on War, Revolution and Peace.* 1962.

Hsüeh, C., *The Chinese Communist Movement, 1937–49. An Anno-*

tated Bibliography of Selected Materials in the Chinese Collection of the Hoover Institution on War, Revolution and Peace. 1962.

Cornell included in its Data paper series (no. 9):

Survey of Chinese language materials on South-East Asia in the Hoover Institute and Library, by Giok Po Oey. Ithaca, May, 1953.

The American Oriental Society's Library was deposited in the library of Yale College in 1855, and has remained there ever since. It was said to contain 15,000 volumes in 1961. A catalogue was published in 1930:

Catalogue of the Library of the American Oriental Society. Edited by Elizabeth Sprout. New Haven, Conn., Yale University Library, 1930.

In this catalogue the titles are classified by subject, beginning with Bibliography, Biography of Orientalists, Periodicals, Transactions of learned societies, etc., the great bulk of the titles being placed by country or race, or by language, in the two sections History of civilization and culture, and Language and literature.

CO-OPERATION AMONG AMERICAN LIBRARIES

Undoubtedly, it must be said to our sorrow and shame, American libraries are more ready to collaborate on projects in the general interest than are their British counterparts. The Library of Congress supplies a leadership in the field of scholarly librarianship that the British Museum could never aspire to. A good instance of this is the *National union catalog of manuscripts* where hundreds of American libraries agreed to catalogue their manuscript collections in a style conforming to a general pattern, so that a minimum of central editing was necessary in order to complete the union catalogue.

Co-operative cataloguing of Oriental books was said by Miss Fukuda to be hardly a success, but nevertheless a number of libraries send copies of their cards to the National Union Catalog, and these are incorporated into the printed accessions lists.

But it is in the field of collecting books that co-operative practices bring the most fruitful results. The Farmington Plan is the obvious example of this.

The Association for Asian Studies which, it will be recalled, is concerned only with what is sometimes called 'Thither Asia', has set up two committees to concern themselves primarily with the development and amelioration of American library collections. These are the Committee for Library Resources on the Far East, and the Committee for American Library Resources on Southern Asia. The latter of these committees owes its inception to a conference held at the Library of Congress in November, 1957, when a number of working papers was submitted by prominent librarians in the United States. These papers give a clear insight into American needs and library practices, and are listed here in full. References to the *Journal of the Oriental Institute of Baroda*, in which journal all of them ultimately found publication, are given:

1. Improvement of American library collections on Southern Asia, with particular reference to research groups and the public. Stephen Hay. 8 (1958–59), pp. 293–304.

2. Reference needs: bibliographies, an assessment and types needed; indexing of periodicals: Southern Asia accessions list and other similar lists. Patrick Wilson. 8 (1958–59), pp. 410–35. [This article was published in a modified form in *J. Asian studies* 8 (1959), pp. 365–76 under the title 'A survey of bibliographies on Southern Asia'. Both versions are valuable, and should be consulted by all concerned with studies of this area.]

3. Primary source materials, the location and acquisition with particular reference to manuscripts, texts and translations. Walter H. Maurer. 9 (1959–60), pp. 76–103.

4. Problems relevant to the acquisition of basic source materials. Andrew D. Osborn. 9 (1959–60), pp. 205–13.

5. Channels of procurement: South Asia. Horace I. Poleman. 9 (1959–60), pp. 321–85.

6. Channels for procurement of publications in South-East Asia. Cecil Hobbs. 9 (1959–60), pp. 460–81.

7. Comparative selection and acquisitions, with special reference to the Farmington Plan and microfilming. Herman H. Fussler. 10 (1960–61), pp. 64–84.

8. Transliteration of vernacular alphabets, co-operative cataloguing of vernacular materials; and cataloguing treatment of pamphlet materials. Sumner Spalding. 10 (1960–61), pp. 184–203.

The articles by Poleman and Hobbs are the most interesting for our present purpose. In them are set out the various methods used by the Library of Congress and other American libraries to acquire publications from 'difficult' countries. A sample Library of Congress blanket order pro-forma is given, as is a list of booksellers throughout the world with whom these orders are placed. Mention is also made of the practice obtaining in many American libraries of sending representatives on book-buying tours to countries producing books which the libraries are desirous of adding to their collections. Detailed (and entertaining) accounts of three such journeys made to the countries of South-East Asia in 1947–48, 1952–53 and 1958–59 were published by Cecil Hobbs in the Cornell Data papers (nos. 3, 11, 40):

An Account of an acquisition trip in the countries of South-East Asia. 1952.

An Account of a trip to the countries of South-East Asia for the Library of Congress, 1952–53. 1953.

South-East Asia publication sources: an account of a field trip, 1958–59. 1960.

Activities of the Committee since the Conference was held are delineated by H. I. Poleman in an article contributed to *Resources for South Asian area studies in the United States*, edited by Richard D. Lambert (1962), and entitled 'American research library resources and needs for support of studies of South Asia.' In it he has listed twenty-four projects proposed for South Asia by the A.A.S. Committee, and ten additional projects proposed in the other working papers. The accomplishments of the Committee up to the date of writing the article are reviewed, and an estimate of the number of titles and annual cost per set of publications from India. These were estimated at 3,745 in the vernacular, costing $2,575 and 1,340 English language publications at a cost of $1,475. These figures are based on entries in the first volume of the *Indian national bibliography*.

Another example of inter-university co-operation is afforded by the Inter-University Committee on South Asia Scholarly Resources. This was set up at a conference held late in 1963 which was attended by American scholars interested in South Asia who felt that there was a need for co-operative efforts in acquiring important collections of primary sources in research materials. The Committee issues the *South Asia microform newsletter* (edited by Mrs Lois Zanow, Department of Indian Studies, University of Wisconsin), which has included in its three issues so far published (January, 1965) lists of microfilms owned by universities in the United States in the Committee's sphere of interest.

But the most significant development in librarianship is without doubt the Public Law 480-supported book acquisition programmes which were inaugurated in 1962.

THE P.L. 480 PROGRAMMES

The Public Law 480 programmes are a device for ensuring that sub-stantial quantities of current publications (government and commer-cial – monographs, periodicals and newspapers) of India, Pakistan, the United Arab Republic, Israel and Indonesia are collected on behalf of a group of American research libraries. The programmes also provide for the central cataloguing by the Library of Congress of the material col-lected. An account of the scheme as it affected the first three countries named was given by the then Co-ordinator. 'United States research library acquisitions in India, Pakistan and the United Arab Republic, by Robert D. Stevens.' *UNESCO Bull. for Libraries*, 17, ii, 1963, pp. 178–80.

The programmes were made possible by funds allocated by Con-gress under the terms of Public Law 83 – 480 (Agricultural Trade, De-velopment and Assistance Act of 1954) as amended by Public Law 85 – 931. Under the amendment (section 104(n)), the Librarian of Con-gress was authorized 'in consultation with the National Science Foundation and other interested agencies, to use foreign currencies, within such appropriations as are made by Congress, for the purchase of foreign publications; for cataloguing, indexing, abstracting and se-lected activities; and for the deposit of such materials in libraries and research centres in the United States specializing in the areas to which they relate'. For the year ending 30 June, 1962 the sum of $400,000 was allocated by Congress for these purposes. The sum made available in 1962–63 was $679,900 of which $630,000 was designed for the purchase of foreign currencies owned by the U.S.

Centres for the collection of local publications were set up toward the end of 1961 in Cairo, Delhi, Karachi and Dacca. Additional centres were established early in 1964 in Tel Aviv and Djakarta. An office in Rangoon is contemplated, but the approval of the Burmese Govern-ment for this undertaking has not yet been received. The only other countries where excess local currencies are owned by the United States Government are Poland and Yugoslavia and it is possible that centres will be set up in these countries in the near future.

THE CENTRES

The centres in Delhi, Cairo, Tel Aviv and Djakarta are each directed by an American employed by the Library of Congress. (The Karachi and Dacca centres are administered from Delhi.) They are run with the aid of a staff recruited locally from the nationals of the country where they are situated. The publications collected are grouped in two main classes, government and commercial, with the three subdivisions of monographs (including pamphlets), periodicals and newspapers. Commercial monographs are secured by placing contracts with booksellers, who undertake to supply a sufficient number of copies of all new publications in all fields of scientific inquiry. The choice is left to the bookseller, and only certain types of children's publications and text-books below university standard are excluded from the terms of reference given him. Periodicals and newspapers are ordered from their publishers.

Government publications are obtained sometimes from official stationery offices or government printers, but Cairo employs an official whose special task it is to visit government departments regularly for this purpose.

All unbound publications are bound locally before being dispatched to the recipient libraries. The items receive preliminary cataloguing in the centres and this forms the basis of accessions lists which are issued at frequent intervals and distributed to all interested libraries whether participating in the scheme or not, including foreign ones. Newspapers are being microfilmed in the centres where this is possible.

Each centre issues accessions lists which are supplied to non-participative libraries on request.

CENTRAL CATALOGUING

The final cataloguing of the material is undertaken by the Library of Congress which supplies sets of printed cards to each of the participating libraries (after a delay of at least three months). These cards are obtainable by other libraries at a cost of seven cents for the first and six for all subsequent cards. A complete set of cards for the publications sent from India and Pakistan is estimated to cost $350 for roughly 5,000 cards annually.

RECIPIENT LIBRARIES

The libraries participating in the scheme number 19 for India and Pakistan, 20 for the United Arab Republic, 12 for Israel and Indonesia; 11 are put forward to receive materials from Burma if the plan to set up a centre there materializes. Some libraries receive material from more than one of the areas, the Library of Congress and Yale being the only ones to receive from all of the areas. All are university libraries with the exception of the Library of Congress and the New York Public Library.

In the year 1962–63 each of the libraries in the India/Pakistan group received 18,000 newspapers, 11,000 serials and 7,000 monographs from India, the figures for Pakistan (West and East) being 5,500, 2,750 and 1,250 respectively. The members of the U.A.R. group each received 5,500 newspapers, 3,000 serials and 2,350 monographs.

For these receipts each library contributes a token sum of $500 for each set of publications to the U.S. Treasury. In addition, in the year 1962–63 each library contributed $7,750 to the Library of Congress for the cost of cataloguing the Indian and Pakistani materials and $1,111 for the materials coming from the U.A.R. The library's total receipts for this purpose were therefore £131,750 and $18,887 respectively.

There is general agreement that a good deal of the material being received is more or less worthless. Some 50 per cent of the U.A.R. monograph material is estimated to be worthy of a place on the shelves of a research library. One university discards about 40 per cent of the material coming in from India and Pakistan. There is some feeling that complete sets of the publications collected ought to be maintained in at least four libraries in the U.S.A., but no library is under an obligation to preserve the whole of its receipts. Opinion is divided on the desirability of having the works selected by experts in the various centres, some librarians preferring to make their own selections.

PUBLICATIONS

The Library of Congress issues an Annual report of the 'Public Law 480 Programs'. *The Library of Congress P.L. 480 Newsletter* has been published since October, 1961.

FOREIGN PARTICIPATION

It is clear that by means of these P.L. 480 programmes American libraries since 1962 have been acquiring a much greater portion of the total amount of publications of India, Pakistan and the U.A.R. than any other libraries, even those inside the countries concerned, and as from 1964 the same statement may be made about publications from Indonesia and Israel. The thought naturally comes to mind as to whether we in this country can participate in these programmes or devise similar ones scaled down to our financial resources. In the first place it may be stated that the cost of these centres is estimated to be $550,000 a year for the Delhi centre, $90,000 for Karachi and $150,000 for Cairo, these sums including the purchase of the books and other materials, binding, postage and payments to staff and other overheads. But even a country as wealthy as the U.S. would not have under-written these expenditures had it not been that it already possessed enormous sums of inconvertible foreign currencies concerned. There is no possibility that a foreign library might participate by paying a share of the total costs for P.L. 480 makes it clear that all the materials collected under this scheme are to be placed in American research libraries. In any case, the contribution which each library is required to make toward the cost of central cataloguing (at present $6,000 for India–Pakistan and $1,900 for U.A.R.) would tax the resources of most libraries in this country beyond endurance.

[13]

Orientalist Libraries in
U.S.S.R.

'Oriental literature in the U.S.S.R. Orientalia in U.S.S.R. libraries, by A. I. Bendik and V. S. Grivnin. Russian translations of Asian and African books, by S. Ivanko.' *UNESCO Bull. for Libraries* 15, 6, November–December, 1961, pp. 322–26.

Libraries and bibliographic centers in the Soviet Union, by Paul L. Horecky. (Indiana University publications, Graduate School, Slavic and East European series, vol. 16, 1959.)

Libraries in the U.S.S.R. with large collections of Eastern literature are described in the short article by Bendik and Grivnin. These are State and Public libraries, libraries of universities, and libraries of institutions dependent upon the Academy of Sciences, and its affiliated branches in the Asian republics. Horecky's book is concerned with libraries in general, but some useful information may be gleaned from it about practices current in some of the libraries with important collections of Orientalia. Thus, for instance, we learn that catalogue cards for printed books in the non-Russian languages of the U.S.S.R. are prepared in the book chambers (*Knizhnaya palata*) of the autonomous republics. This central cataloguing operates in the Armenian, Azerbaidzhani, Georgian, Kirghiz, Tadzhik and Uzbek republics: the cards are distributed through library supply agencies or direct to libraries. We learn also that catalogues of the non-Russian language publications have been prepared in several of the republics, as for example, a union catalogue of Georgian books in fifteen libraries prepared by the Georgian Book Chamber (*Gruzinskaya kniga; bibliyografiya. 1627–1945*. Tbilisi, 1941–51. 2 vols. More than 2,000 entries), and bibliographies of Armenian books from the nineteenth century to the beginning of Soviet rule (*Bibliyografiya armyanskoy literatury*. Erevan, 1953) and the Armenian press (*Bibliyografiya armyanskoy pechati*. Erevan, 1956).

Supplement 34 in Horecky's book (pp. 248–56) is a 'Directory of principal U.S.S.R. libraries, bibliographic centers, and institutes of librarianship', their names being given in transliterated Russian form and in English translation. Libraries in the Asian part of Russia are listed under the following towns: Alma-Ata (Kazakh SSR), Ashkhabad (Turkmen SSR), Baku (Azerbaidzhani SSR), Barnaul (Altai), Cheboksary (Chuvash ASSR), Erevan (Armenian SSR), Frunze (Kirzhiz SSR), Iakutsk, Irkutsk, Karaganda, Kazan (Tatar SSR), Novosibirsk, Samarkand (Uzbek SSR), Tbilisi (Tiflis, Georgian SSR), Ufa (Bashkir SSR) and Vladivostok (Far Eastern State University).

Much more information on Orientalist collections in the U.S.S.R. is given in the following work, written entirely in Russian. It is thought useful to give a detailed list of its contents in English, marking with the letters BG those libraries which are also mentioned in the article by Bendik and Grivnin.

Vostokovednye fondy krupneyshikh bibliotek Sovetskogo Soyuza; stat'i i soobshcheniya. (Akad. Nauk SSSR, Institut narodov Azii.) Moskva, 1963. (Orientalist collections in the most important libraries in the Soviet Union.)

LIBRARIES OF SCIENTIFIC RESEARCH INSTITUTIONS

Institute of the Peoples of Asia, Leningrad section (BG).
Printed books: Arabic, Persian, Turkic languages of the U.S.S.R., Hebrew, Indian, Mongolian, Chinese. *MSS*.: Turkish, Arabic, Persian and Tajik, Syriac, Ethiopian, Hebrew, Mongolian MSS. and xylographs, MSS. of the Central Asian collection, Chinese, Tangut (Hsi-hsia) MSS. and xylographs, Manchu MSS. and xylographs, Tibetan MSS. and xylographs.

Institute of the Peoples of Asia in Moscow (BG).
General, Arabic, Iranian, Turkish, Indian, Mongolian, Korean, Vietnamese, Indonesian, Philippine, Japanese, the Sinological Library.

Institutions in the republics.
Oriental manuscripts in the Academy of Sciences of the Uzbek SSR (BG).
Manuscript collections in the Matenadaran, Erevan (BG).
Tibetan collection of the Buryat Scientific Research Institute.
BG adds the Institutes of Oriental Studies in the Academies of Science of the Tajik and Georgian SSRs, and the Central Scientific Library of the Kazakh SSR of the Siberian section of the Academy of Sciences, Ulan-Ude (BG, also Manchu MSS.).

STATE PUBLIC LIBRARIES

Collections on the peoples of the non-Soviet East in the Lenin State Library, Moscow (BG).

Manuscripts and printed books in Eastern languages in the Saltykov-Shchedrin Public Library, Leningrad (BG).

Oriental collections of the All-Union State Library of Foreign literature (BG).

The Reading Room for the history of the peoples of Asia in the State Public Historical Library of the R.S.F.S.R. (BG).

UNIVERSITY LIBRARIES

M. V. Lomonosov State University Library, Moscow (BG).
A. A. Zhdanov State University Library, Leningrad (BG).
Kazan University Library (BG).
BG adds Central Asian University (Tashkent), Alma-Ata University, University of Azerbaidzhan (Baku).

Seven institutions in Moscow have joined together to bring out a monthly bulletin of books and periodicals on the non-Soviet East (*Novaya sovetskaya i inostrannaya literatura po stranam Zarubezhnogo Vostoka*) received in their libraries. The bulletin is reproduced from catalogue cards sent in by the seven libraries, which are:

1. Fundamental Library of the Social Sciences.
2. All-Union State Library of Foreign Literature.
3. Lenin State Library.
4. Institute of the Peoples of Asia.
5. Research Institute for Conjunctural Studies.
6. Institute of World Economics and International Relations.
7. State Public Historical Library.

[14]

Rest of Europe

FRANCE

The *Répertoire des bibliothèques de France (1950)* indicates the following French libraries as possessing collections of Oriental and African printed books or manuscripts:

Bibliothèque Nationale

Libraries in the University of Paris:
Bibliothèque d'art et d'archéologie.
Institut de civilisation indienne.
Institut des études islamiques.
Institut des études sémitiques.
Institut des hautes études chinoises.

Other libraries in Paris:
Collège de France [important collections on Egyptology and Assyriology].
Institut catholique [Oriental MSS.].
Académie des sciences coloniales.
Agence économique des colonies.
Alliance israélite universelle [Hebraica. Judaica. MSS.].
Association amicale franco-chinoise.
Banque de Syrie et du Liban.
Centre de documentation juive contemporaine.
École nationale de la France d'Outre-Mer [Linguistics. African languages. Malagasy. Asiatic languages].
École nationale des langues orientales vivantes.
École pratique des hautes études [Oriental studies, especially Assyrian and Egyptian].
Maison du Japon.
Ministèrē de la France d'Outre-Mer.
Musée Guimet.
Musée de l'Homme.
Séminaire israélite de France.
Société asiatique de Paris.

P

PROVINCIAL LIBRARIES

Arabic language and literature: Bordeaux, Bibl. Univ.; Marseilles.
Chinese language and literature: Lille.
Hebrew language and literature: Cavaillon.
Oriental languages and literatures: Rouen.
Arabic MSS.: Dole; Marseilles; Montpellier; Montpellier, Bibl. univ. médicale.
Oriental MSS.: Lyons; Montpellier, Bibl. univ. médicale; Nimes; Reims.
Oriental MSS.: Algiers, Bibl. Nat.; Algiers, Government général; Lyons; Montpellier, Bibl. univ. médicale; Nîmes; Reims.
Oriental studies (Orientalisme): Angers; Strasbourg, Institut de linguistique.
Orient latin: Lyons.

DOCUMENTATION CENTRE

Institut de recherche et d'histoire des textes. [This institution is building up documentation sources for the history of medieval manuscripts, including Arabic.]

Most of the Oriental MSS. contained in libraries in Paris and the provinces are included in the great series entitled: *Catalogue général des manuscrits des bibliothèques publiques*.

A short description of the East Asian collections in the Bibliothèque Nationale will be found in the article by Paul Demiéville: 'Organizations of East Asian studies in France', *J. Asian studies*, 18, 1 November, 1958, pp. 172–3. Printed books and periodicals in Western languages are kept mainly in the Département des Imprimés, while those in Eastern languages, either printed or manuscript, are kept in the Départment des Manuscrits, in the charge of Mme M. R. Guignard, head of the Cabinet Oriental. There is a special reading room for Oriental studies. The Bibliothèque National has published many catalogues, principally of its manuscript collections: those which appeared before 1953 are listed in:

> *Les catalogues imprimés de la Bibliothèque Nationale. Liste établie en 1943 suivie d'un supplément (1944–52).* Paris, 1953.

The École nationale des langues orientales vivantes, founded in 1795, managed for some seventy-five years without a library of its own. The history of the library founded by Charles Schéfer in 1868, has been told by its chief librarian, Colette Meuvret, in the School's sesquicentenary volume published in 1948, *Cent-cinquantenaire de l'École des langues orientales*. Paris, 1948. At the time this article was written, the library, which caters for Slavonic languages as well as Oriental, contained 150,000 volumes, more than 30,000 pamphlets, about a thousand manuscripts, and 3,240 periodicals, living and dead. The first part of a catalogue of the Library, containing books on linguistics (philology and Arabic) was compiled by E. Lambrecht, and published in 1897. It took the form of a subject catalogue, with indexes of titles of Arabic works (both in Roman and Arabic characters), and authors. It contains entries for 3,533 works:

> *Catalogue de la Bibliothèque de l'École des langues orientales vivantes.* Tome premier: Linguistique. I. Philologie. II. Langue arabe. Par E. Lambrecht. Paris, 1897.

GERMANY

In 1961 the Deutsche Staatsbibliothek (formerly the Preussische Staatsbibliothek) celebrated the three-hundredth anniversary of its foundation: in honour of the occasion two handsome volumes were published, entitled:

> *Deutsche Staatsbibliothek 1661–1961.* VEB Verlag für Buch- und Bibliothekswesen, Leipzig. I. Geschichte und Gegenwart. II. Bibliographie.

The first volume contains an article by Guido Auster, formerly Director of the Oriental Department, on 'Die Orientalische Abteilung', in which are traced the early history of the collections and the foundation of the Department: this was formed in 1918 through the separation of the Oriental MSS. from the Manuscript Department and the merging with it of the Oriental printed books. The manuscript collections, with the catalogues produced for them, and the various collections of printed books are then described, together with the Oriental Reading Room and its contents and the administration of the Department. The greater part of the Oriental manuscripts, which were sent away for safe keeping during the Second World War, have not yet been returned to Berlin: as the Staatsbibliothek found itself after the war in the Eastern Zone and the places of deposit were in West Germany, these manuscripts remain in the Westdeutsche Bibliothek in Marburg and in the

University Library in Tübingen. Ninety-eight MSS. must be regarded as having disappeared without trace.

The second volume (pp. 116–20) furnishes the bibliography relevant to this article, including a list of the catalogues. The works included are arranged in chronological order, and references to the main collections acquired at various dates are fitted into the same chronological scheme.

The library of the German Oriental Society (Deutsche Morgenländische Gesellschaft) in Halle (now East Germany) published a catalogue, the second edition of which appeared in 1900. It contains a section for the manuscripts owned by the Society and is therefore still of more than mere antiquarian interest.

The *Denkschrift zur Lage der Orientalistik*, like the Hayter Report, devotes some space to the subject of libraries. The two most substantial collections in Western Germany are those incorporated in the Bayerische Staatsbibliothek in Munich (BSM, founded 1558) and the Westdeutsche Bibliothek in Marburg, which has recently changed its name to Staatsbibliothek der Stiftung preussischer Kulturbesitz Marburg und Berlin (SPK). BSM possesses more than 3,500 manuscripts in Oriental languages, SPK more than 6,800, while a further 14,500 volumes, now in the University Library at Tübingen are destined to be added to the latter's collection. BSM's collection of Oriental printed books numbers 80,000, SPK's 60,000: the two libraries collect all literature relating to the Orient (SPK's collection numbers 40,000 volumes) and each has a special Oriental Reading Room. The Oriental reference collection ('Handbibliothek') of the former Preussische Staatsbibliothek is preserved intact in SPK and is kept up to date. A catalogue of this collection was published in 1929:

> Preussische Staatsbibliothek. *Katalog der Handbibliothek der Orientalischen Abteilung*. Leipzig, 1929.

Important collections of Oriental manuscripts and printed books exist in the university libraries of Göttingen, Tübingen, Hamburg, Frankfurt a. M., Bonn, Erlangen, Mainz and Marburg; in the Landes- und Hochschulbibliothek Darmstadt, the Badische Landesbibliothek in Stuttgart; while some manuscripts are to be found in the libraries of the academies of Göttingen, Heidelberg and Mainz.

Mention is made of a subject specialization scheme, by which some libraries have agreed to collect assiduously in certain subjects, viz.:

> SPK – General Oriental studies, Central Asia (Tibet, Mongolia), East and South-East Asia including Indonesia, Polynesia, Melanesia and Micronesia.

Tübingen – Assyriology and related subjects, Semitics, Islamic studies including Turkey, Armenia and the peoples of the Caucasus, Indology.

Frankfurt a. M. – Judaica, Hebraica, Aboriginal languages (Eingeborenensprachen), Colonial studies.

The *Denkschrift* declares it to be of the utmost importance that BSM and SPK should be empowered to collect all Oriental books required for teaching and research, and all writings on the East. University libraries are recommended to co-ordinate their purchases with those of the Seminar or Institute libraries.[1] A series of folding plates in the *Denkschrift*, one for each of the universities surveyed, gives estimates in round figures for the collections in both of these types of library.

A central union catalogue for Oriental books is maintained in two copies in Germany, the University Library in Mainz and the Deutsche Staatsbibliothek in Berlin. This records additions in Asian and North African languages made to the collections of twelve libraries in East and West Germany since 1959, and in March, 1965 contained some 11,000 cards.

OTHER EUROPEAN COUNTRIES

Some information on Oriental collections in the national libraries of European (and extra-European) countries may be gleaned from Esdaile's *National libraries of the world* (2nd ed. by F. J. Hill, London, 1957). Oriental collections are specifically mentioned in the chapters dealing with libraries in the following places:

Aberystwyth, p. 39, Books on Hebrew and other Semitic literature, bequeathed by Professor Witton Davies.

Copenhagen, pp. 208–10, 150 MSS. in Hebrew, Arabic, Persian, in the Niebuhr collection; Rask collection of 150 Pali, Sanskrit, Sinhalese MSS.; Hebrew and Judaic collections (Simonsen, Goldschmidt – 40 Hebrew incunabula); complete set of books printed in Ethiopic from 1513 to the twentieth century; Tibetan MSS.; Mongolian collection; Tibetan Kanjur.

Madrid, pp. 192–93, 197 Turkish, Arabian and Armenian works from the library which Antonio Lopez de Cordova collected in Constantinople, 1869; Hebrew and Arabic MSS.

[1] The traditional pattern in German universities is for each chair to have a seminar or institute associated with it, with a reference library attached.

Oslo, p. 220, Far East collection (Chinese and Japanese MSS. and block prints; Narthang Kanjur and Derge Tanjur; Sørensen collection of Tibetan texts, with other MSS. and block prints; 150 Mongolian and Manchu works; palm-leaf MSS. in Indian and Indonesian languages).

Sofia, p. 271, MSS. relating to the period of Turkish rule in Bulgaria; Turkish archives; printed books, mainly Turkish and Arabic, from eighteenth and nineteenth centuries.

Stockholm, pp. 225–27, Nordenskiöld collection of Japonica; Chinese MSS. acquired by Sven Hedin.

Turin, p. 183, Volperga collection of Hebrew books.

Vienna, pp. 80, 82–83, Oriental and Hebrew MSS. of S. Tengnagel (Librarian 1608–36), foundation of the Oriental collection; collection of Joseph von Hammer-Purastall: MSS. of Eduard Glaser; papyri added under the prefectship of Joseph Karabaček.

The Library of the Hungarian Academy of Sciences at Budapest contains in its Oriental Department the following collections: Tibetan MSS. of Sándor Körösi Csoma, Turkish MSS. given by Armin Vámbéry, the David Kaufmann collection of Hebrew books and MSS., Sándor Kegl's library of Persian and Sanskrit books, the private library of Aurel Stein, reliquia of Sándor Körösi Csoma, and the scientific correspondence of Ignác Goldziher, amounting to more than 10,000 items.

Switzerland has a union catalogue of Judaica and Hebraica, known as the 'Zentralkatalog der Judaica und Hebraica in Schweizer Bibliotheken. It is housed at the Israelitische Cultusgemeinde, Lavaterstr. 33, Zürich; in 1961 it contained 30,000 titles.

15

Asia

The *UNESCO Statistical yearbook* for 1963 gives, in the three tables numbered 23–25, particulars of libraries of all types in a large number of countries. Table 23 gives the number of libraries and the estimated quantity of the holdings in the categories of national, university, school, special and public libraries for 30 countries in Asia, and 11 in Oceania (including Australia and New Zealand). In Table 24 are given figures for circulation (loans) and readers in national and university libraries for 23 Asian and 4 Oceanic countries, and in Table 25 similar figures for public libraries in 25 Asian and 11 Oceanic countries. The statistics relate in the main to the year 1960, but those for 1953 or a year around that time are also given whenever possible to indicate rate of growth.

THE MIDDLE EAST

Joseph A. Dagher, formerly a Conservateur at the National Library of the Lebanon in Beirut, published in 1951 a list of libraries in the Near and Middle East, for which he had been collecting information for over ten years:

> *Répertoire des bibliothèques du Proche et du Moyen-Orient.* Préparé par Joseph A. Dagher. Paris, 1951.

The regions covered are Aden (1), Arabia (Saudi) (7), Egypt (55), Iraq (9), Israel (41), Jerusalem (17), Lebanon (29), Persia (11), Syria (14), Turkey (72), and Yemen (1), the numbers in brackets indicating the entries for each region, which total 259. Of these 259 entries, some refer to a clutch of small or less important libraries, i.e. item 72, 'Bibliothèques Mineures d'Irak', mentions eight private libraries and gives bibliographical references for many other libraries in Baghdad, Najaf, and other towns, and item 159 mentions twelve smaller libraries in the

Lebanon. Many others are mentioned in bibliographies attached to the sections on Egypt (p. 38) and Iraq (p. 43). Included in the information given for each library is the general character of the collections, the number of printed books and manuscripts, and the catalogues, printed and unprinted, of these collections. Details of administration and organization are also supplied.

See also my review of this book in *Bull. S.O.A.S.* 16, 1, 1954, p. 190.

TURKEY

İstanbul kütüphaneleri ve yazma tıp kitapları. Libraries of Istanbul and their medical manuscripts. Muzaffer Gökman. (İstanbul Üniversitesi Tıp Tarihi Enstitüsü Neşriyatından Sayı: 56.) İstanbul Matbaası, 1959.

This is the fifth edition of this very useful booklet. Istanbul abounds in libraries, most of which possess valuable collections of rare manuscripts in the languages of Islam (Arabic, Persian and Turkish). There are thirty-two independent libraries, and others located in mosques, medresses and palaces. Since the First World War many of these have been merged with other libraries, so that today the number of general libraries and special historical libraries in the city is thirteen. Gökman gives the addresses of eighteen libraries, the number of manuscripts and printed books in their collections (135,328 MSS., 539,120 printed books), the present location of the various libraries, and a list of the numbers or shelf-marks of the medical manuscripts in the various libraries (3,604 works in 2,796 volumes).

ISRAEL

The Hebrew University of Jerusalem, 1963. (Jewish National and University Library, pp. 199–222.)

The Jewish National and University Library. Report on the activities in the year 1961. Dr Curt Wormann, Director. February, 1962.

The National Library of Israel is combined with that of the Hebrew University and the joint library is known as the Jewish National and University Library. The Library issues a quarterly journal known as *Kirjath Sepher*, which serves as the Israel national bibliography, as it regularly lists Israel imprints. In addition, each issue contains lists of Judaica and Hebraica published abroad, and of articles on Jewish and Hebrew subjects published in scholarly journals. Articles are also published on Hebrew printing and other bibliographical subjects, as well as on important items in the Library's collections. The Institute for Hebrew Bibliography, which has embarked upon a project to compile a bibliography of all books printed in Hebrew characters from 1475 to 1959/60, is housed in the Library, as is the Institute of Microfilms of Hebrew Manuscripts.

The report for 1961 shows that nearly 57,000 books and periodicals were added to the Library. The number of Hebrew manuscripts was 5,119, of which 289 were in non-Hebrew characters. The contemplated Hebrew bibliography is estimated to run to twelve or thirteen volumes, of which two or three will be given up to detailed indexes. Accessions to the Oriental (i.e. presumably non-Hebrew) Department were 696 books and 2,287 periodicals. The report mentions that a survey of Israel's libraries was prepared for the Bureau of Statistics of UNESCO.

INDIA, PAKISTAN, BURMA, CEYLON

Indian library directory. S. R. Ranganathan, S. Das Gupta, Magnanand. Edition 3. Indian Library Association, Delhi, 1951. [Edition 1 was published in 1938, edition 2 in 1944, both under the title *Directory of Indian libraries*.]

New India directory of libraries and educational institutions. New Book Society of India, New Delhi [1955]. [Reprint of the sections containing alphabetical lists of the libraries in India, Pakistan, Burma and Ceylon, and alphabetical lists of universities and colleges in the same four countries, from *Indian book trade & library directory 1950–51*.]

Directory of special and research libraries in India. Compiled by IASLIC. Calcutta: Indian Association of Special Libraries & Information Centres, 1962.

Baroda and its libraries, by Newton Mohun Dutt. Baroda, Central Library, 1928.

The Indian library directory gives a list of 363 libraries with book stocks of at least 5,000 volumes, except that the libraries of government departments are included whatever the size of their book stocks. For each library a good deal of miscellaneous information is given in tabular form and the list is rearranged so as to provide an index to the libraries by type and by geographical location. Other features included are descriptions of nine library associations and of ten courses in library service provided by universities and other organizations, a classified list of library literature produced in India, and biographical data on members of the library profession in India. It is estimated that a third of the total number of libraries is not included because they did not return questionnaires sent to them.

The New India directory is a bare inventory of libraries in India, Pakistan, Burma and Ceylon, giving names and addresses only. No figures are given, but the number for India probably amounts to 5,400, that for Pakistan to about 130, while Burma has 5 and Ceylon 19.

The *IASLIC Directory* gives information about 173 special and research libraries, that is, libraries which specialize in a particular subject and those academic libraries which possess sufficient source materials for research as well as those belonging to research and learned bodies. Questionnaires were sent out to more than 500 libraries in all, and the work also contains a list of other libraries with specialized collections, with no further information given, these being, presumably, the libraries which did not respond to the questionnaire. We are given in every case, the subjects covered, the resources in books, periodicals, manuscripts, and other library materials and a good deal of other useful information. In fact it may well have been the complexity of the questionnaire that deterred so many libraries from replying to it.

Baroda and its libraries was written to provide a souvenir for visitors to the Baroda Library, a handbook for the staff of the Library and for librarians, educationists and social workers in general, and a record of the achievements of the previous seventeen years in the provision of free public libraries and newspaper reading rooms in town and village in the state. It contains a chapter on the Oriental Institute, formerly the Sanskrit section of the Central Library, lists of periodicals in Baroda institutions, and (in the advertisement pages) a list of the Sanskrit works edited by scholars and published in the Gaekwad's Oriental Series.

NATIONAL LIBRARY OF INDIA, CALCUTTA

The former Librarian of the National Library of India, B. S. Kesavan, published a description of the library (*India's National Library*. Calcutta, 1961). The first four chapters give an account of the history and growth of the library and a prognostication of its future, and describe its printed catalogues, the services it provides and its administrative set-up. Chapter 5, which deals with the technical divisions of the library, lists the numbers of publications received by language and state in which published for the years 1958–59, 1959–60 and 1960–61 (up to February, 1961) as legal deposits under the provision of the Delivery of books

(Public libraries) Act, 1954 and furnishes a statement of the total number of printed books and manuscripts in Arabic, Persian and Urdu in the Buhar Library and other collections under the charge of this Division.

The Indian language collections are described in chapter 6: these comprise 103,041 items in thirteen languages. For each of these languages the total number of books is given and rare and valuable works described.

In chapter 7 is given a survey of the major gift collections, including those named after their donors, Asutosh, Ramdas Sen, Dr Barid Baran Mukherji, Sir Jadunath Sarkar, Dr S. N. Sen, Professor Vaiyapuri Pillai and the Sapru papers.

Chapter 8 is concerned with the *Indian National Bibliography* and the Division responsible for compiling it. Here we may find useful statistics by language and subject of the books and government publications included in the annual volumes of the *I.N.B.*

Among the Appendices are listed the fifty-six sections of a proposed bibliography of Indology, and a list of the sixty publications issued by the library and in the press. The total contents of the library are stated to be 1,007,298 books.

A Guide to Pakistan libraries, learned and scientific societies and educational institutions, biographies of librarians in Pakistan. Revised edition. (Pakistan Bibliographical Working Group Publication no. 3.) Karachi, 1960.

This Pakistan list includes some 250 libraries arranged by type (national, public, university, college, government, learned and scientific societies), giving a good deal of information for each. A who's who of librarians in Pakistan is also provided.

The history of libraries in Ceylon was the subject of a thesis submitted for Part II of the Diploma in Librarianship in the University of London:

T. G. Piyadasa: *The Origin and history of libraries in Ceylon.* 1964.

THE FAR EAST

HONG KONG

Libraries in Hong Kong; a directory compiled by Kan Lai-bing. Hong Kong Library Association, 1963.

For Hong Kong we have an alphabetical list of 215 libraries, with a classified list arranged by type of library, and the names of members of the Hong Kong Library Association.

FORMOSA

University and college libraries in Taiwan: 1961 directory. (Prepared by Yung-hsiang Lai, National Taiwan University Library, Taipei, Taiwan, for the *Bulletin of the Library Association of China*, no. 13, 10 December, 1961.)[1]

CHINA

Libraries in China; papers prepared on the occasion of the tenth anniversary of the Library Association of China. Peiping, Library Association of China, 1935.[2]

JAPAN

Libraries in Japan. Edited by J. L. A. 2nd edition. Japan Library Association, Tokyo, 1958.[3]

LIST OF LIBRARY ASSOCIATIONS IN ASIA AND THEIR PUBLICATIONS

The list which follows has been compiled from a large number of sources which it would be tedious to mention here. It is probably not complete.

Burma Library Association.

Ceylon Library Association. Publ. *Journal.*

Library Association of China.

Egyptian Library Association (founded 1946). Publ. *Proceedings* (in English and Arabic). (The Cairo Library Association issued *Proceedings*, 1950–53.)

Hong Kong Library Association, c/o University Library, University of Hong Kong.

[1] Details of 10 university, 5 college, and 9 junior college libraries in Taiwan are given in a 'directory' published in 1961.

[2] There is little information available in Western languages about libraries in Mainland China. The volume noted above contains a collection of nine essays by Chinese librarians, now somewhat outmoded through the march of political events, dealing with the modern library movement in China, with problems of classification and cataloguing, professional training of librarians, library legislation, co-operation between libraries in that country, and descriptions of libraries of the national, provincial, medical and public types.

[3] The Japanese library's pamphlet sketches the history of Japanese libraries, their present situation and problems, and providing much other useful information, in a rather quaint form of English.

India

IASLIC (Indian Association of Special Libraries and Information Centres, c/o Geological Survey of India, Calcutta, 1. Publ. *Iaslic Bulletin*, quarterly.

Indian Library Association, c/o The Ramakrishna Mission.

Institute of Culture, Gol Park, Calcutta, 29. Publ. *Journal of the Indian Library Association*, bi-monthly.

Andhra Pradesh Library Association, Hyderabad.

Bengal Library Association, c/o Central Library, Calcutta University, Calcutta.

Delhi Library Association, c/o Marwari Public Library, Chandni Chowk, Delhi. Publ. *Library Herald*, quarterly.

Kerala Library Association, Calicut.

Kerala Granthalya Sangam, Trivandrum.

Madras Library Association, 32 Sami Pillai Street, Triplicane, Madras, 5. Publ. *Annual Report*.

Madya Pradesh Library Association, Bhopal.

Maharashtra Library Association, Poona.

Panjab Library Association, c/o Panjab University Library, Chandigarh, Panjab.

Rajasthan Library Association.

Uttar Pradesh Library Association, c/o Banaras Hindu University Library, Varanasi, U.P.

Iran Association of Librarians (founded 1962). (The University of Teheran has set up a Bibliographical research centre, whose functions, as set out in *Bibl. doc. term.* 4, 1 January, 1964, pp. 9–10, include the preparation of bibliographies and catalogues and the supply of information to all organizations and individuals.)

Israel Library Association. (Histadrut ha-Pekidim ha-Ivrim be-Israel.) Publ. *Yad la-koré* (in Hebrew, with English summaries of important articles).

Japan Library Association, c/o Ueno Library, Ueno Park, Tokyo. Publ. *Toshokan zasshi*.

Korean Library Association, Sogong-dong 6, Seoul. (The Korean Bibliographical Society shares this address.)

The Lebanese Library Association, National Library of Lebanon, Beirut. Publ. *Official journal* (annual).

Persatuan Perpustakaan Malaysia (Library Association of Malaysia). Formed in 1964 by merger of the Library Association of Malaya and Singapore. Publ. *Perpustakaan Malaysia*, formerly the *Malayan*

Library Journal and the *Majallah Perpustakaan Singapura/Singapore Library Journal.*

Pakistan Library Association, Dacca University Library, Dacca, 2. Publ. *Quarterly journal.* (There is also a Pakistan Bibliographical Working Group, P.O. Box 534, Karachi, 1, which has several bibliographies and directories to its credit.)

Pakistan Association of Special Libraries, F. 35/7 Federal Capital Area, Karachi, 19.

East Pakistan Library Association, c/o Dacca University Library, Dacca, 2.

The Bibliographical Society of the Philippines, c/o Unesco National Commission of the Philippines, 1580 Taft Avenue, Manila.

Philippine Library Association.

Association of Special Libraries of the Philippines. (Described in *UNESCO Bull. for Libraries*, 16, 9, March–April, 1962, pp. 90–92.) Publ. *ASLP Bulletin.*

Türk Kütüphaneciler Derneği (Association of Turkish libraries). P.K. 175, Yenişehir, Ankara. Publ. *Türk Kütüphaneciler Derneği Bülteni.*

The Asian Federation of Library Associations was formed at an inaugural conference held in Tokyo in November, 1957. For a description of the events which led to its formation, and for its agreed constitution, see 'The Asian Federation of Library Associations' by M. Siddiq Khan, *Library Association record*, 60 (1958), pp. 123–25.

16

Special problems affecting Orientalist Libraries

The special problems with which the custodian of an Orientalist library has to grapple are threefold: those of acquisition of books, processing, and appointment of personnel competent to handle the books.

ACQUISITION OF BOOKS

Without books a library cannot exist. The first problem, therefore, is to obtain the necessary books. These will be published in most of the fifty-four countries of Asia, the fifty-six countries of Africa, many of the islands of Oceania, and in practically all of the countries of Europe, North America and Australasia. Even the Orientalist production of Latin America can no longer be regarded as negligible.

How much is being published at the present day which provides information on Asia, Africa and Oceania, the scholarly writing and imaginative belles-lettres that the student of these regions and the library providing for his needs will wish to obtain and hold available? And how much does this cost? These are questions which were investigated at S.O.A.S. in the summer of 1964. The number of useful and significant books and pamphlets and periodicals published in a single year and the estimated cost of obtaining one copy of each of the monographic publications is shown in Table I.

The figures given in the table are at best only very rough approximations, especially for countries in Asia, Africa and Oceania, where few regularly published national bibliographies are available, and other sources of information, sometimes quite unreliable, have had to be used. It may be of some value to readers of this book to list here the printed sources that were used in making the survey, together with a note of the period of time on which the statistics are based whenever figures for a complete year were not available.

TABLE I

Place of publication	Number of useful Books and pamphlets	Cost £	Estimated Number of Periodicals published
Near and Middle East	1,750	800	250
South Asia	3,300	1,500	8,750
South-East Asia	900	500	1,450
Far East	4,600	3,600	6,200
Africa	2,750	1,350	1,350
Europe	2,400	3,400	
America, Australasia, etc.	600	1,350	

Total 12,500

AFRICA

ANGOLA: *Boletim de Bibliografia Portuguesa.*

CAMEROUN: *UNO Statistical Yearbook, 1963.*

CAPE VERDE ISLANDS: *Boletim de Bibliografia Portuguesa.*

COMORO ARCHIPELAGO: *Biblio.*

EGYPT: Library of Congress Public Law 480 Project (Middle East) *Accessions-lists.*

ETHIOPIA: *UNO Statistical Yearbook, 1963.*

GAMBIA: Colonial Office Library's *Monthly List of Official Colonial Publications.*

GHANA: Commercial: List of books on legal deposit in the Commercial and Industrial Bulletin Supplement to the *Ghana Gazette; Official*: Publications price-list of the Government Printer. 3 months.

HIGH COMMISSION TERRITORIES: *Monthly List of Official Colonial Publications.*

IFNI: *El Libro Español.*

KENYA: *Commercial: UNO Statistical Yearbook,* 1963 and Accessions-lists of the Library of Makerere College; *Official:* Accessions-lists of the Library of Makerere College.

LIBERIA: *Basic Facts and Figures* (Unesco, 1961).

LIBYA: Estimates supplied by Mr Philip Ward, co-ordinator of the Library Services Division of the Oasis Oil Company of Libya, Inc.

MALAWI: *Commercial:* 'List of Publications deposited in the Library of the National Archives, 1961'; *Official: Monthly List of Official Colonial Publications.*

MAURITIUS: *Colony of Mauritius – Annual Report on the Archives Department for the year 1962.*

MOROCCO: *UNO Statistical Yearbook,* 1963.

MOZAMBIQUE: *Boletim de Bibliografia Portuguesa.*

NIGERIA: *Nigeria Publications,* 1962.

PORTUGUESE GUINEA: *Boletim de Bibliografia Portuguesa.*

REUNION: *Biblio.*

SOUTHERN RHODESIA: *List of Publications deposited in the Library of the National Archives,* 1961.

RWANDA: *UNO Statistical Yearbook,* 1963.

ST. HELENA: *Monthly List of Official Colonial Publications.*

SÃO TOME AND PRINCIPE: *Boletim de Bibliografia Portuguesa.*

SENEGAL: *UNO Statistical Yearbook,* 1963.

SEYCHELLES: *Monthly List of Official Colonial Publications.*

SIERRA LEONE: *List of Sierra Leone Publications received by the Sierra Leone Library Board.*

SOUTH AFRICA: *Africana Nova.*

SOUTH-WEST AFRICA: *Africana Nova.*

SPANISH GUINEA: *El Libro Español.*

SPANISH SAHARA: *El Libro Español.*

SUDAN: Information received from Mr A. R. Nasri, Librarian, University of Khartoum.

TANGANYIKA: *Commercial:* Accessions-lists of University College, Dar-es-Salaam; 6 months. *Official:* Accessions-lists of Makerere College.

TUNISIA: List of Tunisian publications supplied by M. Mohammed al-Zlaoui, Administrateur de la Bibliothèque Nationale de Tunisie.

UGANDA: *Commercial:* Makerere College Accessions-lists. *Official:* Uganda Gazette and Makerere College Accessions-lists.

ZAMBIA: *Commercial:* Publications Bureau of Northern Rhodesia's lists in *African Education: Annual Summary for 1962. Official: List of Government Publications,* 1963.

ZANZIBAR: *UNO Statistical Yearbook,* 1963, and Accessions-lists of the Library of Makerere College.

MIDDLE EAST

ADEN: *Monthly List of Official Colonial Publications.*

CYPRUS: *Kypriake Bibliografia.*

Q

IRAN: *Rahnema-yi Ketab. Monthly Journal of the Book Society.* 10 months.
IRAQ: *Al-Kutub al-matbūaʻh fiʼl-ʻIraq liʻām 1963.*
ISRAEL: *Kirjath Sepher.*
LEBANON: List of Lebanese publications of 1963 supplied by Sophia Grotzfeld, Münster.
SAUDI ARABIA: Estimates supplied by Mr Mohammed Amin al-Tamimi, Director-General of Libraries for the Saudi-Arabian government: *UNO Statistical Yearbook, 1963.*
TURKEY: *Türkiye Bibliografyası.*

SOUTH ASIA

CEYLON: *Ceylon National Bibliography.* 3 months.
INDIA: *Indian National Bibliography.*
PAKISTAN: Library of Congress Public Law 480 Project Accessions-lists (Pakistan). 9 months.

SOUTH-EAST ASIA

BRUNEI: *Monthly List of Official Colonial Publications.*
BURMA: *Commercial: Sa-ok Io-ka* World of Books. 3 months. *Official: Monthly List of Government Publications.* 2 months.
CAMBODIA: *UNO Statistical Yearbook, 1963.*
INDONESIA: *Berita Bulanan dari Kantor Bibliografi National.* 11 months.
MALAYA: *Malayan Government Gazette; Malaysian Government Gazette.* 9 months.
SINGAPORE: *Singapore Government Gazette.*
NORTH BORNEO: *Monthly List of Official Colonial Publications.*
SARAWAK: *Monthly List of Official Colonial Publications.*
PAPUA NEW GUINEA: *Australian National Bibliography.*
PHILIPPINES: Information supplied by Mr Severino I. Velasco, Acting Director of the Bureau of Public Libraries, Manila.
THAILAND: *UNO Statistical Yearbook, 1963.*
PORTUGUESE TIMOR: *Boletim de Bibliografia Portuguesa.*
SOUTH VIETNAM: *UNO Statistical Yearbook. 1963.*

FAR EAST

CHINA (PEOPLE'S REPUBLIC): *Chʼüan-kuo hsin shu-nan.*
CHINA (TAIWAN): *Monthly List of Chinese Books (Select Bibliography).* Total figures supplied by the National Central Library of Taiwan.

HONG KONG: Commercial: *Hong Kong Government Gazette*. Official: *Monthly List of Official Colonial Publications*.

JAPAN: Commercial: *Shuppan Nenkan/Japanese Publications Yearbook*. Official: *Zen Nihon Shuppan – Butsu Sō. Mokuroku*.

MONGOLIA: 'Books to be published in 1962 by the Academy of Sciences of the Mongolian People's Republic.' *Mongolia Society Newsletter*, Fall, 1962.

NORTH KOREA: *Korean Books*.

SOUTH KOREA: *Korean Publications Yearbook*.

MACAO: *Boletim de Bibliografia Portuguesa*.

SOVIET ASIA: *Noviye Knigi*.

OCEANIA

FIJI: *Monthly List of Official Colonial Publications*.
GILBERT AND ELLICE ISLANDS: *Monthly List of Official Colonial Publications*.
NEW HEBRIDES: *Monthly List of Official Colonial Publications*.
PITCAIRN ISLAND: *Monthly List of Official Colonial Publications*.
SOLOMON ISLANDS: *Monthly List of Official Colonial Publications*.
TONGA: *Monthly List of Official Colonial Publications*.

EUROPE

ANDORA: *Biblio; El Libro Español*.
AUSTRIA: *Österreichische Bibliographie*.
BELGIUM: *Bibliographie de Belgique*.
BULGARIA: *Bulgarski Knigi*.
CZECHOSLOVAKIA: *České Knihy; Slovenské Knihy*.
DENMARK: *Dansk Bogfortegnelse*.
FINLAND: *Suomessa Ilmestyneen Kirjallisuuden Vuosiluettelo*.
FRANCE: *Biblio*.
GERMANY (E.): *Deutsche Nationalbibliographie*.
GERMANY (W.): *Deutsche Nationalbibliographie*.
GREECE: *Greek Bibliography*. 6 months.
HOLLAND: *Brinkmans Catalogus van Boeken*.
HUNGARY: *Magyar Szerzök Ázsiáról és Afrikáról, 1950–62*. (Hungarian Publications on Asia and Africa, 1950–62. A selected bibliography.)
ICELAND: *Árbók (Landsbókasafn Íslands)*.
ITALY: *Bibliografia Nazionale Italiana*.

LUXEMBURG: *Bibliographie Luxembourgeoise.*

MONACO: *Biblio.*

NORWAY: *Norsk Bokfortegnelse.*

POLAND: *Quarterly Review of Scientific Publications* (Polish Academy of Sciences Distribution Centre for Scientific Publications.)

PORTUGAL: *Boletim de Bibliografia Portuguesa.*

RUMANIA: *Bibliografia Republicii Populare Romíne.*

SPAIN: *El Libro Español.*

SWEDEN: *Svensk Bokförteckning.*

SWITZERLAND: *Der Schweizer Buchhandel.*

U.S.S.R.: *Noviye Knigi.*

UNITED KINGDOM AND EIRE: *British National Bibliography.*

YUGOSLAVIA: *Bibliografija Jugoslavije.*

OTHER COUNTRIES

AUSTRALIA: *Australian National Bibliography.*

BRAZIL: *Boletim international de bibliografia luso-brasiliera.*

CANADA: *United States and Canadian publications on Africa, 1960.*

LATIN AMERICA: *Fichero bibliográfico hispano-Americano.*

NEW ZEALAND: *Copyright publications, 1963.*

U.S.A.: *American Book Publishing Record.*

Some information on trends in scholarly publishing and the difficulties faced by academic publishers in Asia may be found in the following volume, which resulted from a conference held in Honolulu:

Trans-Pacific scholarly publishing; a symposium. Thomas Nickerson, editor. University of Hawaii Press, East West Center Press, 1963.

But the difficulty of discovering what is being published is not all, even when the necessary funds are at the librarian's disposal. There remains the problem of obtaining the material. In the developing countries of Asia and Africa, the business of bookselling is often at a rudimentary stage. Few practitioners of this art are organized to send books overseas, or are able to wait for the inevitably long periods necessary to receive payment for these books, even when this can be done without direct government prohibition or discouragement and in the absence of undue formalities required by those who control international trade. A list of booksellers in developing countries who have been found most satisfactory in dealings with American libraries has been published by Philip J. McNiff:[1] a British counterpart to this list, so far as Asia is concerned, has been compiled by K. B. Gardner. This latter list is printed as an Appendix to this book. Procedures that have been devised and adopted by American librarians in seeking to overcome difficulties of book supply, such as the blanket order, the book-buying tour, the Farmington Plan and Public Law 480 Book Acquisition Program are described in the section dealing with American libraries.

PROCESSING

But if the difficulties and as a consequence the cost of book acquisition work is so much greater for the Orientalist librarian than for those only concerned with areas where Western languages only are spoken, the cost of 'processing' the material when it is received is also much greater by comparison. The S.O.A.S. Library estimated in 1964 that the average cost per book of all the processes through which a book has to pass after it is received in the Library until such time as it finds a permanent home on the shelves, and an entry in the catalogue, was 16s. 7½d. This figure takes no account of money which may have to be spent on binding the book, a form of protection required by perhaps 25 per cent of the books received from Asia and Africa.

This high cost of cataloguing and other processes is directly attributable to the use in Oriental languages of scripts other than the Roman. (The only Asian languages which habitually employ the Roman script are Turkish – since 1928 – Malay to some extent, Indonesian and the Philippine languages.) This factor necessitates the employment of an expert in a rare field, and leads to the necessity for transliterating the script if entries for these titles are to be incorporated in the general catalogue with all the entries for works in European languages. Some libraries try to overcome these difficulties by using separate catalogues for each of the languages using a non-Roman script, arranging the entries in them in accordance with the alphabetical or other rules of arrangement appropriate to the language in question. The principal disadvantage of this system is that translations of an author's works, and biographies and criticisms of his work in other

---

[1] *A list of book dealers in underdeveloped countries.* Compiled by Philip J. McNiff for the Policy and Research Committee of the Acquisitions Section, Resources and Technical Services Section, American Library Association, 1963.

languages, do not appear together with the works in the original language.

So that if it is wished to support the Lubetzky canon of arrangement of all the works by or about a given author together in one place, it becomes essential to transliterate the titles from a non-Roman script. Transliteration, like classification, is an art to which the Latin tag 'Quot homines tot sententiae' might well apply. Every scholar thinks that to show himself worthy of his salt he must devise a system better than any other system already in use. Agreement to use a standard system thus becomes extremely difficult to reach, even on a national plane, and how much more so on an international one?

The main difficulty in this very inexact science stems from the fact that most, if not all, languages employ symbols for phonemes which have no exact counterpart in the language of the transliterator, and an approximation has to be made using the symbols available in the language of the reader. Thus the Arabic *jīm* has its exact counterpart in the English j, but not in the French j, which is pronounced differently, and is a sound completely unknown to German speakers. So that whereas an Englishman might write the name of the Umayyad viceroy as Hajjaj, a Frenchman might write Hadjdjadj, a German Hadschdschadsch, and a Russian Khadzhdzhadzh (this last form a palimpsest transliteration).

Another difficulty is caused by the practice of the Northern Semitic languages (especially Hebrew and Arabic) of not indicating vowel signs. These signs, when they are written, are placed above or below the consonant to which they are attached, but in most cases, other than in printing the Old Testament in Hebrew and the Koran in Arabic, they are totally omitted. Although the structure of these languages is such that no insuperable difficulty results from this omission in reading an ordinary printed text, it does mean that frequently one can only tell from inside information whether a name is pronounced, say, 'Ashsh or Ushsh'. Yet another difficulty arises from the fact that names may be written exactly the same in different languages or dialects using the same script, but pronounced differently. This means that the decision has to be taken whether to transcribe the characters one by one into Roman alphabetical symbols chosen from a standard list, or to indicate the pronunciation of the word by writing it in Roman characters which as nearly as possible indicate the original pronunciation.

In a scientific treatise or a library catalogue the former method may be appropriate, in a work designed for popular consumption the latter.

But when an author transliterates his own name in a way which suits him best (assuming that, which is not invariably the case, that he is consistent in his choice), it is obviously desirable to prefer the spelling adopted by him.

All of these problems of transliteration have been under consideration for some years now by the Orientalia Processing Committee of the Library of Congress, which has devised transliteration systems for several languages. These systems have gained the approval of the American Library Association and have been adopted by many libraries with Asian collections.

NAMES

Much difficulty is also caused the cataloguer by the many varied styles of nomenclature used by Asian peoples. In many of these countries family names or surnames are still not the common practice, and personal names may be compounded of many diverse parts. Again, in some parts of India 'house names' and caste names exist, and Arabic names take on modified and sometimes unfamiliar forms the further eastward they occur. But this problem was considered in detail by the International Conference on Cataloguing Principles held in Paris in 1961 and much useful information on this topic may be extracted from the Conference *Report*, published in 1963. It contains reports of sectional group meetings which were held to consider Arabic, Indonesian and Malayan names; Hebrew names; Indic names of persons (non-Muslim); Iranian names; and Muslim names in India and Pakistan. The paper on Malayan names presented on behalf of the Library Association of Singapore was published in an expanded version by Kho Lian Tie in the *Singapore Library Journal (Majallah Perpustakaan Singapura)*, vol. 2, no. 1, April, 1962. The Report also contains the following working papers submitted to the Conference:

'Rendering of Indic names-of-person in catalogue entries, by Benoyendra Sengupta (pp. 255–65).

'Treatment of Arabic names, by Mahmūd Shenīti' (pp. 267–76).

'The treatment of names in Hebrew characters and title entry for Hebrew books, by R. Edelmann' (pp. 277–79).

For Arabic names, ancient and modern, Muslim and Christian, one may consult with profit two articles published by Daniel Eustache of the Bibliothèque Nationale.

'Catalogue d'imprimés ou de manuscrits arabes, choix de la vedette-auteur.' *Bulletin des bibliothèques de France* 3, 2, 1958, pp. 99–111 (ancient Muslim); 3, 9, 1958, pp. 619–28 (ancient Christian).

Although the second instalment of the article carries a note to the effect that it is to be continued, nothing has in fact appeared in the Bulletin since that time.

The Conference resolved on 'The publication with the minimum of delay of a statement of the practice approved in each country for the entry of the personal names of its nationals'. This statement was published under the following title:

International Conference on Cataloguing Principles (I.C.C.P.), 1961. *National usages for the entry of names of persons*. A survey by A. H. Chaplin. Provisional edition. Organizing Committee, I.C.C.P., c/o National Central Library, London, 1963.

This volume gives information on names in three main categories – elements normally forming part of a name, additional elements included in catalogue headings, and order of elements in catalogue headings – for a number of countries and language regions, viz. Arabic names, Burma, Ceylon, China, India, Indonesia, Iran, Israel, Japan, Korea, Malaya, Turkey, U.S.S.R. (Armenian, Georgian, Central Asian Republics and Kazakhstan, Azerbaijani) and Vietnam. It is, however, marred by a number of misprints and inexact transliterations which will no doubt be remedied in a future definitive edition.[1]

Perhaps the only other problem which afflicts the cataloguer of Asian books is caused by the use by many Asian countries and cultural regions of different systems of chronology, so that dates have to be translated into the equivalent Christian era dating. Calendars and systems of dating in the Near and Middle East, India and Pakistan, South-East Asia, China and Japan are explained in the *Handbook of Oriental history*, ed. C. H. Philips (1951), which gives also a comparative table for A. H.

---

[1] Other works on cataloguing that may usefully be consulted are:

Regeln für die alphabetische Katalogisierung von Druckschriften in den islamischen Sprachen (arabisch, persisch, türkisch). Auf Grund von Beratungen eines Gremiums von Fachbibliothekaren zusammengesteut von Ewald Wagner. Wiesbaden: Harrassowitz, 1961. (Reviewed in *Zentralblatt für Bibliothekswesen*, 76, 1962, pp. 25–27, by Irmgard Engelke.)

'The cataloging of Arabic books, by G. R. Tibbetts.' *Library Q.* 29 (1959), pp. 113–32.

Cataloging of Persian works, including rules for transliteration, entry and description, by Nasser Sharify. American Library Association, Chicago, 1959.

'Zur Titelaufnahme chinesischer Werke. Von Arthur Matthies.' *Zentralblatt für Bibliothekswesen*, 76, 1962, pp. 481–87.

(Anno Hegirae, the Islamic era) and A.D. dates. Not included in the Hand-book, however, is the Jewish or A.M. (Anno Mundi) system, which is frequently met with in imprints in older Hebrew books. Here the situation is even more complicated, as dates are often given in the form of a chronogram, a Biblical or other phrase in which the numerical value of the letters has to be computed.

Having catalogued the books, the librarian must now arrange these on the shelves in a way convenient to users of the library. Here a special problem is caused by Chinese books, which even to this day are sometimes published in a form requiring them to lie flat in a bundle on the shelves, the title of them being printed on the fore-edge of the individual fascicles constituting a book. Such books obviously have to be stored in a sequence separate from the books bound in European style, if economy in use of space is an important consideration, and when is it not, in a library?

It is common practice in a large general library with extensive collections of Orientalia for the books in Oriental languages (especially those in Chinese and Japanese) to be kept together in a special section, whatever the subject of the books. Books in Western languages, however, are classified in accordance with one of the well-known systems that have been devised for this purpose: of these probably the Library of Congress scheme makes the most satisfactory provisions for Orientalia collections, but none of them is entirely satisfactory for use by a specialist library. Some libraries, on the other hand, argue in favour of complete classification by subject, irrespective of language, on the grounds that separation of books dealing with the same subject on the basis of language (even when this is an Oriental one written in an unfamiliar cript) is arbitrary and offends against general philosophical principles. But there are many sound practical reasons why such a separation has much to commend it: those relatively few people who do read an Oriental language are best served by having all books in these languages kept together in a block irrespective of subject, and the great majority of people conversant only with European languages derive no advantage from finding individual volumes, or small blocks of volumes, interspersed among the books which they can read.

With the development of centres of area studies in many countries, where students of all academic disciplines are brought together into groups, there is much to be said for an arrangement of books by area rather than by subject. For in classification by subject borderline cases occur with great frequency, and very arbitrary decisions constantly have to be taken. As an example of this, it may be mentioned that in the Library of Congress the five journals used by every devotee of Islamic studies are classified in four different places. And even in universities where no centres of area studies have been established, many of the academic staff holding posts in a discipline such as law, economics, sociology, ethnology, linguistics, literature, history, geography and many more tend to spend most of their time concentrating on a particular area rather than being engaged in comparative studies.

This separation by Oriental language, and primary classification by area or country has been adopted to a very large extent by S.O.A.S., as already briefly mentioned above, but even here it has been found desirable purely for practical reasons, to make exceptions in the cases of art and law. In these two fields, at any rate in S.O.A.S., lawyers and art historians tend to be comparatists rather than regionalists.

RECRUITMENT OF STAFF

We have left until the last consideration of what is probably the greatest problem of all, that of recruiting competent expert staff. Few people combine competence in an Oriental language with training in librarianship, and the first of these requirements cannot be dispensed with. The expert when found, too, will have to perform many varied duties from the time before the book reaches the library till it finds its final home on the shelves. For only he can detect it in the first place, write out the order, check the invoice, enter it in the accessions register, catalogue it, classify it and advise a reader about it. So that when many Oriental languages are covered by a library, centralization of these varied activities becomes impossible, and a vertical division of work organization rather than a horizontal one becomes imperative.

Booksellers in Asia

Compiled by K. B. GARDNER

Most libraries in Western Europe and the United States experience difficulties, to a greater or lesser degree, in obtaining books promptly and efficiently from booksellers in the countries of Asia. Until the book trade in these countries becomes more highly organized and is geared to a world market, it is unreasonable to expect the same standard of service in book supply as that provided by book dealers in the West. In the meantime, it may be of some interest to librarians to know which dealers in the three areas of the Near East, South Asia and the Far East. have proved most satisfactory in the experience of British libraries. The following list has been drawn up by the British Museum, with the assistance of the principal libraries in Great Britain specializing in the acquisition of books from Asia. Book dealers most strongly recommended are marked with an asterisk.

NEAR EAST

IRAN
   *Tahoori,   (Persian)
    P.O. Box 804,
    Avenue Shah-abad,
    Teheran, Iran.

    Ketab-Khaneh Danesh,   (Persian)
    293–295 Saadi Avenue,
    Teheran, Iran.

IRAQ
   *K.M. al-Rajab,   (Arabic)
    Maktabat al-Muthanna,
    Shar' al-Mutanabbi,
    Baghdad, Iraq.

ISRAEL
   *Rubin Mass,   (Hebrew)
    P.O. Box 990,
    Jerusalem, Israel.

*Nathan Steiner,   (Hebrew)
43 Geulah Street,
Tel Aviv, Israel.

Ludwig Mayer,   (Hebrew)
P.O. Box 1174,
Jerusalem, Israel.

LEBANON

*Librairie Orientale,   (Arabic)
B.P. 1986,
Place de l'Étoile,
Beirut, Lebanon.

Ras Beirut Bookshop,   (Arabic)
P.O. Box 2796,
Beirut, Lebanon.

SYRIA

Mr J. G. Zakhour,   (Arabic)
B.P. 2776,
Damascus, Syria.

TURKEY

*Elif Kitabevi,   (Turkish)
Sahaflar Carsisi 4,
Beyazit,
Istanbul, Turkey   .

Sella Dilacar,   (Turkish)
63–5 Omer Hayyam Cad.,
Hamalbasi-Beyoglu,
Istanbul, Turkey.

UNITED ARAB REPUBLIC

*Dr M. Morad,   (Arabic)
Dar al-Ma'arif,
15 Sh. Sabri Abu 'Alam,
Cairo, U.A.R.

Al-Arab,   (Arabic)
28 Kamel Sidky Street,
Cairo, U.A.R.

Sirovic,   (Arabic)
P.O. Box 615,
Cairo, U.A.R.

SOUTH ASIA

INDIA (NORTH)

*Chowkhamba Sanskrit Series Office,
Gopal Mandir Lane,
P.O. Box 8,
Varanasi – 1, India.
(Hindi, Sanskrit, Pali, Prakrit)

*Deccan Bookstall,
Deccan Gymkhana,
Poona – 4, India.
(Marathi)

*Lawyers Bookstall,
Gauhati,
Assam, India.
(Assamese)

*K. L. Mukhopadhyay,
6/1a Banccharam Akrur Lane,
Calcutta – 12, India
(Bengali, Sanskrit)

*Munshi Ram Manoharlal,
P.O. Box 1165,
Delhi – 6,
India.
(Hindi, Sanskrit, some south Indian languages, Panjabi)

*Poona Oriental Book House,
1015 Sadashiv Peth,
Poona – 2, India.
(Marathi, Sanskrit)

N. M. Tripathi, Ltd.,
164 Princess Street,
Bombay – 2, India.
(Gujarati, Sanskrit, Tamil, Malayalam)

Danish Mahal,
Aminuddaula Park,
Lucknow, India.
(Urdu in India)

Granthaloka,
5/1 Ambika Mookherjee Road,
Belgharia, 24 Paraganas,
West Bengal, India.
(Good for second-hand books and books in English from Calcutta region)

Lyall Book Depot,
Chaura Bazaar,
Ludhiana, Punjab, India.
(Panjabi)

Maktaba Jama'a Ltd.,
Jama'a Nagar,
New Delhi – 25, India.
(Urdu in India)

Rajpal & Sons,   (Hindi)
Kashmere Gate,
Delhi – 6, India.

R. R. Sheth,   (Gujarati)
Princess Street,
Keshar Baug,
P.O. Box 2517,
Bombay – 2, India.

INDIA (SOUTH)

National Book Stall,   (Malayalam)
Kottayam,
Kerala, India.

Sathyashodhana Pustaka Bhandar, (Kannada)
The Fort,
Bangalore – 2, India.

South India Saiva Siddhanta   (Tamil)
    Works Publishing Society,
1/140 Broadway,
Tinnevelly,
Madras, India.

PAKISTAN

*Ferozsons Ltd.,   (Urdu)
60 The Mall,
Lahore, Pakistan.

*Iqbal Book Store,   (Urdu)
Somerset Road,
Saddar,
Karachi, W. Pakistan.

Maktaba Jadeed,   (Urdu)
6 Fateh Mohammed Road,
Lahore – 7, W. Pakistan

Peoples Publishing House,   (Urdu)
Alminar Market,
Chowk Anarkali,
Lahore, W. Pakistan.

Nawroze Kitabistan,   (Urdu)
Dacca,
E. Pakistan.

FAR EAST

HONG KONG

*Apollo Book Company,   (Chinese)
42 Wellington Street,
(P.O. Box 471),
Hong Kong.

C. M. Chen Book Company,   (Chinese)
324 King's Road, 1st floor,
Hong Kong.

Chiao Liu Publication Service,   (Chinese)
P.O. Box 5734,
(6a Cameron Road, 2nd floor),
Kowloon, Hong Kong.

Kai Man Bookstore,   (Chinese)
23 Wellington Street, or
264 Des Voeux Road Central,
Hong Kong.

*Lau Siew Sing,   (Chinese)
52 High Street, 2nd floor,
Hong Kong.

Modern China Book Company, (Chinese)
188 Tung Chau Street, 10th floor,
Kowloon, Hong Kong.

Oriental Book Company,   (Chinese)
81 Grenville Road, 2nd floor,
Tsim Sha Tsui,
Kowloon, Hong Kong.

*Universal Book Company,   (Chinese)
17 Gilman's Bazaar, 1st floor,
Hong Kong.

Wai Man Book Store,   (Chinese)
105 Portland Street, 3rd floor,
Kowloon, Hong Kong.

PEKING

Guozi Shudian,   (Chinese)
P.O. Box 88,
Peking.

JAPAN

> Far Eastern Booksellers,   (Japanese)
> No. 2, 2-chōme Jimbo-chō,
> Kanda, Chiyoda-ku,
> Tokyo, Japan.

> *Japan Publications Trading   (Chinese)
>   Company,
> Central P.O. Box 722,
> Tokyo, Japan.

The above are suitable for new books. For second-hand books the number of suppliers offering reasonably satisfactory service is legion. Most of them, however, can supply only books from their own immediate stock, offered through printed catalogues. The only ones in our experience which can also offer a search service of even limited effectiveness are:

> *Isseidō Shoten,
> 7 1-chōme, Jimbo-chō,
> Kanda, Chiyoda-ku,
> Tokyo, Japan.

> *Shibunkaku,
> Nishitera-machi,
> Shimokyō-ku,
> Kyoto, Japan.

List of works referred to in the text

Arranged under authors, compilers, etc. (personal or corporate) or titles.

The final number following each entry gives the page number of this book in which the reference appears.

Actes des deux premiérès rencontres des orientalistes belges sous le titre "Journée des orientalistes belges" 1963 et 1964. 64.

Afshar, Iraj: *Bibliographie des catalogues des manuscrits persans.* Tehran, 1958. 81.

Afshar, Iraj: *Index Iranicus.* Tehran, 1961. 113.

Ahmed bin Ali, *Syed*: 'Buku² panduan (reference) dalam bahasa Melayu.' *Malayan Libr. J.* 1, 4, 1961, pp. 17–21. 91.

Akademiya Nauk SSSR. Institut narodov Azii: *Vostokovednye fondy krupneyshikh bibliotek Sovetskogo Soyuza; stat'i i soobshcheniya.* Moskva, 1963. 81, 207.

Akademiya Nauk SSSR. Institut Vostokovedeniya. *Ocherki po istorii russkogo vostokovedeniya.* 5 vols. Moskva, 1953–60. 25.

All-India Oriental Conference: [*Proceedings*], 1919–   . 65.

The American Historical Association's *Guide to historical literature.* New York, 1961. 93.

American Universities Field Staff: *A Select bibliography: Asia, Africa, Eastern Europe, Latin America.* New York (1960), suppls. 1961, 1963. 156.

Amzalak, M. B.: *The Oriental studies in Portugal.* Lisbon, 1928. 29.

Anderson, B. R.: *Bibliography of Indonesian publications; newspapers, non-government periodicals and bulletins 1945–1958 at Cornell University.* Ithaca, 1959. 197.

Annual bibliography of Oriental studies. 1934–   . 140.

Annual Report of the Registrar of Newspapers for India. 107.

Apor, E. and Ecsedy, H.: *Hungarian publications on Asia and Africa, 1950–1962; a selected bibliography.* Budapest, 1963. 144.

Arberry, A. J.: *British contributions to Persian studies.* London (1942). 30.

Arberry, A. J.: *British Orientalists.* London, 1943. 31.

Arberry, A. J.: *The Cambridge School of Arabic.* Cambridge, 1948. 31.

Arberry, A. J.: *The Library of the India Office. A historical sketch.* London, 1938. 176.

Arberry, A. J.: *A Second supplementary hand-list of the Muhammadan manuscripts in the University & colleges of Cambridge.* Cambridge, 1952. 77.

Arberry, A. J.: *Specimens of Arabic and Persian palaeography.* London, 1939. 75.

The Asia Who's Who. 3rd ed. Hong Kong, 1960. 103.

R

Asian bibliography. 1949.

Asien-Bibliographie. 149.

Association of British Orientalists: [*Conferences*]. 60.

Axelbrod, J. and Bigelow, D. L.: *Resources for language and area studies.* Washington (1962). 48.

Aufrecht, T.: *Catalogus catalogorum: an alphabetical register of Sanskrit works and authors.* 3 vols. Leipzig, 1891–1903. (Reprinted Wiesbaden, 1962.) 84.

Aziya Seikei Gakkai: *Asian studies in Japan.* Tokyo, 1964. 53.

Babinger, F.: 'Ein Jahrhundert morgenländischer Studien an der Münchener Universität.' *ZDMG* 107, 2 (N.F. 22, 1957), pp. 241–269. 28.

Balfour, E. G.: *The Cyclopaedia of India and of Eastern and Southern Asia.* 3rd ed. 3 vols. London, 1885. 97.

Baqai, I. H.: *Books on Asia.* Delhi (1947). 156.

Barthold, V.: *La découverte de l'Asie. Histoire de l'orientalisme en Europe et en Russie.* Traduit du russe en annoté par B. Nikitine. (Bibliothèque historique.) Paris, 1947. 22.

Barthold, V.: *Materialy dlya istorii Fakul'teta Vostochnykh Yazykov.* Tom 4. *Obzor deyatel'nosti Fakul'teta 1855–1905.* St. Peterburg, 1909. 27.

Beeston, A. F. L.: 'The Oriental manuscript collections of the Bodleian Library.' *Bodleian Library record* 5, 2 (Oct. 1954). 79, 170

Bendik, A. I. and Grivnin, V. S.: 'Orientalia in U.S.S.R. libraries.' *UNESCO Bull. for Libraries* 15, 6, 1961, pp. 322–26. 206.

Bernheimer, C.: *Paleografia ebraica.* Firenze, 1924. 75.

Bibliographia Asiatica, 149.

Bibliographie des principales publications éditées dans l'Empire japonais. Tokyo, 1931. 110.

'Bibliographie sommaire des ouvrages d'orientalisme en langue japonaise (parus entre 1938 et 1950).' *Bull. Maison Franco-Jap.,* nouv. sér., 1 (1951). 146.

Bibliografiya Vostoka. Leningrad, 1932–37. 137.

Bibliography of Asian studies (formerly *Bulletin of Far Eastern bibliography*). 1936– . 148.

Bibliography of the humanistic studies and social relations. Tokyo, 1952– . 146.

Bibliothèque Nationale: *Les Catalogues imprimés de la Bibliothèque Nationale.* Paris, 1953. 79.

Birnbaum, S. A.: *The Hebrew scripts.* London, 1954– . 75.

Borovkov, A. K.: 'Vostokovedenie v SSSR za 30 let.' *Izv. Akad. Nauk SSSR, Otd. lit. i yaz.* 6, 5 (1947), pp. 395–407. 145.

Bowen, H.: *British contributions to Turkish studies.* London (1945). 30.

Brockelmann, C.: *Geschichte der arabischen Litteratur.* 2 vols., 3 suppl. vols. Weimar, 1898; Berlin, 1902; Leiden, 1937–42. (—— 2. Aufl. 2 vols. Leiden 1943–49.) 85.

Brown, W. N.: *Resources for South Asian language studies in the United States.* Philadelphia (1960). 49–50.

Browne, E. G.: *A Literary history of Persia.* 4 vols. Re-issue, reprinted. Cambridge Univ. Press, 1928–29. 21.

Bühler, G.: *Indische Palaeographie von circa 350 a. Chr. – circa 1300 p. Chr.* Strassburg, 1896. 76.

Bühler, G.: *Indian palaeography.* Bombay, 1904. 76.

California (University of): *Asiatic and Slavic studies on the Berkeley campus, 1896–1947.* Univ. California Press (1947). 30.

Cambridge history of the British Empire. 7 vols. 1929–36. 152.

Carson, P.: *Materials for West African history in the archives of Belgium and Holland.* London, 1962. 73.

Cataloghi dei codici orientali di alcune biblioteche d'Italia . . . 1878–1904. 80.

Catalogus der Koloniale Bibliotheek van het Kon. Instituut voor de Taal-, Land- en Volkenkunde. 's-Gravenhage, 1908, supplements 1915, 1927, 1937. 154.

Ceadel, E. B.: *Classified catalogue of modern Japanese books in Cambridge University Library.* Cambridge (1961). 174.

Centre for East Asian Cultural Studies, Tokyo: *A Survey of Japanese bibliographies concerning Asian studies.* Tokyo, 1963. 145.

——*East Asian cultural studies.* Vol. 1. 1962. 47.

Ceylon yearbook. 1959– . 7.

Chaplin, A. H.: *National usages for the entry of names of persons.* (International Conference on Cataloguing Principles, 1961.) Provisional ed. London, 1963. 232.

Chatterjee, Sir A. and Burn, Sir R.: *British contributions to Indian studies.* London (1943). 30.

Chicago University. Committee on Far Eastern Civilizations and Committee on Southern Asian Studies: *The University of Chicago doctoral dissertations and masters' theses on Asia 1894–1962.* Chicago, 1962. 58.

The China yearbook (formerly *The China handbook*). 1957–58– . 10.

Cinq-cinquantenaire de l'École des Langues Orientales. Histoire, organisation et enseignements de l'École Nationale des Langues Orientales Vivantes. Paris, 1948. 24.

Collison, R.: *Encyclopaedias; their history throughout the ages.* New York, London, 1964. 97.

Colomiès, P.: *Gallia Orientalis.* 1665. 23.

Columbia University Library: *Index to learned Chinese periodicals*. Boston, 1962. 197.

Columbia University members' essays and doctoral dissertations on Asia 1875–1956. New York, 1957. 58.

Commissione nazionale italiana per l'UNESCO: *Contributo italiano alla conoscenza dell' Oriente: repertorio bibliografico dal 1935 al 1948*. Firenze (1962). 57, 142.

Conover, H. F.: *Serials for African studies*. Washington, 1961. 106.

Couling, S.: *The Encyclopaedia Sinica*. Shanghai, 1917. 97.

Cramer, M.: *Koptische Paläographie*. Wiesbaden, 1964. 75.

Craster, Sir E.: *History of the Bodleian Library, 1845–1945*. Oxford, 1952. 170.

Crick, B. R. and Alman, M.: *A Guide to manuscripts relating to America in Great Britain and Ireland*. London, 1961. 72.

Cyprus: a handbook on the island of Aphrodite. Nicosia, 1964. 6.

Dagher, J. A.: *Répertoire des bibliothèques du Proche et du Moyen-Orient*. Paris, 1951. 215.

Dandekar, R. N., Raghavan, V.: *Oriental studies in India*. New Delhi, 1964. 54.

Dani, Ahmad Hasan: *Indian palaeography*. Oxford, 1963. 76.

Daniels, F. J.: *Japanese studies in the University of London and elsewhere*. London, 1963. 31.

De Gubernatis, A.: *Matériaux pour servir à l'histoire des études orientales en Italie*. Paris, 1876. 24, 142.

Demiéville, P.: 'Organization of East Asian studies in France.' *J. Asian Studies* 18 (1958), pp. 163–181. 55.

Deutsche Morgenländische Gesellschaft: *Wissenschaftliche Jahresberichte* 1846– . 131.

Deutsche Staatsbibliothek 1661–1961. 2 vols. Leipzig, 1961. 211.

Directory of the cultural organizations of the Republic of China. Taipei, 1961. 53.

Directory of the Republic of Cyprus. London, 1962–63. 6.

Diringer, D.: *The hand-produced book*. London (1953). 69.

'Dix années d'études orientales en Pologne populaire.' *Rocznik orient*. 20 (1956), pp. 7–14, 29, 141.

Döbeln, E. von: 'Nordisk orientalisk bibliografi för åren 1911–20 (—— 1921–25).' *Svenska Orientsällskapets Arsbok* 3 (1925), pp. 51–88; 1926–27, pp. 93–133 144.

Dobson, W. A. C. H.: *The Contribution of Canadian universities to an understanding of Asia and Africa*. (Ottawa, 1964.) 50.

Dobson, W. A. C. H.: *A Select list of books on the civilizations of the Orient*. Oxford, 1955. 156.

Dugat, G.: *Histoire des orientalistes de l'Europe du XIIe au XIXe siècle, précédée d'une esquisse historique des études orientales.* 2 vols. Paris, 1868–70. 22.

Duignan, P. and Glazier, K. M.: *A Checklist of serials for African studies ...* Stanford, 1963. 106.

Dutt, Newton Mohan: *Baroda and its libraries.* Baroda, 1928. 217.

Echols, J. M.: *Preliminary checklist of Indonesian imprints during the Japanese period (March 1942–August 1945), with annotations.* Ithaca, 1963. 197.

Editions Scientifiques de Pologne: *Catalogue des publications orientalistes.* [1964?]. 142.

Elahi, Khwaja Nur, Moid, A., and Siddiqui, Akhtar, H.: *A Guide to works of reference published in Pakistan.* Karachi, 1953. 91.

Ellis, A. G. and Edwards, E.: *A Descriptive list of the Arabic manuscripts acquired by the Trustees of the British Museum.* London, 1912. 77.

Encyclopaedia of Buddhism. Ceylon, 1961– . 97.

The Encyclopaedia of Islam. 4 vols. Leiden, London (1908–) 1913–36. (–Suppl. 1934–38.) (– New ed. 1954–) 1960– . 95.

Encyclopaedia Judaica: das Judentum in Geschichte und Gegenwart. 10 vols. Berlin, 1928–34. 95.

Enoki, K.: *Japanese researchers in Asian studies.* Tokyo (1963). 52.

Enoki, K.: *Research institutes and researchers of Asian studies in the Republic of Korea.* Tokyo, 1963. 54.

Enoki, K.: *Research institutes for Asian studies in Japan.* Tokyo, 1962. 51.

Esdaile, A.: *The British Museum Library; a short history and survey.* London (1946). (2nd impr., 1948.) 164.

Esdaile, A.: *National libraries of the world.* (2nd ed. by F. J. Hill.) London, 1957. 213.

Eustache, D.: 'Catalogue d'imprimés ou de manuscrits arabes, choix de la vedette-auteur.' *Bull. bibliothèques France* 3, 2, 1958, pp. 99–111; 3, 9, 1958, pp. 619–628. 232.

External research, 59.

Falkenstein, A.: *Denkschrift zur Lage der Orientalistik.* Wiesbaden, 1960. 56.

Favitski de Probobysz (Cte de): *Répertoire bibliographique de la littérature militaire et coloniale française depuis cent ans.* Paris, Liège, 1925. 154, *note* 1.

Favre, G.: *les études orientales à la Société d'Histoire et d'Archéologie de Genève 1838–94.* Genève, 1894. 30.

Fawcett, Sir C. *See* Foster, Sir W.

Foster, Sir W.: *The English factories in India, 1618(-1669). A calendar of documents* . . . 13 vols. Oxford, 1906–27. (New series, vols. 1–3, 1670–1684, by Sir Charles Fawcett. Oxford, 1936–54.) 73.

France. Ministère des Colonies: *Cinq cent livres sur la Communauté française.* Paris, 1945. 154, *note.*

Francis, F. C.: *The Catalogues of the British Museum.* 3. *Oriental printed books and manuscripts.* London, 1951. 79, 164–5.

Franke, H.: *Sinologie.* Bern, 1953. 33.

Friederici, K.: *Bibliotheca Orientalis* . . . London, etc., n.d. 133.

Frykholm, L.: *Oversikt over samhällsvetenskapliga bibliografiska hjälpmedel.* Stockholm, 1960. 123.

Fück, J.: *Die Arabischen Studien in Europa bis in den Anfang des 20. Jahrhunderts.* Leipzig, 1955. 32.

Fukuda, N.: *Libraries for Japanese studies; a report of a survey.* Tokyo, 1963. 192.

Gabrieli, F.: *Gli Studi orientali.* Napoli, 1950. 24.

Gabrieli, G.: *Bibliografia degli studi orientalistici in Italia dal 1912 al 1934.* Roma, 1935. 24, 142.

Gabrieli, G.: *Manoscritti e carte orientali nelle biblioteche e negli archivi d'Italia.* Firenze, 1930. 79.

Garde, P. K.: *Directory of reference works published in Asia.* UNESCO (1956). 89.

Gardner, K. B., Grinstead, E. D., and Meredith-Owens, G. M.: 'The Department of Oriental Printed Books and Manuscripts of the British Museum'. *J. Asian Studies* 18, 1959, pp. 310–18. 79, 165.

Gibb, Sir H. A. R.: *Area studies reconsidered.* London, 1963. 49.

Gibb, Sir H. A. R., and Kramers, J. H.: *Shorter encyclopaedia of Islam.* 1953. 96.

Giles, L.: *Descriptive catalogue of the Chinese manuscripts from Tunhuang in the British Museum.* London, 1957. 167.

Giok Po Oey: *Survey of Chinese language materials on Southeast Asia in the Hoover Institute and Library.* Ithaca, 1953. 199.

Giuseppi, M. S.: *Guide to the contents of the Public Record Office.* Revised and extended (to 1960) from the *Guide* by the late M. S. Giuseppi. 2 vols. London, 1963. 70.

Gökman, Muzaffer: *Istanbul kütüphaneleri ve yazma tıp kitapları.* Istanbul, 1959. 216.

Gonçalves, J.: 'Bibliografia do Ultramar portugues, existente na Sociedade da Geografia de Lisboa.' *Bol. Soc. Geog. Lisboa.* ser. 78–80. 155.

Grinstead, E. D.: *Chinese periodicals in British libraries.* London [1962]. 108.

Grousset, R.: *Histoire de l'Asie.* (Que sais-je?) Paris, 1941. 19, *note.*

Grousset, R.: *A History of Asia*; translated from the French by D. Scott. New York (1963). 19, *note*.

Grundriss der indo-arischen Philologie und Altertumskunde. Berlin, Leipzig, 1896–1920. 101.

Guboglu, M.: 'Quarante ans d'études orientales en U.R.S.S. (1917–57.)' *Studia et Acta Orient*. 1(1958), pp. 281–316. 145.

Guppy, H.: *The John Rylands Library, Manchester: 1899–1935* . . . Manchester, 1935. 186.

Hadi, M. M. el-: *Arabic library resources in the United States* . . . 192.

Hale, R. W.: *Guide to photocopied historical materials in the United States and Canada*. Ithaca (1961). 74.

Hamer, P. M.: *A Guide to archives and manuscripts in the United States*. New Haven, 1961. 74.

Haupt, R.: *Internationales Taschenbuch für Orientalisten*. 2. Aufl. Leipzig, 1910. 66.

[Hayter report.] University Grants Committee: *Report of the Sub-Committee on Oriental, Slavonic, East European and African Studies*. London, 1961. 35.

Hazra, Niranjan K., Lee Siew Cheng, Edward: *Malayasian* [sic] *serials; a check list of current official serials of the Malaysian governments*. Singapore [1964?]. 108.

The Hebrew University of Jerusalem, 1963. 216.

Herrmann, C. H.: *Bibliotheca orientalis et linguistica* . . . Halle a/S., 1870. 141.

Hervouet, Y.: *Catalogue des périodiques chinois dans les bibliothèques d'Europe*. Paris, 1958. 108.

Hewitt, A. R.: *Guide to resources for Commonwealth studies in London, Oxford and Cambridge, with bibliographical and other information*. London, 1957. 152.

Hewitt, A. R.: *Union list of Commonwealth newspapers in London, Oxford and Cambridge*. London, 1960. 120, 153.

Heyne, A.: *Orientalistisches Datenbuch*. Leipzig, 1912. 66.

Hobbs, C.: *An Account of an acquisition trip in the countries of Southeast Asia*. 1952. 201.

Hobbs, C.: *An Account of a trip to the countries of Southeast Asia for the Library of Congress, 1952–53*. 1953. 201.

Hobbs, C.: *Southeast Asia publication sources: an account of a field trip, 1958–59*. 1960. 201.

Hong Kong. Union Research Institute: *Catalogue of Mainland Chinese magazines and newspapers* . . . 1962. 108.

Hoover Institution on War, Revolution and Peace. Stanford Univ., 1963. 198.

Hooykaas, J. C.: *Repertorium op de koloniale literatuur, of systematische inhouds-gaaf van hetgeen voorkomt over de Koloniën (beoosten de Kaap) in mengelwerken en tijdschriften* . . . Amsterdam, 1877 & suppls. 154.

Horecky, P. L.: *Libraries and bibliographic centers in the Soviet Union*. Indiana Univ., 1959. 206.

Ike, Nobutaka: *The Hoover Institution collection on Japan*. Stanford Univ., 1958. 198.

The India Office Library: its function, scope and resources. London, 1962. 70. *See also* Sutton, S. C.

Indian Association of Special libraries and Information Centres: *Directory of special and research libraries in India*. Calcutta, 1962. 217.

Institut International des Civilisations Différentes: *Répertoire international des centres d'étude des civilisations et de leurs publications*. Bruxelles, 1955. 45.

International African Institute: *Handbook of African languages*. 1952– . 18.

International Conference of Orientalists in Japan: *Transactions*. 1956– . 63.

International Congress of Orientalists: [*Proceedings*]. 1874– . 62–3.

International Congress of Orientalists: *Doklady Sovetskoy delegatzii na XXIII (–XXVI) Mezhdunarodnom Kongresse Vostokovedov*. Moskva, 1954– . 63.

Inter-University Committee on South Asia Scholarly Resources: *South Asia micro-form newsletter*. 201.

Ishida, Mikinosuke: *Bibliographie de l'orientalisme japonais*. Tokyo, Paris, 1958, 1962. 146.

Islam ansiklopedisi. Istanbul, 1941– . 97.

Janert, K. L.: *An Annotated bibliography of catalogues of Indian manuscripts*. Wiesbaden, 1965. 81.

Janert, K. L.: *Verzeichnis indienkundlicher Hochschulschriften: Deutschland-Österreich-Schweiz*. Wiesbaden, 1961. 58.

Japan Library Association: *Libraries in Japan*. 1958. 220.

Japan. Ministry of Education: *Bibliographical list of Japanese learned journals—humanities and social sciences*. Tokyo (1960). 109.
—— *natural and applied sciences*. Ib., 1962. 109.

Japan. National Diet Library *and* Ministry of Education: *Directory of Japanese scientific periodicals 1962*. Tokyo, 1962. 109.

Japanese science review: economic sciences. No. 8 (1962). 53.

Japanese universities and colleges 1963, with major research institutes. Tokyo. 53.

The Jewish encyclopaedia. New ed. 12 vols. New York, London, 1901–6. (Reprints 1916, 1925.) 95.

The John Rylands Library, Manchester; a brief descriptive account. Manchester (1954, repr. 1955, 1958). 186.

Joshi, V. C.: *Guide to sources of modern Indian history project* [1963?]. 72.

Kan Lai-bing: *Libraries in Hong Kong; a directory.* Hong Kong, 1963. 219.

Kesavan, B. S.: *India's National Library.* Calcutta, 1961. 218.

Khan, Shafaat Ahmad: *Sources for the history of British India in the seventeenth century.* London, 1926. 73.

Köhler, J.: *Deutsche Dissertationen über Africa; ein Verzeichnis für die Jahre 1918–59.* Bonn, 1962. 58.

Kokusai Bunka Shinkokai: *K.B.S. bibliography of standard reference books for Japanese studies with descriptive notes.* Tokyo, 1959– . 92.

Krymsky, A. E. i Minorsky, V. F.: *Ocherki iz istorii orientalistiki v XVI i XVII veke.* Moskva, 1903.

Kublin, H.: *An Introductory reading guide to Asia.* New York, 1958. 156.

Kuhn, E. und Klatt, J.: *Literatur-Blatt für orientalische Philologie.* Leipzig, n.d. 134.

Lai, Yung-Hsiang: *University and college libraries in Taiwan* (1961). 220.

Lambert, R. D.: *Resources for South Asian area studies in the United States.* Philadelphia (1962). 50.

Lambrecht, E.: *Catalogue de la Bibliothèque de l'Ecole des Langues orientales vivantes.* Paris, 1897. 211.

Lev, D. S.: *A Bibliography of Indonesian government documents and selected Indonesian writings on government in the Cornell University Library.* Ithaca, 1958. 197.

Lewin, E.: *Subject catalogue of the Library of the Royal Empire Society, formerly Royal Colonial Institute.* 5 vols. (London) 1930–61. 184.

Lewis, B.: *British contributions to Arabic studies.* London, 1941. 30.

Library of Congress: *African newspapers currently received in selected American libraries.* Washington, D.C., 1956. 120.

Library of Congress: *Japanese scientific and technical serial publications . . .* Washington, 1962. 109.

Library of Congress: *A List of American doctoral dissertations on Africa.* Washington, 1962. 58.

Library of Congress: *The National Union catalog of manuscript collections 1959–61* (— *1962—Index 1959–62*). Ann Arbor, Mich., 1962 (—Hamden, Conn., 1964). 73.

Library of Congress: *Newspapers on microfilm.* 5th ed. Washington, 1963. 120.

Lim Wong Pui Huen: 'Current Malay serials.' *Majallah Perpustakaan Singapura* 2, 2, October, 1962, pp. 75–94. 107.

Littmann, E. *See* Paret, R. and Schall, A.

Livotova, O. E.: 'Bibliografiya izdaniy Aziatskogo musea i Instituta vostoko- vedeniya.' *Ocherki po ist. russkogo vostokoved.* 3 (1950). 145.

Livre jubilaire composé à l'occasion du 4e centenaire du Collège de France. Paris, 1933. 24.

Ljunggren, F. and Geddes, C. L.: *An International directory of institutes and societies interested in the Middle East.* Amsterdam, 1962. 46.

Lust, J.: *Index Sinicus.* Cambridge, 1964. 113.

McNiff, P. J.: *A List of book dealers in underdeveloped countries.* 1963. 229.

Macray, W. D.: *Annals of the Bodleian Library, Oxford.* 2nd ed. Oxford, 1890. 170.

Malalasekera, G. P.: *See* Encyclopaedia of Buddhism.

Malaysian year book 1963–64. (*The Malaya Mail*, Kuala Lumpur.) 8.

Malclès, L. N.: *Les Sources du travail bibliographique.* 4 vols. Genève, Lille, 1950–8. 87.

Malleret, L.: 'Aperçu d'un demi-siècle de travaux scientifiques à l'Ecole Française d'Extreme-Orient.' *France-Asie* 125–7, oct.–déc. 1956, pp. 217–306. 24.

Mansoor, M.: *Oriental studies in Ireland and Irish Orientalists.* Dublin (1943). 28.

Marakuev, A. V.: *Desyat' let vostokovedeniya na sovetskom Dal'nem Vostoke (1922–32).* Vladivostok, 1932. 28.

Marburg. Westdeutsche Bibliothek: *Orient-Literatur in Deutschland und Österreich, 1945–50.* Marburg (Lahn) (1950). 141.

Margoliouth, G.: *Descriptive list of the Hebrew and Samaritan MSS. in the British Museum.* London, 1893. 77.

Margoliouth, G.: *Descriptive list of Syriac and Karshuni MSS. in the British Museum acquired since 1873.* London, 1899. 77.

Martineau, A., Roussier, Tramond: *Bibliographie d'histoire coloniale (1900–30).* 150.

Matthews, W. K.: *Languages of the U.S.S.R.* London, 1951. 17.

Mattison, F. C.: *A Survey of American interests in the Middle East . . .* Washington, 1953. 47.

Meillet, A. et Cohen, M.: *Les Langues du monde, par un groupe de linguistes.* Nouv. éd. Paris, 1952. 17.

The Middle East and North Africa. 10th ed. London: Europa Publications, 1963. 6.

Morhouse, W.: *American institutions and organizations interested in Asia. A reference directory.* 2nd ed. New York, 1961. 47, 192.

Morgan, K. W.: *Asian religions; an introduction to the study of Hinduism, Buddhism, Islam, Confucianism and Taoism.* New York, London, 1964. 18.

Moritz, B.: *Arabic palaeography . . .* Cairo, 1905. 75.

Moses, L.: *Language and area study programs in American universities.* Washington, 1964. 48, 192.

Müller, A., *et al.*: *Orientalische Bibliographie* . . . Berlin, etc. 1888–1928, 134.

Munby, A. N. L.: *Cambridge college libraries; aids for research students.* Cambridge (1962). 175.

Muramatsu, Y.: *Japanese studies of contemporary China.* Los Angeles, 1959. 52.

Musiker, R.: *Guide to South African reference books.* 3rd rev. ed. Grahamstown, 1963. 93.

New Book Society of India, New Delhi: *New India directory of libraries and educational institutions.* New Delhi (1955). 217.

New York Public Library: *Cumulative list of national and local gazettes.* 122.

Nickerson, R.: *Trans-Pacific scholarly publishing; a symposium.* Univ. of Hawaii, 1963. 228.

Nifor guide to Indian periodicals 1955–56. Poona, 1956. 106.

Nihon no sankyō henshū iinkai. Nihon no sankō tosho. Tokyo, 1962.

Nunn, G. R., and Tsien, Tsuen-hsuin: 'Far Eastern resources in American libraries.' Repr. from *Library Q.* 29, 1(1959), pp. 27–42. 192.

Pakistan Bibliographical Working Group: *A Guide to Pakistan libraries, learned and scientific societies and educational institutions, biographies of librarians in Pakistan.* Karachi, 1960. 219.

Paret, R. und Schall, A.: *Ein Jahrhundert Orientalistik: Lebensbilder aus der Feder von Enno Littmann und Verzeichnis seiner Schriften.* Wiesbaden: Harrassowitz, 1955. 23.

Pearson, J. D.: *Index Islamicus 1906–55 (– Suppl. 1956–60.)* Cambridge, 1958, repr. 1961 (– 1962). 113.

Pearson, J. D.: *Oriental manuscript collections in the libraries of Great Britain and Ireland.* London. 1954. 79.

Pearson, J. D.: 'The Rôle of the library in Oriental studies.' *Proc. XXIII Int. Cong. Orientalists,* 1954, pp. 34–42. 163.

Peking, Library Association of China: *Libraries in China,* Peiping, 1935. 220.

Philips, C. H.: *Handbook of Oriental history.* London, 1951. 20, 103.

Piyadasa, T. G.: *The Origin and history of libraries in Ceylon.* [Thesis.] London, 1964. 219.

Poleman, H. I.: *A Census of Indic manuscripts in the United States and Canada.* New Haven, 1938. 84.

Polska Akademia Nauk: *Bibliografia polskich prac orientalistycznych (1945–55).* Warszawa, 1957. 141.

Predari, F.: *Origine e progresso dello studio delle lingue orientali in Italia.* Milano, 1842. 24, 142.

Preussische Staatsbibliothek: *Katalog der Handbibliothek der Orientalischen Abteilung.* Leipzig, 1929. 212.

Průšek, J.: 'Desat let naší orientalistiky.' *Archiv. orient.* 23(1955), pp. 271–311. 145.

Public Record Office: *Guide to the contents of the Public Record Office.* 2 vols. London, 1963. 70.

Public Record Office: *The Records of the Colonial and Dominions Office.* 1964. 70.

Public Record Office: *List of Cabinet papers 1800–1914.* 1964. 70.

Public Record Office: *List of papers of the Committee of Imperial Defence to 1914.* 1964. 70.

Quan (L. King): *Introduction to Asia: a selective guide to background reading.* Washington, 1955. 156.

Quatre esquisses détachées relatives aux études orientalistes à Leiden. Leiden [1932]. 29.

Ragatz, L. J., and J. E.: *A Bibliography of articles, descriptive, historical and scientific, on colonial and other dependent territories, appearing in American geographical and kindred journals.* Washington (1951). 151.

Ragatz, L. J.: *A List of books and articles on colonial history and overseas expansion published in the United States 1900–1930 (– 1935).* Ann Arbor, Mich., 1939. 150.

Raghavan, V.: *New catalogus catalogorum: an alphabetical register of Sanskrit and allied works and authors.* Madras, 1949. 84.

Ranganathan, S. R., and Sivaraman, K. M.: *Bibliography of reference books and bibliographies.* Madras, 1941. 91.

Ranganathan, S. R., Das Gupta, S., Magnanand: *Indian library directory.* Edition 3. Delhi, 1951. 217.

Rau, W.: *Bilder hundert deutscher Indologen.* Wiesbaden, 1965. 66.

[Reay report:] *Report of the Committee appointed by the Lords Commissioners of His Majesty's Treasury to consider the organization of Oriental studies in London . . .* London, 1909. 34–.

[Reay report:] *Minutes of evidence . . .* Ib., 1909. 34–.

Roberts, R. A. *See* Royal Commission on Historical Manuscripts.

Rodgers, F.: *Directory of Japanese learned periodicals.* (2nd ed.) Urbana, Ill., 1957. 109.

Roff, W. R.: *Guide to Malay periodicals 1876–1946, with details of known holdings in Malaya.* Singapore, 1961. 107.

Royal Asiatic Society: *A Catalogue of printed books published before 1932 in the library . . .* London, 1940. 183.

Royal Commission on Historical Manuscripts: *Guide to reports on collections of MSS. of private families, corporations and institutions in Great Britain and Ireland.* 3 vols. London, 1914–38. 71.

Royal Commission on Historical Manuscripts: *The Reports of the Historical MSS. Commission,* by R. A. Roberts. London, 1920. 72.

Royal Commission on Historical Manuscripts: *Reports ... revised to 31st August 1956.* London. 72.

Sardesai, R. N.: *Picturesque Orientalia.* Poona, 1958. 66.

Sayle, C.: *Annals of Cambridge University Library, 1278–1900.* Cambridge, 1916. 173.

[Scarbrough report:] *Report of the Interdepartmental Commission of Enquiry on Oriental, Slavonic, East European and African studies.* London, 1947. 35– .

Schmidt, E. R.: *Preliminary list of Ph.D. dissertations on South Asia, 1933–60 (unedited).* Madison, Wisconsin, n.d. 58.

Schwab, M.: *Répertoire des articles relatifs à l'histoire et à la littérature juives parus dans les périodiques de 1783 à 1898.* Paris, 1900. 113.

Seaholm, F.: 'Winchell, Walford, or Malclès?' *College and Research Libraries* 25, 1 January, 1964, pp. 21–26. 89.

Shabad, T.: *Geography of the U.S.S.R.; a regional survey.* 10, *note.*

Siddiq Khan, M.: 'The Asian Federation of Library Associations.' *Library Association Record* 60 (1958), pp. 123–5. 222.

Simmonds, E. H. S.: *Asia and Africa; a select bibliography for schools.* 2nd ed. London (1963). 156.

Singer, Cyrus A. E. *et al. See* The Jewish encyclopaedia.

Sinor, D.: 'Dix années d'orientalisme hongrois (1940–50).' *J. asiatique* 239 (1951), pp. 211–35. 144.

Skeat, T. C.: *The Catalogues of the manuscript collections in the British Museum.* Rev. ed. London, 1962. 71.

Société asiatique: *Le Livre du centenaire (1822–1922).* Paris, 1922. 23.

Société des études indochinoises: *Cinquante ans d'orientalisme français.* 1951. 24.

Somadasa, K. D. [: *A Catalogue of Ola leaf manuscripts in the temple libraries of Ceylon.* Colombo] 1959. 84.

Soviet Orientalogy between the XXV and XXVI Congresses of Orientalists. Moscow. 1963. 145.

Sparn, E.: *Las Mayores colecciones de manuscritos orientales existentes en las bibliotecas del mundo.* Cordoba, Argentina, 1935. 78.

Sprout, E.: *Catalogue of the library of the American Oriental Society.* New Haven, 1930. 199.

Spuler, B.: *Handbuch der Orientalistik.* Leiden, 1952– . 98.

Stamp, L. D.: *Asia; a regional and economic geography.* 9th ed. London (1957). 4, *note.*

Standing Conference of Libraries with Materials on Africa: *Theses on Africa.* Cambridge, 1964. 58.

Stegemann, V.: *Koptische Paläographie.* 75.

Stephens, R. E.: *Library collections for area programs.* 1964. 192.

Stevens, R. D.: 'United States research library acquisitions in India, Pakistan and the United Arab Republic.' *UNESCO Bull. Libraries* 17, 1963, pp. 178–80. 202.

Storey, C. A.: *Persian literature, a bio-bibliographical survey.* London, 1927– . 85.

Strelcyn, S., Lewicki, M., Zajaczkowski, A.: *Katalog rekopisow orientalnych ze zbiorów polskich.* 1959– . 83.

Strelcyn, S.: *Szkice z dziéjow polskiej orientalistyki.* 1957. 29.

Stucki, C. W.: *American doctoral dissertations on Asia, 1933–58* . . . Ithaca, 1959. 58.

'Gli Studi orientali in Italia durante il cinquantenario 1861–1911 (bibliografia). *RSO* 5, 1913–27. 142.

Survey of humanistic studies in Japan, 1960. 51.

Sutton, S. C.: *A Guide to the India Office Library.* London, 1952. 71, 176.

Sutton, S. C.: 'The India Office Library.' *J. Asian Studies* 18 (1959), pp. 425–8. 79, 176.

Taiwan National Central Library: *Handbook of current research projects in the Republic of China.* Taipeh, 1962. 58.

Têng, Ssŭ-yü and Biggerstaff, K.: *An Annotated bibliography of selected Chinese reference books.* Harvard U.P., 1950. 91.

Ternaux-Compans, H.: *Bibliothèque asiatique et africaine ou catalogue des ouvrages relatifs à l'Asie et à l'Afrique qui ont paru depuis la découverte de l'imprimerie jusqu'en 1700.* Paris, 1841. 129.

Tikhvinskiy, S. L.: *A Soviet view of Chinese studies in Japan.* Los Angeles, 1959. 52.

The Times of India directory and yearbook. Bombay, etc., London, 1954–5– . 6.

Ting, J. C.: *British contributions to Chinese studies.* 1951. 31.

Tōhō Gakkai: *Books and articles on Oriental subjects published in Japan during 1954– .* 146.

'Trends of Asian studies in postwar Japan.' *Developing Economies,* prelim. issue no. 1, 1962, pp. 75–105. 52.

Twitchett, D.: *Land tenure and the social order in T'ang and Sung China.* London, 1962. 31.

United Nations. ECAFE Library: *Asian bibliography.* 1952– . 149.

United States. Department of State: *External research.* 59.

United States National Commission for UNESCO: *A Selected bibliography of books, films, filmslides, records and exhibitions about Asia.* (Washington, 1957). 156.

University College, London, School of Librarianship and Archives: *Report on the work of the School for the period 1956–62.* (Occasional publications, no. 11.) xi, *note* 1.

Urdu encyclopaedia of Islam. Lahore, 1959– . 97.

Vajda, G.: *Album de paléographie arabe.* Paris, 1958. 76.

Vajda, G.: *Répertoire des catalogues et inventaires de manuscrits arabes.* Paris, 1949. 81.

Venkateswara Sarma, K.: *Index of papers submitted to the All-India Oriental Conference, sessions I–XII (1919–44).* Poona, 1949. 65.

Voegelin, C. M., and F. M.: 'Languages of the world'. *Anthropological linguistics* 6, 3 (1964)– . 17.

Vogel, J. Ph.: *The Contribution of the University of Leiden to Oriental research.* Leiden, 1954. 29.

Voigt, W. *Verzeichnis der orientalischen Handschriften in Deutschland.* Wiesbaden, 1961– . 82.

Voorhoeve, P.: 'Het Beschrijven van oostersche handschriften.' *Bibliotheekleven* 41, no. 11, Nov. 1956, pp. 321–34. 77.

Vostokovedenie v Leningradskom Universitete. Leningrad, 1960. 28.

Wainwright, M. D., and Matthews, N.: *A Guide to manuscripts and documents in the British Isles relating to South and South-East Asia.* London, 1965. 72.

Walford, A. J.: *Guide to reference material.* (– Suppl.) London, 1959(– 1963). 86.

Wensinck, A. J., und Kramers, J. H.: *Handwörterbuch des Islam.* 1941. 96.

West Pakistan yearbook. 1956– . 7.

Winchell, C. M.: *Guide to reference books.* 7th ed., and Suppl. 1–4. Chicago, 1951–63. 86.

Windisch, E.: *Geschichte der Sanskrit-Philologie und indischen Altertumskunde.* Berlin, Leipzig, 1917, 1920. 32.

Windisch, E.: *Philologie und Altertumskunde in Indien.* Leipzig, 1921. 32.

Wormann, C.: *The Jewish National and University Library. Report on the activities in the year 1961.* 216.

Yearbook of international organizations. 44.

Zaehner, R. C.: *The Concise encyclopaedia of living faiths.* 1959. 18.

Zajaczkowski, W.: 'Die Polnischen orientalistischen Arbeiten in den Jahren 1951–58.' *Folia Orient.* 1 (1959), pp. 163–173. 141.

Zbavitel, D.: *Oriental studies in Czechoslovakia.* Prague, 1959. 55.

Zenker, J. T.: *Bibliotheca orientalis*. Pars I. *Libros continens arabicos persicos turcicos inde ab arte typographica inventa ad nostra usque tempora impressos.* Lipsiae, 1840. 129.

Zenker, J. T.: *Bibliotheca orientalis, Manuel de bibliographie orientale.* 2 vols. Leipzig, 1846, 1861. 129.

1872–1902. Tridtzatiletie spetzial'nykh klassov Lazarevskogo Instituta Vostochnykh Yazykov. Pamyatnaya knizhka. Moskva, 1903. 27.

INDEX

Acquisition of books 223–9
Afghanistan 6
Africa 12–13
    newspapers 120
    periodicals 106
    West, materials for history 73
African Studies Association
    U.K. 61
    U.S.A. 61
America (United States of). *See*
    U.S.A.
American Historical Association
    93
Arabia 4
Arabic
    MSS. 81
    palaeography 75
Art and archaeology 20, 125
Asia 4
    boundaries 4
    European MSS. 69
    libraries 215–20
Asian studies 3
    See also Oriental studies
Association for Asian Studies 61
Association of British Orientalists
    59–61

Belgium
    African territories 13
    Conferences 64
Bhutan 7
Bibliografiya Vostoka 137–40
Bibliographies
    general 123–40
    national 140–7
    parts of Asia 148–55
    select 156–60
Bibliography of Asian studies 148–9

Bibliothèque Nationale
    catalogues 79
Birmingham, Selly Oak Colleges
    Library 187–8
Bodleian Library 170–2
    MSS. 79
Booksellers 235–40
Borneo 8
British Commonwealth 13
    bibliography 151–4
    newspapers 120
British Museum 71, 164–70
Brunei 8
Bulletin of Far Eastern bibliography
    148
Buddhism 97
Burma 7
    libraries 217–19
Burma Office
    records 70

C.I.P.S.H. 44
Cambodia 9
Cambridge libraries 175–6
Cambridge University Library
    173–5
Canada
    Indic MSS. 83–4
    Organizations 50
Ceylon 7
    libraries 217–19
    MSS. 84
Chester Beatty Library 188–9
China 9
    libraries 220
    periodicals 108
    reference books 91
Colonial bibliographies 150–5
Congresses 62–5

Coptic
    palaeography 75
Cyprus 6
Czechoslovakia
    bibliographies 145
    organizations 55

Durham University Library 185–6
Dutch East Indies. *See* Indonesia

East India Company
    records 70
Eire. *See* Ireland
Encyclopaedias 95–8
England. *See* U.K.
European MSS. 69

Far East 9
    libraries 219–20
    newspapers 120
Formosa. *See* Taiwan
France
    African territories 13
    colonial bibliographies 154
    conferences 64
    libraries 209–11
    organizations 55–6
    Oriental studies 23–4

Gardner, K. B. 235–40
Gazettes 122
Geography 125–6
Germany
    African territories 13
    bibliographies 140–1
    conferences 64
    libraries 211–13
    organizations 56–7
    Oriental studies 28
Great Britain. *See* U.K.
Guide to historical literature 93

Handbuch der Orientalistik 98–101
Hayter Sub-Committee 35, 137–
    42, 189–91

Hebrew
    palaeography 75
Historical Manuscripts Commission
    71–2
History 19–20, 103, 126
History of religion 124
History of science 125
Holland. *See* Netherlands
Hong Kong
    libraries 219–20
Hungary
    bibliographies 144

Indexes to periodicals 115
India 6
    conferences 65
    libraries 217–18
    organizations 54
    periodical articles 113–14
    periodicals 106–7
    reference books 91
India House Library 185
India Office Library 176–8
    MSS. 79
    records 70
Indian MSS. 81, 83–4
Indian palaeography 76
Indo-China 7, 9
Indonesia 8
    periodical articles 114
Institute of Historical Research
    guides to materials for history of
    West Africa 73
International Congress of African-
    ists 65
International Council for Philo-
    sophy and Humanistic Studies 44
International organizations 43–7
International Union of Orientalists
    44, 61
Iran 6
Iraq 5
Ireland
    MSS. 79
    Oriental Studies 28
Islam 96–7
Israel 5
    libraries 216–17

Italy
    African territories 13
    bibliographies 142–4
    MSS. 79–80
    organizations 57
    Oriental studies 24–5

Japan 10
    bibliographies 145–7
    congresses 63
    libraries 220
    organizations 51–3
    periodical articles 114–15
    periodicals 109–10
    reference books 91–3
John Rylands Library 186–7
Jordan 5

Korea 10
    organizations 54
Kuwait 5

Languages 15–18, 128
Laos 9
Law 20, 127–8
Lebanon 5
Libraries 163–234
Library associations 220–2
Library co-operation 189–91,
    199–205
Library of Congress 194–5
Library problems 223–34
Linguistics 128
London University. School of Ori-
    ental and African Studies. *See*
    School of Oriental and African
    Studies

Malay
    reference books 91
    periodicals 107–8
Malaya 8
Malaysia 8
Malclès, L. N. 86–9
Maldive Islands 7
Manuscripts 69–85
    cataloguing 74

Middle East 4–5, 6
    institutes and societies 46
    libraries 215–16
    newspapers 119
Mongolia 10
Mudge–Winchell 86–9
Muscat and Oman 5

N.D.E.A. 49
Names 231–2
National Defense Education Act.
    See N.D.E.A.
National Historical Publications
    Guide to photocopied historical
    materials 74
National Library of India, Calcutta
    218–19
National Register of Archives 72
National Union Catalog of manu-
    scripts 74
Near East 4–5
Nepal 7
Netherlands
    colonial bibliographies 154
    Oriental studies 29
News summaries 120–1
Newspaper cuttings 121–2
Newspapers 119–20

Oceania 11–12
Orientalische Bibliographie 134–5
Orientalists 66
Organizations 43–65
Oriental studies 3, 14–15, 15–20,
    21–34, 34–42
    organizations for 43–66
Oxford libraries 172–3

Pakistan 7
    libraries 217–19
    reference books 91
Palaeography 75–6
Periodical articles 113–15
Periodicals 104–22
Persia 6
Persian Gulf states 5
Persian MSS. 81

Philippines 9
  periodical articles 114
Philosophy 125
Poland
  bibliographies 141–2
  MSS. 82–3
  Oriental studies 29
Portugal
  African territories 13
  colonial bibliography 154–5
  Oriental studies 29–30
Processing 229–31
Professional associations 59
Public Law 480 202–5
Public Record Office 69
Pushtu MSS. 84

Reay Committee 34, 35
Reference books 86–103
Religions 18, 124–5
Reviewing journals 105–6
Royal Asiatic Society 183
Royal Commonwealth Society
  bibliographies 153
  library 183–5

Sabah 8
Sanskrit MSS. 84
Sarawak 8
Scandinavia
  bibliographies 144
Scarbrough Commission 34, 36–7
Scholars. *See* Orientalists
School of Oriental and African
  Studies 35, 37–42
  Library 178–83
Selly Oak Colleges Library, Bir-
  mingham 187–8
Siam. *See* Thailand
Sikkim 6
Social sciences 126–7
Societies 61–2
South Africa
  periodical articles 114
  reference books 93
South Arabia, Federation 4
South Asia 6–7
  newspapers 119

South-East Asia 7–9
  newspapers 119
Soviet Asia 10
Spain
  African territories 13
Straits Settlements 8
Switzerland
  Oriental studies 30
Syria 5

Taiwan 9
  libraries 220
  organizations 53–4
Thailand 9
Times, The
  cuttings 122
Timor 8
Transjordan 5
Turkey 5
  libraries 216
  periodical articles 113

U.K.
  conferences 59–60
  libraries 164–91
  MSS. 73, 79
  organizations 51
  Oriental studies 30–32, recent
    developments 34–42
  Pushtu MSS. 84
U.S.A.
  history of Oriental studies 30
  Indic MSS. 83–4
  libraries 192–205
  MSS. collections 73–4
  organizations 47–50
U.S.S.R. 10
  bibliographies 145
  conferences 64–5
  libraries 206–8
  MSS. 81
  Oriental studies 25–8
Union catalogues
  MSS. 82
Union of Socialist Soviet Republics.
  See U.S.S.R.

United Kingdom of Great Britain and Ireland. *See* U.K.
United States of America. *See* U.S.A.
Universities 57–9

Vietnam 9

Walford, A. J. 86–9
Who's Who
    Asian 103
Winchell, C. M. 86–9
Wissenschaftliche Jahresberichte 131–2

Yemen 4